THE LONGEST LINE

THE LONGEST LINE

Broadway's Most Singular Sensation:
A Chorus Line

Gary Stevens and Alan George

APPLAUSE
THEATRE BOOK PUBLISHERS
NEW YORK • LONDON

AN APPLAUSE ORIGINAL

THE LONGEST LINE
by Gary Stevens and Alan George

Copyright © 1995 Gary Stevens and Alan George

PLAYBILL® covers reprinted by permission of PLAYBILL Incorporated. PLAYBILL® is a registered trademark of PLAYBILL Incorporated, New York, NY.
Back Stage casting notice reprinted with permission of Backstage, © 1995 BPI Communications.
Martha Swope photos courtesy Martha Swope © Time Inc. Herb Migdoll photos courtesy © Herb Migdoll.
Excerpt from *The Way I Was* reprinted with permission of Marvin Hamlisch (©1992 by Marvin Hamlisch and Gerald Gardner), Charles Scribners Sons.
Trois Acrobates: Folies-Bergère used with permission of David Douglas Duncan reproduced from his book *Prismatics* (Harper & Row).
Advertisements and radio copy reproduced with permission of Serino Coyne Inc. Group Sales material courtesy of Shubert Group Sales,
   Group Sales Box Office, Cliff Scott and Susan Frank.

Design and production by Sue Knopf.
Front and back jacket photos by Herb Migdoll.

Library of Congress Cataloging-in-Publication Data

Stevens, Gary, 1962-
         The longest line : fifteen years of Broadway's most singular
sensation / by Gary Stevens and Alan George.
         p.   cm.
         Includes index.
         ISBN 1-55783-221-8
         1. Hamlisch, Marvin. Chorus line. I. George, Alan,   1956-   .
II. Title.
ML410.H1745S74   1995
792.6'42--dc20   95-35885
                                                      CIP
                                                       MN

British Cataloging-in-Publication Data
A catalogue record of this book is available from the British Library

ISBN: 1-55783-221-8 – hard cover   ISBN: 1-55783-238-2 – 1997 paperback

APPLAUSE BOOKS

211 W. 71st St.   406 Vale Road
New York, NY 10023   Tonbridge KENT TN9 2XR
Phone: (212)595-4735   Phone: 073 235-7755
Fax: (212)765-7875   Fax: 073 207-7219

Acknowledgments

Sincere gratitude to all those we interviewed for sharing your A CHORUS LINE experiences with us. Without your recollections and anecdotes this book would not have been possible, and we are forever grateful.

Very special thanks to Troy Garza, Baayork Lee, Fran Liebergall, Herbert Harris, and Alyce Gilbert for verifying the accuracy of our lists of actors, musicians, and related data.

To: Susan Frank, Cliff Scott, Jack Thomas, Ronnie Lee, and Janet Robinson for contributing the wonderful Group Sales materials. Nancy Coyne and Nancy Gerber of Serino Coyne Inc. for digging out from storage (twice!) those glorious ads and for an unforgettable afternoon looking through your archives. Merle Debuskey for access to the publicity files. Bill Jones for the costume plot. Angelique Ilo for the Shubert backstage tour. Jim Manfredi of Artkraft Strauss for sharing the blueprint.

Wayne Sapper for pulling out the sign. Michael Yaccarino of TDF for the data. Ann Walker of Local 802 Musician's Union for access to fifteen years of ACL logs. Steve Elish of *Backstage* for access to back issues. Jordan Harris of *Variety* for allowing us to research 767 weeks of back issues — and Suzi Germano for your help in this task.

Warm appreciation to all those who sent us their personal photos, mementos and keepsakes: Scott Allen, Cheryl Clark, David Diamond, Lois Englund, Steve Gardner, Troy Garza, Deborah Geffner, Bernard Gersten, Bob Giraldi, Abe Jacob, Betty & Bernard Jacobs, Bob Kamlot, Fran Liebergall, DeLee Lively, Kevin McCready, William Mead, Otts Munderloh, Don Pippin, Wanda Richert, Marvin Roth, Loida Santos, Bill Schelble, Reinhold Schwenk, Michael Serrechia, Bobby Thomas, Robert Valli, and Mitchell Weiss. A great big THANK YOU to all!

A picture is worth a thousand words and the words in THE LONGEST LINE are unequivocally complimented by the great work of the contributing photographers and artists: Sunny Bak, Paul Davis, David Douglas Duncan, Bernard Fox, Steve Friedman, Troy Garza, Gerry Goodstein, Michael Harvey, Roberta Hershenson, Jack Hoffman, Cliff Lipson, Mike Norcia, George Rios, Ron Scherl, Peter Stanford, Martha Swope, and especially Herb Migdoll.

Personal thanks are extended to: Bernard Jacobs and Gerald Schoenfeld of The Shubert Organization — from the plaque to this book, we thank you for your ongoing support. Maryann Chach of The Shubert Archive for all your cooperation. Dennis Rhodes for helping get this book off the ground. Ron Feiner, Esq. and Pamela Golinski, Esq. for your assistance. Howard I. Golden, Esq. for your guidance, advice and generosity. The fantastic team at Applause: Rachel Reiss for dotting the "i"s and crossing the "t"s, Kay Radtke for such positive energy and genuine interest, and Paul Sugarman for picking up the loose ends. Joel Avirom for the input. Sue Knopf, our designer, for an incredible job. And to our Editor and Publisher, Glenn Young, for trust, confidence, freedom, collaboration, and painstakingly treating this book with such TLC.

And Allison Casement — for opening the door.

DEDICATION

To my mother, Elayne Kaplan, always in my heart,
who knew how much I loved this show.
— Gary

To my partner on this book and in life,
whose passion, inspiration, and undying determination
always fill me with wonder, awe, and much love.
— Alan

And to everyone associated with A CHORUS LINE
for fifteen years of THE BEST!

Contents

Authors' Notes

Since its opening in July 1975, A CHORUS LINE has been an integral part of our lives. Between the two of us, we have seen practically every Broadway show since 1969, but nothing has left the impact of or affected us as deeply as A CHORUS LINE. During its New York run, we saw the show over seventy-five times between us, followed by countless tour and stock performances, including a trip overseas specifically to see a company touring through Germany.

Going back to A CHORUS LINE over and over again was like visiting an old friend. Not only was it riveting theatre, but we were fascinated by the nuances and changes in interpretation that occurred over the years. And, of course, it was always fun to be in attendance if something out of the ordinary happened on stage.

Our favorite seats were always front row center orchestra. Yet we enjoyed getting different perspectives of Michael Bennett's brilliant staging and Tharon Musser's extraordinary lighting by sitting in various sections of the house. There was a certain pride in our knowledge of the show, and what a thrill for us to have had the opportunity, through this book, to expand that knowledge in areas which could not have been explored from our seats in the Shubert Theatre.

Because of its legacy to and importance in the history of American musical theatre, when the show closed in 1990 we felt there should be a permanent tribute at the Shubert, its home of fifteen years. With the blessing of the Shubert Organization, and the support of the eight Broadway Cassies, producer Joseph Papp, and the three New York drama critics who originally reviewed the show in 1975, we ventured into a year-long fund-raising drive to dedicate a cast bronze plaque honoring the show. Fans from all over the country contributed to this effort, giving something back to the show that had given them so much pleasure over the years. On October 30, 1991, the plaque was unveiled in the Shubert Theatre lobby, packed with A CHORUS LINE alumni. Absent from the festivities was Joseph Papp, who sadly and ironically passed away the next day.

It was our intention to learn about all aspects of the run of the show and to document that information. We interviewed 125 people. This book is in *their* words. It is a chapter in history told to us by the people who lived it. Everyone we spoke with had passionate feelings and emotions tied to the show, whether positive or negative. Several refused to be interviewed because "it was too personal" or they didn't want to "rehash the past," but that, too, is an expression of passion. Everyone interviewed, however, agreed there will never again be anything like the A CHORUS LINE experience — the energy, the creativity, the teamwork.

THE LONGEST LINE delves deeply into the creative and technical work done on the show, and chronicles in unsparing detail the legacy of innocence, savvy, and consummate artistry that made A CHORUS LINE the longest running show in Broadway history. Accompanied by a myriad of never-before-seen photos, illustrations, and memorabilia from our private collection as well as those of others associated with the show, this book pays tribute to *everyone* affiliated with A CHORUS LINE from beginning to end. It is not a story about Michael Bennett, but you will find many observations of him and the way he operated, as he inarguably was the backbone of the show. Because it was a long time ago, we had the unenviable task of digging deep into memory banks. There are the inevitable discrepancies and recollections that are not always in synch. What we have presented is how the people who were there remembered and experienced it.

Elegant in its simplicity, A CHORUS LINE represents an era of Broadway long gone. This book is a historical documentation of all the elements that went into making a show work in that era — a time before the marketing blitz that is critical to the longevity of today's Broadway spectacles.

In the pages ahead, you will experience A CHORUS LINE during its heyday and its leaner times, followed by its resurgence through the "end of the line." You will experience A CHORUS LINE to its fullest — onstage, backstage, and offstage.

Gary Stevens & Alan George
New York City, October 1995

Who's Who: The Voices in THE LONGEST LINE

CAST

*Although many of the actors played different roles on tour,
only their Broadway role is listed below.*

MEMBER	BROADWAY ROLE
SCOTT ALLEN	Original Understudy
KEITH BERNARDO	Don (Final Company)
STEVE BOOCKVOR	Zach
KERRY CASSERLY	Kristine
CHERYL CLARK	Cassie
KAY COLE	Original Maggie; Diana
MURPHY CROSS	Judy
PATTI D'BECK	Understudy
RON DENNIS	Original Richie
FRASER ELLIS	Understudy
LOIS ENGLUND	Val
DIANE FRATANTONI	Diana; Understudy
VICKI FREDERICK	Cassie
LAURIE GAMACHE	Cassie (Final Company)
PATRICIA (TRISH) GARLAND	Original Judy
DEBORAH GEFFNER	Kristine
MICHAEL GRUBER	Mike (Final Company)
DEBORAH HENRY	Cassie; Val
ANGELIQUE ILO	Judy (Final Company); Cassie
ANTHONY INNEO	Zach
BRADLEY JONES	Greg
DeLEE LIVELY	Val
BETTY LYND	Understudy
ROBIN LYON	Understudy (Final Company)
GAY MARSHALL	Diana
KEVIN NEIL McCREADY	Larry (Final Company); Al
WAYNE MELEDANDRI	Paul
JACK NOSEWORTHY	Mark (Final Company; last cast member ever hired)
CYNTHIA ONRUBIA	Connie; Understudy
SCOTT PEARSON	Zach
ANN REINKING	Cassie
WANDA RICHERT	Cassie; Val
JUSTIN ROSS	Greg
LOIDA SANTOS	Diana
MICHAEL SERRECCHIA	Original Understudy
DONN SIMIONE	Al; Larry; Understudy
PAMELA SOUSA	Cassie
RON STAFFORD	Bobby
JANE SUMMERHAYS	Sheila
LYNNE TAYLOR-CORBETT	Cassie
CLIVE (CLERK) WILSON	Original Larry; Zach
JANET WONG	Connie
KATHYRYNANN (KATE) WRIGHT	Sheila
KAREN ZIEMBA	Bebe; Understudy

MUSICIANS

LARRY ABEL	Chief Music Copyist
RALPH BURNS	Orchestrator
BILL BYERS	Orchestrator
VINCENT FANUELE	Musician; Assistant Conductor
BERNARD FOX	Music Copyist
JERRY GOLDBERG	Conductor
MARVIN HAMLISCH	Composer
HERBERT HARRIS	Contractor
FRAN LIEBERGALL	Original Pianist; Vocal Supervisor
AL MATTALIANO	Musician
DON PIPPIN	Original Musical Director & Vocal Arranger
BOB ROGERS	Conductor
MARVIN ROTH	Musician
ALPHONSE STEPHENSON	Conductor
BOBBY THOMAS	Music Coordinator
JONATHAN TUNICK	Orchestrator
HAROLD WHEELER	Orchestrator

BOOK

NEIL SIMON	Script "doctor"

PRODUCTION MANAGEMENT

EMANUEL AZENBERG	General Manager (Original Road Companies)
RICHARD BERG	Assistant General Manager
PATTI D'BECK	Assistant Dance Captain
FRASER ELLIS	Assistant Stage Manager
TROY GARZA	Dance Captain
BERNARD GERSTEN	Associate Producer, NYSF
JEFF HAMLIN	Original Production Stage Manager
BOB KAMLOT	Original General Manager
BOB MacDONALD	Company & General Manager
BOB REILLY	Company Manager
RON STAFFORD	Assistant Stage Manager
PETER VON MAYRHAUSER	Stage Manager
MITCHELL WEISS	Company Manager
CLIVE (CLERK) WILSON	Dance Captain

SALES & MARKETING

SUSAN FRANK	NYSF Freelance Graphic Designer
BILL FRIENDLY	Shubert Theatre Box Office
STEVE GARDNER	President: Hit Show Club
ALISON HARPER	NYSF Subscription Director
NANCY HELLER	NYSF Audience Development; Marketing
ARNOLD KOHN	Lerman Graphics: Souvenir Program Printer
RONNIE LEE	Group Sales Box Office
JOE McLAUGHLIN	Shubert Theatre Box Office
MICHAEL MILIONE	Shubert Theatre Box Office
NOREEN MORGAN	Shubert Theatre Box Office
JANET ROBINSON	Group Sales Box Office
CLIFF SCOTT	NYSF GroupTix; Marketing
ED SHERIDAN	Shubert Theatre Box Office
JACK THOMAS	Director of Shubert Group Sales and Subscription
MITCHELL WEISS	NYSF GroupTix

PHOTOGRAPHY

HERBERT MIGDOLL	Souvenir Program Photographer & Designer
MARTHA SWOPE	Photographer

ADVERTISING

GENE CASE	Creative Director: Case & McGrath
NANCY COYNE	Creative Director: Serino Coyne Inc.
PAUL DAVIS	Freelance Artist for Case & McGrath
RICK ELICE	Associate Creative Director: Serino Coyne Inc.
PAUL ELSON	Freelance Photographer
BOB GIRALDI	Director of A CHORUS LINE's first TV commercial
DON JOSEPHSON	Account Executive: Blaine Thompson
MIKE MONES	Account Executive: Serino Coyne Inc.
NICK NAPPI	Art Director: Serino Coyne & Nappi
MORRIS ROBBINS	Art Director: Blaine Thompson
JAMES RUSSEK	Account Executive: Case & McGrath
REINHOLD SCHWENK	Art Director: Case & McGrath
MATTHEW SERINO	President: Serino Coyne Inc.

PUBLICITY

MERLE DEBUSKEY	Press Agent
BILL SCHELBLE	Press Agent
BOB ULLMAN	Press Agent

LIGHTING

TONY D'AIUTO	Spotlight Operator
THARON MUSSER	Designer

COSTUMES

THEONI V. ALDREDGE	Designer
ALYCE GILBERT	Wardrobe Supervisor
BILL JONES	Dresser
BARBARA MATERA	Costume Executor
WOODY SHELP	Finale Hat Maker

SOUND

ABE JACOB	Designer
OTTS MUNDERLOH	Original Sound Mixer

SET

ARTHUR SICCARDI	Production Carpenter

SHUBERT THEATRE

BERNARD B. JACOBS	President, Shubert Organization
BETTY JACOBS	Plum Productions / Mrs. Bernard Jacobs
GENE KORNBERG	Artkraft Strauss Signs
JIM MANFREDI	Artkraft Strauss Signs
KEITH MARSTON	Shubert Organization Projects Coordinator
FRED OLSSON	Shubert Organization Facilities Director
WAYNE SAPPER	King Displays
GERALD SCHOENFELD	Chairman, Shubert Organization
PHILIP J. SMITH	Vice President, Shubert Organization

The Show in "Line Lingo" from Start to Finish

The Opening
    In the Mirror
    Away from the Mirror
    The Ballet mark (marking the combination)
    Hanging out (waiting stage right
        before getting called into groups)
    Putting in groups (*I Hope I Get It*)
    Ballet Combinations
    Jazz Combinations
    Larry clump (getting pictures and back to
        center stage to listen to Larry)
    The Back-Up and the Come-Down
        (also known as the Surge or Line Charge)
    Resume

The Names

The Diana Name (we first hear underscoring
    during her name section)

The Line Bounce (spotlights head to head down the
    line)

I Can Do That

And
    The Internals (Internal thoughts are a theme
        that is repeated throughout the entire Montage)

At the Ballet:
    Ballet Backup
    Ballet Barre
    Ballet Blaze

Sing!

Hello Twelve, Hello Thirteen, Hello Love
    (The Montages)
    Montage I begins with Mark
    Montage II begins with Connie

Nothing
    Montage III begins with Don Kerr
        Bah dah's and *Mother* Montage
    Montage IV (also known as Monster
        Montage) begins with Greg
        Wah wah's & Gimme the Ball sections

Val monologue

Tits & Ass (*Dance:10, Looks:3*)

Short Paul scene

The First Cassie/Zach scene

The Cassie dance (*The Music and the Mirror*)
    First dance section
    The small mirrors (slow section)
    Accelerando (small mirrors raise up)
    Swan Lake
    Red
    Heat wave
    The pirouettes
    The back-ups (handshake)
    Layout (final pose)

Paul Monologue

The *One's*:
    One Re-entrance
    One Mistake chorus
    One First internal
    One Second internal (groups of four)
    Girls chorus
    Boys chorus
    Smile & Sing chorus (boys and girls together)
    Follies section / The Cassie/Zach confron-
        tation scene
        The cast become ghosts à la FOLLIES.
        The Internals in this section are called
        "Schmoozes" with the cast's voices
        echoing, counting, and chanting in the
        background
    Final chorus

The Tap Combination
    Big Group tap
    Groups of 4 tap
    4th group of tappers is when Paul falls —
        "The Accident"

The Accident scene

The Alternatives Scene
    (after Paul is carried off, Zach asks the question
    "What are you going to do when you can't
    dance anymore?" which begins the scene)

What I Did For Love

The Elimination Walk (one at a time back in line)

The Final Elimination

The end of the show

Finale *One*
    The bows: Men's bows and Ladies' bows
    Shuffle along section (the partnering)
    The parade (in cake walk)
    The Wedge
    Grapevine Circle (expands into the Jeté Circle)
    Final lineup
    The Backup
    Final chorus
    The Kicks

FADE TO BLACK

Glossary of Relevant Terms Used in THE LONGEST LINE

ABC's - alphabetical Broadway show listings in a newspaper, usually *The New York Times*

Actor's Equity Association; Equity - theatrical union for stage actors

audition - interview or tryout

back of house - area of the theatre behind the orchestra seats

billing - printed credit of actor, producer, writer, etc. on programs, posters, etc.

booth singers - offstage singers (the understudies) who were not performing on the line

call back - the second stage in an audition process that only those under consideration are asked to attend

Cassie fly mirrors - seven small mirrors lowered for slow section of the Cassie dance

cattle call - mass audition drawing a large number of performers

choreographer - creator of the dance steps

company - cast of a show as a whole

company manager - attends to the performer's production-related needs and is involved with the show's operations on a daily basis

copyist - copies and distributes the musical score for individual instruments

cover / second cover - understudy or standby

covered pit - the orchestra pit that was covered by a black scrim

cue - a signal for an upcoming entrance, set or light change, movement, etc.

dance arranger - creates the dance music that is derived from the songs

dance captain - supervisor of dance work, once choreography is in place; usually member of the chorus

dance bag - the shoulder bag that dancers use to carry their rehearsal attire

deck - the stage floor

doctoring - enhancements to the script by someone other than the playwright

dolly - a low, wheeled platform on which a camera is mounted for moving about a set

doubler - musician who plays more than one instrument during a performance

downstage - the area of the stage closest to the audience

dress rehearsal - run-through of the show in full costume and tech, usually without stopping, that takes place at the end of the rehearsal period prior to beginning performances

dresser - member of the wardrobe staff who assists the performers with their costume changes

dressing room - room or area for the actor to costume and make-up for performance

favored nations - a form of contract, or clause within a contract, for the actors in a company which decrees that all cast members receive equal treatment and salaries

footlights - a row of lights along the front of stage, level with the actors' feet

front lights - the spotlights, manually operated from the lighting bridge near the balcony, which follow performers' movements around the stage

front of house - the area of the theatre used by the audience, including seating sections and lobby; also referred to as the exterior of the theatre

general manager - supervises the financial and business related transactions of the production

gypsy - a chorus member who generally moves from show to show

hard stock - theatre tickets printed on a cardboard stock used prior to computerization

house seats - tickets set aside per performance for VIPs, guests, etc.; generally the prime locations

Local 1 - the stagehands' union

mark - the specific place on the stage floor for a performer's position

masking - flats or drapes used to conceal the backstage area from the audience

milliskin - thin, shiny, spandex-like fabric

notes - comments and criticisms given to the cast by the director or stage management after rehearsal or performance

open call - non-private, open audition, usually advertised in the trade papers

orchestration - the composition or arrangement of music for an orchestra

papering the house - distribution of complimentary tickets

periaktcid - a three-sided set device dating back to ancient Greece that, as it turns, reveals a different scene on each side. A CHORUS LINE utilized eight sixteen-foot periaktoids: one side was black velour; one side was mirror; one side was the sunburst seen only in the Finale.

photo call - the time when a show is professionally photographed for publicity and exterior display purposes

preset board - a programmed lighting board that allows each scene's lighting cues to be preset

press agent - the publicist assigned to the show for media relations

previews - the period of performances preceding opening night, during which changes are usually made

proscenium arch - the structural frame around the stage

put-in rehearsal - a replacement actor's final rehearsal, the only one with the entire cast, just prior to his/her first performance, done cue to cue primarily for proper placement of the new actor

raked - sloped

scalper - a person who buys theatre tickets for purposes of reselling them at a significantly higher price

screen test - the test film of an actor to see if he/she is suitable for the role

set-ups - the recreation of specific positions by actors for a photo shoot

Shubert Alley - the landmark strip connecting 44th and 45th Streets alongside the Shubert and Booth Theatres.

special, a - lighting that highlights and defines a particular area of stage

spotlight - a strong beam of light used to prominently illuminate a particular person, thing, or group

stage manager - person who runs the performance from backstage and signals the cues of the show; also oversees rehearsals, scheduling, and props

standby - an understudy who is "on call" and must be prepared to perform at the last minute if needed

standing room - the area behind the last row (usually of the orchestra seating) designated for standees

subtext - the interpretation of thoughts and feelings implied but not stated in the script, usually developed by the performer

swing - an understudy who does not perform in the show unless replacing an actor who is out

take-in - the installation of sets and lights in a theatre.

tech rehearsal - rehearsal for the purpose of testing the technical aspects of the production

three sheets - three paper sheets, put together to create a poster, usually 41" x 81", used for displays in train stations, bus depots, and other large, prominent areas

TKTS - Theatre Development Fund's (TDF) half-price ticket booth, also known as the booth, the wagon, and Duffy Square.

underscoring - music that is heard under dialogue

understudy - an actor who is ready to perform a role in case the actor playing the role misses a performance; in A CHORUS LINE the understudies perform the opening number, are eliminated, and become "booth singers" for the duration of the show

upstage - the stage area farthest from the audience

wing space - the area directly off the stage on either side

workshop - the creative period during which A CHORUS LINE was developed and staged for presentation, while continuous changes were made

Prologue

How did A CHORUS LINE begin? How did it get from being an idea in Michael Bennett's mind to those legendary tape sessions to a workshop at the New York Shakespeare Festival Public Theatre? The answer is nobody knows. Suddenly it was there. Why was it there? What brought Michael Bennett and Joe Papp's lives into this historic conjunction?

In late spring of 1974, we were doing a musical at the Festival called MORE THAN YOU DESERVE by Michael Weller and Jim Steinman, a kind of send-up of SOUTH PACIFIC, but about the war in Vietnam. Simultaneously, on a whole other planet known as Broadway, Michael Bennett had achieved a new level of stardom by virtue of having fixed SEESAW. I was amazed by the turn-around the show had achieved under Michael's ministrations. We were having our own trouble with MORE THAN YOU DESERVE, and one day I said to Joe, "You know the problem with this show? It needs a show doctor." "Like who?" asked Joe. "Like Michael Bennett," I replied. "Michael who?" "Michael Bennett," and I told him about SEESAW. Joe said, "No, don't worry about it; Kim Friedman is the best director in the world for this and she's gonna be perfect." And that was the end of that. Until a few days days later, when Joe did call Michael Bennett and asked if he might be interested in directing KNICKERBOCKER HOLIDAY by Maxwell Anderson and Kurt Weill for the Beaumont at Lincoln Center, which the NYSF was running. Michael said, "Why don't you send me the script and score and I'll think about it." A couple of days later Michael called and said, "I really don't want to do KNICKERBOCKER HOLIDAY — but I have an idea."

That was the beginning. Michael came down and played Joe the edited version of the tapes and said, "I want to workshop it." And Joe said, "Sure. Why don't you do it here?"

Bernard Gersten, Associate Producer,
New York Shakespeare Festival

Photo by Herb Migdoll

Doctoring the Book

BERNARD JACOBS [President, Shubert Organization]: I was standing in the back of the theatre during a preview with Michael and Jimmy Kirkwood, and the valium line came across. The audience went hysterical, and Jimmy was laughing. Michael poked me and said, "You know, he thinks he wrote that line!" Neil Simon's involvement was strictly between Michael and Neil, and I think Michael did it in such a way that he really made Jimmy Kirkwood think he was rewriting the lines. Michael was very good at that, in terms of manipulating people.

NEIL SIMON: Michael and I had been friends and we worked together on PROMISES, PROMISES and THE GOOD DOCTOR. Michael asked me to come down to the Public and just see the show. And I did. I thought it was wonderful, and he said, "Can we talk about it after the show?" I said, "Yes," and we went to some little Chinese restaurant, I think with Bob Avian. Michael said, "It needs to be funnier." I said, "I don't really think so, whatever is up there is working." "No, I want more laughs in it." I told him that I couldn't help him because of the Dramatists Guild rule of not being able to put new material in unless you get the consent of the authors, and he said, "I have the con-

sent." "But I'm not positive about that," I replied. "Don't worry about that, I'll take care of Jimmy and Nick." So I agreed. I went back and saw it again, and asked Michael for a script.

I went home and wrote maybe twenty-five or so new lines throughout the play. I just put them in willy-nilly, where I thought it could be funnier, and always trying to stay with the characters. I can't remember exactly how many of my lines he used. But what he did was to take the sheet of paper containing my lines, sit down on a chair and put it between his legs. And as he was talking to the cast, he'd say, "You know, you ought to say ..." Then he'd look down on the paper, with his hand covering his forehead, and say, "Why don't you say this," and would give them my line. Then the actor would say the line and everyone would laugh, and say that Michael was really coming up with them today! Michael would give me reports, telling me what worked and what didn't. I couldn't be there, obviously, when he was putting them in. This was all during previews. And that's how he got the lines in. I would say it took me maybe a week or so. For me, it was kind of a challenge. It was fun to be able to attach myself to something that I knew was going to be such a

big hit — to be able to add something, just to see if the lines worked. And when they did, I was pleased.

Bob Avian knew of my involvement, and I guess Jim and Nick knew. But then it got around in Shubert Alley somehow. People knew about it, well, reporters knew about it. They would ask me if I did help on A CHORUS LINE, and at the beginning I wanted to play it down, I didn't want to say anything because I thought it would be trouble for everybody. Later on I admitted to it. I don't think anybody wanted to talk about it, really. In a way, I didn't want to horn in on Michael's success. I knew it was going to be huge, whether they had the extra lines or not. They do help, God knows, but the show was just so original for its time, and the reaction was so enormous, I knew nothing was going to stop this thing.

See, I didn't even know how much work Jim and Nick had done because from what I had heard, Michael had all these conversations with the actors and just wrote down what they had to say, and a lot of those speeches were intact. Michael wasn't really a writer, I knew that, and so he got Jim and Nick, but I have no idea even what their contribution was. I never got any complaints from Jim or Nick. They knew that it wasn't Michael who put the material in, and

in a sense I knew I was breaking the Dramatists Guild Rule. I assumed that he told them that I was going to put in lines, but I think they didn't want it known.

It did seem to me in places that you could go along and have somebody saying dramatic things while moving the story, but when they're attempting jokes and they're not working, it pulls the show down a little bit. So those were the glaring spots, and I said that really has to be fixed. We spent about three hours in that restaurant talking about things. But for me, all I really needed was to say, "Give me the script, I'll go home and send you what I can." Also I knew a lot of those dancers, and I knew what they could do. I knew Kelly Bishop could land a line like anybody, so I wanted to give her a lot. There's some people you don't give the jokes to because they're not going to do it very well.

I'll never remember what lines I put in, honestly, but "Uptown and to the right" I would know is mine; it sounds like me. I've written twenty-eight plays, God knows how many movies, and people say lines to me, and I say, "That's funny, where is that from?" They say, "It's one of your plays." When you write so much, and you take a line out of context, especially since I wasn't there from the beginning

and working on that, I would never know. The joke about Buffalo, sometimes I think I wrote it, and then I'm pretty sure that Mark Twain wrote it. I sometimes think it was in the show before me, and yet, there's a part of my mind that says I wrote it, and there's part of my mind that says it's an old joke that was written by somebody like Mark Twain, and it wasn't Buffalo, it was someplace else, like Philadelphia or something.

I didn't have a right to say what they would or wouldn't use of my work — I just offered. I was foolish enough to read the books by Moss Hart where he said authors went out to help other authors in trouble. It was sort of an unwritten custom that you help your friends. I didn't very often doctor up shows. Despite the fact that my nickname is Doc, I rarely have done it. I've done it only when I got something in return. For example, at one point I owned the Eugene O'Neill Theatre, and we needed a play in there and David Merrick had ROSENCRANTZ AND GUILDEN-STERN ARE DEAD. They were looking for a theatre, so I said, "Move it to the Eugene O'Neill," and he said, "I will if you will help and fix up HOW NOW DOW JONES." So I did.

I never got paid for A CHORUS LINE. I was doing very well on my own, making a lot of money, and who knew it was going to run for fifteen years? The only thing that Michael sent me, which was a very weird gift, was a pair of satin pillow cases. I don't know what I was going to do with a pair of satin pillow cases, unless I joined a fancy club of the Ku Klux Klan. But then I remember asking Michael Bennett to help me on a play I was doing. And he charged me! I don't think if anybody asked me to fix something up, I would ever again do it for free.

Looking back, my most vivid memory isn't the writing so much, but the night that I went to see the show. I was married to Marsha Mason, the two of us went and outside afterwards, Marsha was just extolling its virtues, saying, "Michael, it's just brilliant, it's going to be sensational." But he was worried, and said, "You've got to come talk to me." So Marsha went home and we went to this little Chinese restaurant, and I kept saying, "You just need a little thing here and there." He said, "No, no, no, I need more, I need more." He kept pushing. Michael had a way of getting his way. He kept calling me and calling me and asking for more and more. I probably would have done it, but by that time I would have asked for something. But I didn't even know it was going to leave the Public Theatre.

"It was sort of an unwritten custom that you help your friends … I never got paid for A CHORUS LINE. I was doing very well on my own, making a lot of money, and who knew it was going to run for fifteen years? The only thing that Michael sent me, which was a very weird gift, was a pair of satin pillow cases … But then I remember asking Michael Bennett to help me on a play that I was doing. And he charged me!

— NEIL SIMON

eft center photo courtesy Robert N. Valli
ther photos by Herb Migdoll

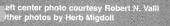

Donna McKechnie, Deborah Henry, Vicki Frederick
Center photo courtesy Robert N. Valli, others by Herb Migdoll

Clockwise from top Laurie Gamache, Cheryl Clark, Pam Sousa

Top right photo by Peter Stanford; others by Herb Migdoll

Top four photos by Herb Migdoll; bottom photo by Jack Hoffman

CHAPTER 1

. . . .

A VIEW FROM THE LINE

. . . .

> *"Kevin Kline read beautifully, but he couldn't dance. Michael said, 'Teach him the opening number, and if he can do it, he's got the job.' And there I was saying, 'Kevin, I'm sorry, I don't think this is going to work out.'"* — CLIVE WILSON

Getting the Job

FRAN LIEBERGALL [Original Pianist; Vocal Supervisor]: We did not want to hear anything from the show. We didn't want somebody singing *What I Did For Love* if we weren't thinking of her as Diana. If it was an open call, we would ask for sixteen bars of their best material. And most people who auditioned had to go through the cattle call process — that's what Michael wanted.

We knew how cold other auditions were, and how people could be cut off and tossed aside. Michael gave every dancer his or her dignity.

TROY GARZA [Dance Captain]: We screened people in groups of ten or so. Each person stepped forward one at a time, said their name, age, and where they were from — just so we could hear them talk. They then performed a time step and double pirouette. Those who survived the first cut would learn the Ballet & Jazz combination of *I Hope I Get It*. We danced everyone in groups of four to compare dancing skills. Those who didn't dance as well, but looked

great, we asked to sing. We were measuring people's talents. All of the superb dancers would stay to sing. Then we gave them sections from the show to read. We would call people back at least once.

RON DENNIS [Original Richie]: When I came to New York in 1964, the dancers of color being hired for Broadway were all fair skinned so they could blend in. When I started getting roles as a darker-skinned dancer, and being short on top of it, it was a radical new thing at the time. Now it's commonplace, but then I was breaking the darker-color barrier and didn't even know it!

When I auditioned for the workshop, Michael wanted to keep me, but it was a woman's role vacated by Candy Brown they needed to fill. Baayork Lee asked Michael, "Why does the character have to be a girl? You like Ron, so why don't you just take him?" And that's what happened.

SCOTT ALLEN [Original Understudy]: I came into the show late to play Al. I was

trying to catch up in rehearsals. But coming from an acting background, it took me a little longer to pick up dance steps. By the end of my first week, my head was spinning. Michael was afraid I was not going to be up to speed by the time the show was ready to open. I was sure I was going to be fired. Michael moved Don Percassi up to Al and made me the understudy.

CLIVE WILSON [Original Larry; Dance Captain]: Bobby LuPone's sister, Patti, was living with a Broadway actor named Kevin Kline, whom Bobby asked me to see for Zach. Kevin read beautifully, but he couldn't dance. According to Michael, anybody could do the *One* number. Including Kevin. He was fine with that. But in those days, Michael insisted that Zach dance the opening number. So he said, "Teach him the opening number, and if he can do it, he's got the job." I met with Kevin every morning for weeks, and it just didn't work. He would have been perfect as Zach, and Kevin wanted to do it. And there I was saying, "Kevin, I'm sorry, I

don't think this is going to work out."

LOIDA SANTOS [Diana]: I couldn't attend when they were creating the book for A CHORUS LINE because I had pneumonia. I could have been the original Diana Morales, but I never became a part of the creative process. Being ill cheated me out of the opportunity. When it finally came time for my audition, four or five months after the Broadway opening, Michael said, "I want you to play Diana, but I want you to take voice lessons for a month." He paid for them out of his own pocket so I would be prepared. He was willing to put his own money and time on the line for me. At my audition, Michael said, "I can't believe you're singing the way you are," which was a compliment because his money paid off. Michael positioned me at the end of the white line in Diana's position. When they let me know I had the part two or three weeks later, I panicked. I was the only character in the show who would be singing two songs!

ANN REINKING [Cassie]: Michael and Bob Avian called and asked if I would be interested in doing Cassie, and I said, "Yeah, absolutely." There was no problem with whether I could dance it, but Michael wanted to know if the song would work in a lower key. Donna is a soprano, and I am almost a tenor. Fran Liebergall transposed it into my key. Michael said it was fine so I went into rehearsal at City Center.

TROY GARZA: Sometimes we would hold auditions in New York for other companies, train people at the Shubert and send them out on the road. That was part of my responsibility. Oftentimes people would have to go out on the road first before we could find a spot for them in the Broadway Company, but occasionally people came straight to New York, depending on the situation.

PAM SOUSA [Cassie]: I auditioned at the time they were planning the tours. They asked me to read for Val. I didn't have a call back, nor should I have; I wasn't right. That summer I did an industrial show where I did a big solo number which Bob Avian saw, and when I got back off the road, they called immediately. "Please join the show and learn Cassie. We don't know where we'll need you, but we'll need you soon." I became a second cover on Broadway in November of 1976 and started playing Lois, as all the Cassies did.

VICKI FREDERICK [Cassie]: I would mop the stage for Michael Bennett just to be part of the show. Finally there was an audition, the mother of all auditions — and they asked me to read for Cassie. I learned a little of the opening scene and was told to come back and learn the number.

There were so many callbacks for the Cassies, with about ten of us learning it. When we were cut down to five, we were asked to perform the vocals and dance

Ron Dennis, the Original Richie

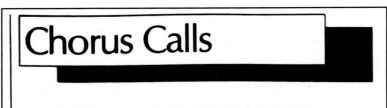

Chorus Calls

EQ. "CHORUS LINE" REPLACEMENTS

3/1 at 10 AM & 2 PM at The Shubert Theatre, 225 W. 44 St., stage door.

An Equity chorus call will be held for possible replacements for "A Chorus Line," at the Shubert Theatre, 225 W. 44 St., stage door entrance. Production contract. New York Shakespeare Festival/Joseph Papp, producer; Michael Bennett, dir. Chorus call procedures in effect.

Thurs. March 1 — Equity male dancers who sing very well at 10 AM.
Thurs. March 1 — Equity female dancers who sing very well at 2 PM.

Opposite:
Eivind Harum as Zach

individually. I'll never forget Michael teaching us the number, and especially the very last sequence backing up down the line — the handshake. His little feet were moving so fast; not even Donna's went that fast. We weren't doing enough of a contraction and Michael would shout, "Give me!" as we'd do the whole sequence pulling back on the line. Then we waited and waited. Finally I heard the news that I would be understudying and off I went to rehearsal at City Center. I really didn't have an idea which Company I would be in because Michael didn't know yet himself where he was going to put everybody.

LYNNE TAYLOR-CORBETT [Cassie]: I had done PROMISES and SEESAW and Michael liked me a great deal. But I had a dance company then and had made the decision to choreograph. I wasn't going to be a dancer anymore. But when I heard about the show and actually got called in to audition for Cassie, my resolve cracked. Everybody knew Donna would do it, but I guess they were reading people to see different qualities. And they really liked me. Michael always said to me, "I don't know what to do with you but I like you so much." I got called back but then firmly decided to focus my life in choreography.

A CHORUS LINE became an incredible hit and they called me again to be a replacement for the tour, but my story was the same. I was beginning to do very well and became more known in the dance world. Sue McNair, Michael's assistant, said, "Why don't we just let her do it when she can do it. Would you want to be the floating Cassie?" That is when the term "floating" came about. I said, "Fabulous!" There has never been a job like this and I'm not sure Equity would allow it now. Donna taught me quite a lot of the show and they told me to come to the Shubert every Friday. That was 1977. I learned Cassie, and Pam Sousa, who had been doing it on the road, was having a knee problem in Miami, so I went on there for the first time. The show was so new there weren't a lot of people old enough to play Cassie; the understudies were all in their early twenties. That's why Michael seized on this "floating" arrangement because I was someone more on their level and experience.

JANET WONG [Connie]: I was offered the job at my audition and ten minutes later, they took it back. They had wanted to send me out to Los Angeles but claimed they had made a mistake; someone else had been hired already. I don't know what really happened but I was devastated. Then they called me the next day saying I had the job after all and could I leave tomorrow for Los Angeles? At the airport, I heard my name paged. It was Peter Von Mayrhauser, the stage manager: "Don't get on the plane, you're going to do the show in New York. Lauren Kayahara is going to L.A." Meanwhile, my trunk had gone to L.A., I had given up my rent-controlled apartment, and my whole world got turned upside down.

MURPHY CROSS [Judy]: At the open call I thought for some reason I had been eliminated. I didn't hear my number and I was crying because I'd thought I was doing great. So I started leaving with my dance bag and Rick Mason came running after me, "No, no, no, you're not supposed to leave." I became so giddy and nervous; I was new to the whole process. When I came back, I saw this handsome guy at the foot of the stage. I thought it was Michael Bennett and it turned out to be Bob Avian. I had them switched in my head from the start of the audition. They asked me to learn some of Judy Turner and I got the show. I realized then that I was perfect for Judy Turner because I *was* Judy Turner at that audition.

"Signing my Broadway contract was very harried and disappointing. I was shaking when I walked out of the office, because I thought what a shame, this is supposed to be one of the glorious times in my career." — CHERYL CLARK

KATE WRIGHT [Sheila]: I went to the biggest cattle call ever on a freezing day in January. When I was on stage with the other hundred girls, I looked out into the audience and saw Bob Avian, who I mistakenly assumed was Michael Bennett. The whole day I danced to Bob Avian thinking he was Michael Bennett.

CHERYL CLARK [Cassie]: I was doing CHICAGO at the time and Bob Fosse had made me understudy to Chita Rivera. A CHORUS LINE was looking for a first replacement for Donna McKechnie and about five of us were there auditioning, including Anita Morris, Lynne Taylor-Corbett, and Vicki Frederick. The audition process was so intense; it lasted about five weeks. They finally called and said because you're so young, Michael wants to groom you. He wants to know if you will understudy Ann Reinking, who got the role to replace Donna. I was very disappointed. As much as I loved Annie, I preferred to stand by for Chita Rivera.

A few months later I got a call that they were going to premiere A CHORUS LINE in Australia. I was to be Cassie, and we were forced to sign a ten-month contract. Scott Pearson, who played Zach, and myself were the only two Americans. It was a fantastic experience. Michael asked me to replace Pam Sousa on Broadway in December 1978.

Signing my Broadway contract was very harried and disappointing. I went down to the Festival and Sue McNair called and said, "Before she signs, we want to see her do the dance again." I was very dismayed, and said, "But Michael Bennett himself called me up to come and do this." Sue was pulling a lot of attitude. I told our general manager, Bob Kamlot, "I'm here to sign my contract." I was shaking when I walked out of the office, because I thought, what a shame, this is supposed to be one of the glorious times in my career. Unfortunately, there were some very unattractive goings-on with management — not the management backstage, and certainly not the company managers.

SCOTT PEARSON [Zach]: I wanted to get to New York very badly. I had come back from Australia after a year opposite Cheryl Clark, and then went into the International Company. I began sending multiple telegrams to Sue McNair, Joe Nelson, Michael Bennett, and Bob Avian. My first telegram read, "Be the first on your block to reunite an Australian couple." At one point Michael called me and said, "I missed your telegram this week." Eivind Harum was playing Zach in New York and had been missing a lot of performances. In my second telegram I wrote, "Norwegians may be tall but Swedes are more reliable." I replaced Eivind on Broadway.

ANGELIQUE ILO [Cassie; Judy]: I had gotten the job of understudy and rehearsed for one week when they called me in for another audition and hired me as Judy. That was quite a coup.

LAURIE GAMACHE [Cassie]: In June of 1980, I was just out of college with a dance degree when the show toured through my home town of Des Moines. One of the local news stations wanted to follow one person through the audition process for a Bus & Truck tour. They got hold of my dance teacher and interviewed me beforehand at the theatre as I did each step of the

audition. I was very young, a ballerina, and danced the jazz combination very much like a ballerina, and so I got hired to play Lois for the tour. I was an understudy for about six weeks and then I played Kristine for about a year and a half.

WAYNE MELEDANDRI [Paul]: I was told by a dance captain, "When they don't know what to give someone, they just give him Larry."

WANDA RICHERT [Cassie]: I was 18 years old, living in Chicago and going to beauty school. The show was going to be coming to the city for a gala opening. The newspaper announced auditions at the Shubert Theatre. We did the whole thing everyone always talks about, the double pirouette and time step, and we learned the jazz and ballet combinations. They had me sing *At The Ballet* and said, "We'll let you know." One day, I was standing at the shampoo bowl with a lady in the sink when I got a call to join the show in L.A. I left my customer in the bowl, rushed home and became a "beauty school dropout."

DEBORAH HENRY [Cassie; Val]: There was nobody left except me at the audition. I remember how deadening the silence was standing on stage. "Well, Deborah, do you want the job?" I said, "Sure." "Well, you got it." They then said, "Oh … we forgot to ask you to dance." I did four pirouettes into the arabesque and held balance. I signed

From left:
Paul Charles as Larry;
Ken Rogers as Richie;
Rene Clemente as Paul;
Diane Fratantoni as Diana

the contract that day to replace Pamela Blair in L.A.

CYNTHIA ONRUBIA [Connie; Understudy]: I put on my padded bra, lashes, and leotards and went to the audition. We danced, they made cuts, and we sang Tricia's *I Really Need This Job* and *At the Ballet*. Clive Clerk, Baayork Lee, and Bob Avian were there. I waited outside in the hall as they took another girl in to audition. When she came out I asked, "Did you get it?" She said, "No, you did."

I was fifteen years old. They knew I was young but never asked exactly how old I was. On my first day of rehearsal, I filled out my card and thought, "I should lie about my age." But I can't lie. I'd been a member of Equity since 1969, and if I lied, it would mess up my pension and insurance. I gave my card to the stage manager the next morning and they said, "Oh my God, we've got a minor on our hands." So my mom had to get me a work permit every month.

MICHAEL GRUBER [Mike]: I had left my picture and résumé at the Shubert stage door before I went off to Alaska for a production of JOSEPH, and they called me in Alaska just before Christmas. I was going to fly directly home to Cincinnati for the holidays but wound up flying to New York for the audition instead. I first saw A CHORUS LINE as a sophomore in high school when it came through Cincinnati. Sachi Shimizu, Ron Kurowski, and Laurie Gamache were in that tour and, ironically, I ended up doing the show with them in New York.

"I was 18 years old, living in Chicago and going to beauty school. We did the whole thing, the double pirouette and time step. They had me sing At the Ballet *and said, 'We'll let you know.' One day, I was standing at the shampoo bowl with a lady in the sink when I got a call to join the show in L.A. I left my customer in the bowl, rushed home and became a 'beauty school dropout.'"* — WANDA RICHERT

Learning the Show

JEFF HAMLIN [Original Production Stage Manager]: The first workshop was predominantly a dance workshop, testing the basic idea of what the show was going to be about, and whether it had merit and could sustain itself. There were hours and hours of dance rehearsals, which I observed and noted in reams of rehearsal logs.

MICHAEL SERRECCHIA [Original Understudy]: All the stories and ninety-nine and nine tenths of the characters were compilations of our lives. James Kirkwood and Nicholas Dante had taken the transcribed tapes and loosely put them together; trying characters on the actors like suits off a rack. The first time we ran book with no dance or music — it was four and a half hours of pure tragedy! We walked out of there wanting to slit our wrists. Everybody's mother had died; it was just the worst of the worst.

But that's when the genius of Michael Bennett really kicked in. He's the world's greatest editor. From four and a half hours of solid book down to one hour and fifty-nine minutes of song, dance, visual, and book. A lot of material came and went, but everything that went flavored what stayed.

RON DENNIS: There were constant changes, along with constant ego trips from various factions. Michael gave more attention to some people than to others — that's just the way it was. Often in group rehearsals, people who were having numbers written for them were asked to rehearse privately with Ed Kleban and Marvin Hamlisch. We always knew when "teacher" was coming in to get the "A" student. The rest of us stood around saying, "Okay, when's my turn coming?"

We were told that this was an ensemble company and we were all going to be treated as individuals, yet special as a group. What really turned the company's head was when Pam Blair came into rehearsal one day and announced that Donna McKechnie was getting more money than anybody else, after being told that we were all on favored-nations contracts. That caused a big rift in the cohesiveness of our company, and that wound never really quite got healed. It was a bit unfair that it was done and the way it came to be known to the rest of us. We didn't blame Donna at all. She had been Michael's darling for a couple of other shows. I totally understood why he was pushing her to the forefront. But the money thing just didn't seem fair. We were lied to.

KAY COLE [Original Maggie]: I'm told my high E at the end of *Ballet* became known as the "money note." That was mine, it was created for me. I remember Marvin saying, "We can keep going." And it just kept soaring and soaring. "Oh, she can sing that? Let's try this ..." The note naturally lives in me, because of the passion of the piece and whom I'm talking about. It was not hard for me to sing that note eight shows a week because it lives there.

BRADLEY JONES [Greg]: I remember T. Michael Reed saying to us, "Take your scripts, get a pencil and write down, I NEED THIS JOB ... I WANT THIS JOB at the top of the first page." He was trying to keep that urgency in the rehearsal period so we would hold on to it on stage.

KATE WRIGHT: Kelly Bishop was really sweet to me and said, "I will give you plenty of notice when I am out." Needless to say, something happened between shows one matinee day and management calls me at dinner and says, "You're on." If I hadn't had Thommie Walsh standing on the line beside me, I would have fallen

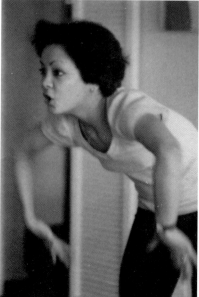

*Troy Garza teaching
Cynthia Onrubia*

LOIDA SANTOS: When it came to singing, I freaked. Especially in *What I Did For Love*. As the orchestra played the intro, I would find my note and hum it until I had to start singing. I tortured myself every night for as long as I worked on that show, because singing was not natural for me.

ROBIN LYON [Understudy]: I was a leader and a team player. At one point the Company was very bad vocally, and I started coaching them.

apart. He was always so wonderful. Although Kelly was going to be leaving soon, Thommie wanted her replacement to be as good as possible. He was very nurturing. The "Sheila/Bobby" relationship was so much a part of him, he wanted to make it work. He gave me everything: subtext, moment-to-moment things. Bobby LuPone and I used to have little sessions where he would talk to me about Zach and Sheila. He was great, too.

CYNTHIA ONRUBIA: Baayork sat me down one day and said, "Tell me about Maggie." It's good I had already started to think about subtext. Baayork went right to that level.

JANET WONG: During my very first performance, in the opening just before *Resume*, I remember lifting up my picture, and all of a sudden I hear this rumbling next to me. I was terrified. Then I realized that Michael Serrecchia, who was on as Greg for Justin Ross, was chanting! I'm sure my picture was shaking, it sent me over the edge and threw me. There were some friendly nudges to get me in the right place that night.

KERRY CASSERLY [Kristine]: Even with two weeks rehearsal, there is no way to be ready for A CHORUS LINE. Suddenly you're in a grid of numbers and wing space with people that want things a particular way.

DEBORAH HENRY: When I was learning the show, they said, "We want you to know your numbers right away." They would turn all of the lights out in the Shubert. I'd make my move in a black-out. And they would flip the lights back on to make sure I was right on the number and not a half an inch off.

LAURIE GAMACHE: Until you're out there with the lights in your face, it's not the same. There are so many things to know about the show that you just have to perform it to feel comfortable. I wouldn't have felt any more ready if I'd had two more weeks of rehearsal. At the time, I was blissfully unaware. I knew my marks, my notes — and I did the show like that! It took about ten years to figure out how to really do it and what the show actually means.

KERRY CASSERLY: They taught us every finger movement, hand gesture — exactly what to do. We would practice the name section forever, where Zach says, "Start with your name and step forward." "That's too far ... that's not far enough ... come on again ..." It would take hours to practice names at rehearsals.

KEITH BERNARDO [Don]: My one "put-in" rehearsal was the most nerve-wracking experience imaginable. It was at 7:00 p.m., only an hour before curtain. I was introduced, "This is the new Don Kerr,"

and then you go from cue to cue to cue. The first time I did the show fully with the company was my opening night.

MICHAEL GRUBER: When I was in the show, the whole thing was "just be you." They were really hip on that and tried to come from a truthful place. I missed the mind trips, that whole era, thank God.

ANTHONY INNEO [Zach]: Everyone on the line was told to look at a blue light underneath the mezzanine, as the "Zach spot."

KEVIN McCREADY [Larry; Al]: Michael was a short man, and his choreography was down. He always wanted everything low. For me, being six feet tall, I like to dance up and balletic. Dancing in the show was definitely harder for a taller person.

Character Interpretation

Kerry Casserly as Kristine

LAURIE GAMACHE: Michael manipulated the original dancers to do great things; he kept them on the edge of their abilities all the time.

Ten years later there wasn't anything on file or tape to teach me how to play Kristine, how to be nervous her way. Nobody ever said, "You are going to forget what you're talking about three times. The first time you forget, you kind of pause for a second and Al tells you; you remember and go right on. The second time you struggle a little bit longer; the third time you really can't find it — Al jumps in — and you go YES!" I figured that out by watching it night after night and doing it over and over again. There's a formula, a way to make that funny. Nobody ever said, "It is because you're thinking ..." I never heard anyone coach that way. You just made it up and if you were an actress, eventually the point would become clear to you. All those years there were people with more of a dance captain mentality directing the show than people with a director/actor mentality.

ANTHONY INNEO: I wasn't told "This is the way you say it, this is how you move," which is how everything usually was done at A CHORUS LINE. I was left alone, and created the Zach I saw. I orchestrated him from beginning to middle to end knowing where I wanted him to go, knowing he's ultimately the villain of the piece because he controls their lives.

WAYNE MELEDANDRI: I was given the freedom to find the part of Paul for myself and that was a real gift to me. I had my own vision of the piece. I wanted to present that character differently than anybody else had. No one showed me how Paul was supposed to fall. I've seen every Paul do it differently. I did it on the hop, hop, turn. I think it's finding what is safest for the individual. I would fall on the fleshy part of my thigh and actually my hand would go first.

DIANE FRATANTONI [Diana; Understudy]: Michael gave people line readings. He didn't know how to get something out of someone without either terrorizing them or mimicking what he wanted. He would do it for you and then you had to do it for him. It wasn't the ideal situation.

MURPHY CROSS: I remember Michael working with Ron Kurowski; he would give him comedian-type notes. He would say, "That Jack Benny beat" or "Rodney Dangerfield thing." He used to give Ron comedian-name beats for his Bobby monologue, because Ron used to do that sort of

Photo by Herb Migdoll

Jack Benny take when he'd turn his head real slow.

ANGELIQUE ILO: Playing Judy Turner was fun because I could never go wrong. I found a comedic side of myself which I didn't know existed. Everyone always said you have to do it exactly the way it was done before but I really don't believe that at all. I pulled a lot of stuff. They never held back my reins as long as I stayed within the framework.

BRADLEY JONES: Michael was very generous to me. I once did something differently in the Greg monologue at rehearsal and Bob Avian said, "No, that's not the way it's done, you've got to do it another way." But Michael said to Bob, "No, no, no ... that's his. Let him do that." Michael didn't usually say that, because the show was a machine, and we all had to fit the mold.

RON STAFFORD [Bobby]: T. Michael Reed influenced me the most. We were in Boston, I had only been playing Bobby for a few weeks, and I was having a hard time with the part. I always thought: this is a well written script, all I have to do is say the lines and the audience is going to laugh. It wasn't the case at all. I thought, "I'm dying out here ... I'm not funny." T. Michael got together with me after the show one evening and he directed me. I started to get better and better and by the time I got to New York, I felt comfortable doing it.

MURPHY CROSS: I didn't exactly know how to get all the laughs in the Val monologue until I was lucky enough to work alone with Michael for about an hour. He was Val, his little hip down in the Val pose, with that attitude. He showed me the dynamics, spelled out the rhythms, rises, and falls and launched into her with a passion and zest. It must have been the best acting class I ever had. I was so blessed to have that time alone with him.

Photo by Herb Migdoll

Above: Broadway's second Sheila, Kate Wright, and Ron Stafford as Bobby. Ron later became assistant stage manager of the Broadway Company.

Left: Lois Englund as Val

Broadway's second Paul, George Pesaturo

LAURIE GAMACHE: If they gave us any leeway, I didn't know it. I wasn't aware of it. Judy Turner always did the same thing, "23" with an up-inflection on the 3. So that's what I did and it never occurred to me to say it with a different inflection. Coming from a dance background and not an acting background, the first thing I did was copy what I saw. It took me a long time to realize I could do whatever I wanted and it still would be Judy if I was being Judy. Management was very specific. They said your hand goes up here, you go like this, you run over here, you do this. But they never told me how or why. They never gave such specific motivations. I had to do that myself.

LOIS ENGLUND [Val]: There was a period when I could do no wrong. And there was a time when I couldn't roll my eyes without Michael telling me I was totally all wrong on stage.

TROY GARZA: Bob Avian was always interested in the show having integrity, but his presence was missed a lot. He would watch the show occasionally. I recall one night he gave such wonderful notes to the Broadway cast after the show. They were all enthralled and the next few performances were just fantastic. But that's what a show needs. They could get precisely the same words from the stage manager or dance captain but when the director comes in, or Bob, who was pretty much synonymous with Michael Bennett in this case, then people respond. They are hungry for that authority.

BRADLEY JONES: Gregory Gardner is compensating for his not very good looks. He's insecure and that's why he is so grand. He is a sad person looking for love and self-esteem. He's been around, and he can see himself and his desires in these younger people, like Mark. I played him as a thirty-two-year-old, so he can see his younger self in all these people. That's why he can say, "Life, darlings, it's tough all over. That's why I have no plans, no alternatives." So many Gregs just blew that off, but it is "Just get me through the day." I've drunk and drugged and had sex. I've been through it all. Now it's not about that, it's about growing up and relinquishing some of that nonsense.

JUSTIN ROSS [Greg]: It wasn't until I went back into the show for a two-week stint before it closed that I was the right age to play Gregory Gardner. And it wasn't until that time that I truly understood who Gregory is, and could honestly say, "Just get me through the day." I usually got my laughs, but never served him as well as when I was really able to understand him, to have lived and been up and down.

CLIVE WILSON: Playing Larry, starting the show and taking the pictures from the kids, was always a very intimate time for

me. The eye contact sometimes was about offstage events, someone I may have had a fight with, a friend I may have had a quarrel with; there were so many dynamics. When somebody was going on for the first time, I could convey assurance to them. I had these moments that sometimes had nothing to do with the show.

ANTHONY INNEO: I never left the back of the house during the Cassie dance. That was my food. Michael once told me, "The movie is on the stage." Michael explained that when Cassie is in her spot and moves back toward the mirror to dance and the lights change into an "internal," she never really leaves that spot. The "internal" is Zach's creation. It's not Cassie's. He imagines how she danced, he remembers her as a fabulous dancer. She's his invention, which is what made it so difficult for him to deal with her. It's almost like a flashback. I started looking at it as the movie, and I saw it. It's amazing. Michael made it very clear you should never see Zach.

WAYNE MELEDANDRI: The show is almost set up for Paul's monologue. What other show allows an actor to be by himself, for ten minutes, seven of which is monologue, on a bare stage in total control of the audience, without the use of music or dance? In musical theatre that just never comes along and in straight drama, rarely, unless it is Shakespeare.

KEITH BERNARDO: There was always the feeling of never knowing who was going to be canned next. They wanted it that way because it kept the show a little desperate. Playing it on the edge all the time, although not good for your digestive system, was great for the show.

Mr. & Mrs. Loida Iglesias

MICHAEL WHITE

REQUESTS THE PLEASURE OF YOUR COMPANY

AT A PARTY

FOLLOWING THE FIRST NIGHT OF

A CHORUS LINE

ON THURSDAY, 22ND JULY, 1976

AT THE LYCEUM, WELLINGTON STREET

LONDON, W.C.2.

Supper 9.45 p.m.
& Dancing

R.S.V.P. 13 Duke Street,

On the Road

ANN REINKING: It was mandatory that the National and International Companies be excellent. We were the first to go out into the world to represent the show. Michael worked with everybody one on one.

JANE SUMMERHAYS [Sheila]: The thing I will never forget about doing the show in London is the raked stage. We had many, many injuries. We had performances where the entire understudy cast was on, there were so many disasters. In the first dance section of the opening combination, when we go forward, I nearly went into the pit. Doing the double pirouette was impossible for us until we got used to the stage. Your whole center of balance shifted.

RON STAFFORD: In London, just to do the ballet back-up required so much effort. We were walking uphill backwards.

JANE SUMMERHAYS: Petra Siniawski, a Cassie replacement in London, couldn't sing the role, so they dreamed up the Cassie chorus. Offstage singers would back her up vocally during *The Music and the Mirror*. One thing they had to reinforce was keeping our American accents. We would slip into a British accent without even knowing it.

SCOTT ALLEN: I went into the National Company for three months in Los Angeles. It was like a concentration camp — horrendous. The stage managers were dictators. The second assistant stage manager sat stage right with a stop watch every night and timed the length of scenes. It just wasn't pleasant. There was a lot of hostility. The International Company was a world of difference. The great thing was they were their own company; they weren't a mixed breed.

TROY GARZA: Some people preferred being on the road because the money was better, some people went on the road because they had no choice and just wanted to do the show. Sometimes the road companies were not good and at other times they were great. There was so much flux in the casts all the time that I think the quality of the show varied to a considerable degree throughout 1977-1983.

MURPHY CROSS: The stage managers were pretty good at keeping the show intact. Martin Herzer, on the road, was great at keeping it from becoming THE GONG SHOW.

SCOTT PEARSON: I had been with the Original Company in California for a year playing Bobby and covering Zach, which I

had eyes for all the time. I originally got the job without auditioning because Michael knew my work. But when I moved from Bobby in L.A. to Zach in Australia, I had to audition and prove myself. In fact, Michael showed up in Australia to direct us after his divorce from Donna. He needed some time to himself, and he chose to take it in Australia with us.

DONN SIMIONE [Al; Larry; Understudy]: If Michael didn't like a person in a certain role on the road, he would tell them to take the night off on an opening night and bring someone in.

DEBORAH HENRY: I premiered A CHORUS LINE all over the United States. It was the golden glory days and I was Cassie. Michael knew I was adaptable and got along with people. I'm great under stress. I think that I was well liked, not bolting in with a fur coat saying, "Excuse me, I'm Cassie tonight." When I would arrive at a Company I always made sure to figure out what was going on and make things comfortable, and let it be known that I'm not there to take somebody's position. I was there for someone who just downright needed a break or was on vacation. It was never removing a girl off-stage and putting me on. It was never that way with me.

PAM SOUSA: When Michael first sent me on the road, he said, "You must play the 'star' for me." It was difficult, but he didn't want me to socialize with the company. In the show, most of the characters don't know Cassie personally and Michael thought it would subconsciously be best if

The International Company, featuring, from left: Ronald Young, Jean Fraser, Troy Garza, Mark Dovey, Sandy Roveta, Jane Summerhays, Ron Kurowski, Miriam Welch, Yvette Matthews, and Wellington Perkins

they did not know me offstage either. He liked his Cassies and wanted them to be the "stars" of his show.

WANDA RICHERT: On the road, because I was Cassie, I got all the attention.

BRADLEY JONES: The fear of Michael was sort of passed down to you from the companies. You'd hear that if he didn't like the way you walked down the hall-way, you were fired, which wasn't true. He was putting together what he called a premier company to play ninety-three cities in nine months. We had to be young and energetic, and I really believe he cared.

WANDA RICHERT: When I was on the road, we sat in places for long periods of time. We were able to have apartments. It was a life.

LAURIE GAMACHE: When we started the Bus & Truck Company, Michael wanted it to be different. Michael updated some of the dialogue and Theoni made changes in the costumes. She gave us brighter colors and higher cut legs on leotards. Instead of wool, she put all the guys in milliskin jazz pants — which turned out to be a fiasco. When we were touring in the midwest, it was hard enough for the audience to see a bunch of people in tights and leotards, but to have that down-light on us, standing on the line, with the audience staring at everyone's genitals all night was just too much. So they went back to the other pants. At the time I joined the company, we updated the character birthdates too. The show was supposed to take place in the present, but in later years they went back to saying it takes place in 1975. But at the time they updated the show, they wanted it to be

more '80s. Instead of saying a character was born in 1945, they would say 1955, because it was almost ten years later. The characters would still be the age they were supposed to be while keeping the time frame in the present. The references changed accordingly. Instead of Judy Turner saying, "I want to be the next Gwen Verdon," she said "the next Ann Reinking." Val used Sandy Duncan instead of June Allyson in her bit. They also changed Steve McQueen to Roger Moore because Steve McQueen had died.

The first replacement cast on Broadway was often referred to as "The 'New' New York Company"

In and Out of the Show

MICHAEL SERRECCHIA: Living through the infiltration of the second cast, we were getting farther from the spirit of the original. We were more and more becoming part of a mega-money-making machine. I rationalized a lot. Looking back, if I could improve my A CHORUS LINE experience, I would have left before we moved to Broadway. When the second cast came in, they were very excited but the Originals that remained weren't because their family was breaking up. It was like going through a divorce and winding up with the in-laws.

I bought a gift for every one of the new people and put it on their dressing room tables with a note that said, "Welcome to the New Chorus Line Experience." We were all dealing with the breakup differently and saying goodbye to our friends. All of the understudies stayed in New York. There we were, training the new people we were trying to be supportive of. I had to teach the roles to new people so I could cover for them. There was a big wad of pride to swallow there. Something you felt entitled to do, but the reality was that you weren't doing it. I made my decision to stay. I was going to make it pleasant and positive and try to recreate some of that wonderful feeling that I got for the new people.

SCOTT ALLEN: I certainly don't think there was animosity toward new people coming in, but there was an unevenness that happened. It wasn't fun or enjoyable to do. Too many people not bothering to dance, not bothering to warm up, not bothering to put themselves into what the show was. There was so much attitude going on, people were suddenly "stars." It wasn't about the show, it was about serving the individual. Most of the Originals that stayed really worked on the show and kept the integrity, Thommie Walsh especially. I really admired him.

PETER VON MAYRHAUSER [Stage Manager]: Michael said very clearly that we have to use what these new people have to offer. When new people brought in something within that very tight structure that was A CHORUS LINE, then it would work. Even on an off day, which was rare, the show never fell apart because it was so tightly knit.

JUSTIN ROSS: Being in the "New, New York Company," the expectation level was very high. Of the Original Cast who stayed in New York, there were people who reached out to us and those that didn't. Certain personalities were more generous than others. Ultimately, everybody became friends. It may have taken a few of them some adjusting, but it worked out to be a very nice environment.

ANN REINKING: Michael had almost an entirely new New York Company, with most of the Originals going to California. We were being treated, and being received, as an original cast. We were re-reviewed and because it had not been open that long, people who were coming to see

Gay Marshall as Diana

Photo by Ron Scherl

21

it were still unbelievably enthusiastic. It was really the first time I was one of the principal parts in a show that was obviously a monumental hit. It was a good learning and growing experience. The Cassie dance is very hard and long and because of that, it keeps you honest. I had to really stay true to myself and be fit. I could enjoy all the wonderful perks that were happening, but there was no way I could buy into them.

KAY COLE: The Originals were supportive of new cast members. New blood is always exciting; it completely puts a different turn on it. Charlene Ryan's Sheila certainly gave *At the Ballet* a different take, a different energy. It was very exciting, and we were all thrilled to be going to L.A. And the newcomers were so grateful

to have gotten through the amazing audition process and gotten the job.

RON DENNIS: In California, there were enough of us as a unit from the Original Cast that we knew what the show was supposed to be. The new people molded themselves around *our* energy. We were the nucleus. I gather the Originals who remained in New York had a harder time, because it was less of them and more new people. We had a breeze.

SCOTT PEARSON: When Michael brought me into the New York Company he said, "I need to rotate the Zachs and I want you here. You deserve to be here, you've done your time on the road, but you won't be here forever. I'll let you know when it's time to leave." Companies

kept intermingling to keep the actors on their toes. You've got to keep changing people, otherwise it gets too complacent; it needs that edge. Zach paces the show. The way he reacts to what is said on stage sets the tone. Always has and always will. I would move from company to company. I was with the Broadway Company maybe five or six times.

JANET WONG: When I first came into the show, I remember Thommie Walsh saying, "Welcome to the Factory."

VICKI FREDERICK: Bob Fosse felt like we were all abandoning him. He was not happy about it, but I think he expected it. A CHORUS LINE was the hit show. Management at PIPPIN had even talked with Michael about staggering us as we

From left:
Vicki Frederick,
Loida Santos,
Pam Sousa

Photo by Herb Migdoll

Photo by Troy Garza

Photo by Troy Garza

left, so as not to lose us all at once. Michael took me, Kate Wright, Justin Ross, Mitzi Hamilton, Chris Chadman, Pam Sousa, and Patti D'Beck. Fosse lost a big group of dancers. The thing that always got Bob was when people would say, "I love you, Bob Fosse, and your show, A CHORUS LINE." It would really irk him.

ANN REINKING: I think Bob Fosse took it as a compliment that Michael picked his people for A CHORUS LINE. Practically everyone Bob touched went on to higher levels. If you worked for Bob, it was a great calling card. It meant you were a good dancer, intelligent, and talented. Even if you couldn't sing, you had the intelligence to make a number work. He was very flattered, and proud of all of us. He thought the show was well structured and saw me play Cassie several times.

DEBORAH GEFFNER [Kristine]: Bob was really annoyed everyone was making such a big fuss out of all these dancers standing around whining. When he had DANCIN' running, he'd say, "Over there they talk about dancing. Here we dance."

KATE WRIGHT: Sometimes it was difficult having people come into the Broadway Company from the road companies, because they had a different style of doing the show. They played huge theatres and therefore sometimes gave huge performances and it wouldn't match. I never did go out with a road company and I think I missed something. It would have given me a little bit more tolerance for some of the new performances. Because if you came to New York and joined the show, you'd get judged by that line. Until you fit in and got all your notes and molded your performance to the New York Company, it could be pretty brutal.

LAURIE GAMACHE: When we were on the road, we had to live up to the standards of Broadway excellence. But then at the same time, I heard stories about the creative staff telling the Broadway Company, "We have this young group of kids on the road doing the show with more energy, more commitment than you." So on one hand we're getting, "Live up to Broadway standards," and the New York people were getting, "Get up off your ass, the kids on the road are more enthusiastic than you." I wanted to be as good as the Broadway people because I always thought someday I would be one of them. That's the plan, that's where you put your head. If you're going to do this, they're going to see that you're good enough and whisk you to New York. After about nine months, the understudies had to sign six-month riders, and the line people had to sign nine-month riders. About this time, one of the understudies from our road company was put into the Broadway cast. Then all of a sudden, everyone felt that at any moment any one

Photo by Herb Migdoll

Broadway's second Val, Barbara Monte-Britton

*Betty Lynd
(crouched),
Pam Sousa,
Jane Summerhays,
and Jeff Hyslop
(standing)*

of us could be on Broadway and be a star. So we all signed our contracts for another six months.

LOIDA SANTOS: I was in London only about a month or two before I got sick and had to come home. A couple of days before I was to head back to rejoin the International Company in London, Michael called me and said, "You're not leaving, you're replacing Carole Schweid as Diana on Broadway." Unfortunately, nobody told Carole she was being fired. I was upset because they were hiding me. They had me come to the theatre, but, "Don't come until after curtain." It was strange. I didn't want her to think I was taking it away from her. It was so deceiving.

DIANE FRATANTONI: They called me a number of times over the years to come back as Diana and I always said no. But I did go back for three months, right before the show closed. It was hard. I had to relearn things. I felt I had done good work in the show before, but I really wasn't pleased with what I was doing then. I was glad I didn't close the show. I didn't want all that hoopla.

DEBORAH HENRY: I used to go back and forth, switching from playing Val to Cassie. I understood them both: Valerie externalized things Cassie felt inside and vice versa. It was no problem going from role to role. The problem I had was the

transition of my friends. That was the hardest part. Because I was still Debbie, just the color of my costume changed.

But people changed and it was very lonely for a while. They thought because I was Cassie, I was really busy and had plans, when I was just sitting in my hotel room. I'd hear all of the groups of kids going out after the show. No one asked me to go anywhere.

GAY MARSHALL [Diana]: I had it set up where I could come and go within a certain framework. I couldn't just take two nights off, but I could work three months, and go away three months. They always sent me out to open a city if they weren't sure of their Diana. I would play the show the night it was being reviewed and then come back to Broadway. You don't know these people in the other company and there's so many people on that stage. But everyone is a plotted point on a piece of graph paper. If everyone did their job right, no one got stepped on.

FRASER ELLIS [Understudy]: Anyone who knew the role could come in to the show, never having rehearsed with that company, and just go on. There was never traffic; they had it down to a science. The masonite panels on stage had the numbers. There were charts for each character, grids showing you where to go. In the Bus & Truck Company, we would have to adapt to old vaudeville houses where

there was no space. Sometimes we had literally eight feet from the line to the mirror, so we had to compact it all, and adjust. On the other hand, at the MUNY, which is huge, they tried to double the grid. We could have done five grids of the stage because it was so large. We felt like little tiny ants running around with party lights strung up.

ANGELIQUE ILO: The last time I went into the New York Company in May of 1988, I called and asked if they needed a Judy. I didn't want to do Cassie again. I had just had two kids and I really needed a job. So they called me in. Now it seems so difficult to get into a show, but A CHORUS LINE made it so simple.

PAM SOUSA: When I came back to the show, there was a spirit that was lost. Michael said to me when I first left the show, "I understand, because you shouldn't do something more than two years. It's very difficult to be fresh and I don't want you to go, but I understand and I think it's good for you." I think he really respected my leaving. So when I came back, I felt a dullness about it, kind of going by the numbers. But it was a different group of people on the line and I loved that, because as Cassie, I knew in my heart, Cassie knows Val, Sheila, Bobby. I don't know this person. I come in knowing those elements, and with different people playing them, it was great fun.

ANTHONY INNEO: I would never say yes. I would always say why and continually found it difficult accepting notes from a dance captain. As the years went on, the dance captains literally ran the show. They were more important than the stage managers. They extended themselves and went into the acting notes. And when a dance captain gives me acting notes, it's trouble! It got to the point where I said, "This is the way Michael said I can do it," and that shut them up. Whenever I was fired, which was two or three times, Michael would always call me back and give me a raise.

KERRY CASSERLY: There were always a lot of sad goodbye parties with people saying, "Oh, so what, it happens to everyone." And sure enough, they would be back in the Broadway Company before you knew it. We wasted so many tears. Just about everybody that was fired was re-hired.

DEBORAH GEFFNER: It was an A CHORUS LINE experience to be fired by Michael; it was just part of the A CHORUS LINE thing.

GAY MARSHALL: When I gave my notice, Michael came walking into the theatre with this fabulous burgundy fedora hat and said, "I hear you are leaving." I said, "Can I have that hat?" "What do you want to stay? I will give you any-

thing you want." "Okay, more money." "Except money." I had heard some people were making fabulous money. The Cassies, Zachs, always. They told me the cut-off for Diana was a grand. "No Diana ever made more than a grand, we can't start with you." I stayed, but the deal was I could leave whenever I wanted and come back, just give a little notice. And I got the hat!

DEBORAH HENRY: I gave my notice just to be able to take a break. I hadn't had a vacation in three years. But Michael said, "You can't do this, please come to New York. There's no spot for Cassie right now, but would you like to do Valerie Clark on Broadway?" There was all this hoopla as if I was stepping down to play Val, but it didn't make any difference. I was so fond of Valerie Clark. And to do it on Broadway! I had been in a red girdle for such a long time. To hang it up and let it all just hang out was a great feeling.

Val was really open and out there and I felt refreshed. During the time I was on Broadway as Val, I would go off to do Cassie somewhere on the road. And later, when I was playing Cassie on Broadway, I'd get a call from Michael, "We are opening in Nashville for the first time, you are the only Valerie Clark that can get by saying 'fuck'." I went out for opening night, everyone was happy and they'd send me back to do Broadway as Cassie.

ANN REINKING: I left the show because Bob Fosse had asked me to replace Gwen Verdon in CHICAGO. I wanted to try something else. I had spent five or six months with the Broadway Company and a couple of months in Los Angeles.

If they had asked me, I probably would have considered going back to A CHORUS LINE. But I was just fortunate at that time to be working, one project after the other. I don't think anybody thought about it, including myself. I wasn't that available.

WAYNE MELEDANDRI: How do you leave something that has given you so much and you've given so much to? It was such a wonderful place. I couldn't just say that's enough, I have to go. Yet it was my choice to leave. On a deeper level, I had to create things wrong with it to make it easier for me to go. And on a practical level, it was hard to leave the paycheck.

JANET WONG: I composed my notice before I decided to give it. I wrote, "After three and a half years of not getting the job, I have decided to stop coming to the audition." People asked me if I was leaving for something, and I said "Yes ... my life." I was really tired of doing it, I wasn't happy. I had been in it too long, it had gotten tedious and I just wasn't enjoying it.

KEVIN McCREADY: People would just go in and do the show; they had their own lives. It wasn't a company that went out together, or a full camaraderie thing. Through the run of the show, some people became jaded, or not as appreciative of what they were doing. Some lost the perspective that even though they were doing the show night after night, there were people in the audience seeing it for the first time.

PAM SOUSA: Those last months before the Gala, it was becoming a job. That was bothering me because I never did it as a job. It was always a love experience. It was time to go.

PETER VON MAYRHAUSER: In September 1978, I said, "I've had enough, this is too much for me." It was over two and a half years, and it was time for me to go. I was offered a Mike Nichols show, which I was thrilled about. Tom Porter was stage managing the Chicago Company and they offered him the job to replace me. He said, "Are you crazy? This show is going to run forever. You won't need another job the rest of your life." I said, "That's what I'm worried about. I'll be an old man and will have done one show." Tom came in, and stayed until it closed. Other than a brief two or three month period with Joe Calvan, it was just Jeff Hamlin, me, and Tom Porter who stage managed A CHORUS LINE on Broadway.

LYNNE TAYLOR-CORBETT: I loved doing it, but I had gotten everything from it. I didn't suffer any of the awful stuff the others did. I got that pizzazz and that moment of being part of a wonderful thing. Some people made careers out of the show. You never knew if you should stay or go. There's no way to know. Some of them stayed way too long. But if there was no other great show to go into, what were you going to do?

Photo by Herb Migdoll

From left: Murphy Cross, Wellington Perkins, Steve Baumann, and Christine Barker

Understudies

SCOTT ALLEN: There wasn't time set aside for the Original Understudies, so we worked by ourselves a lot. I don't think there was one of us who didn't know our stuff. We worked at proving ourselves to everybody. When we moved uptown, all the understudy dressing rooms were downstairs. The separation between what we called "upstairs" and "downstairs" grew that much greater. But we played our own mind games on those people too.

MICHAEL SERRECCHIA: It was truly the glory days in the workshop. Everyone was treated equally, everyone was important. We were dependent upon one another and drew upon each other for support. A CHORUS LINE peaked at the Public Theatre; every aspect of it was perfect. It was pure creative energy directed by a man who was a genius orchestrator. Each of us equally felt the excitement, glory and thrill. There was no derision and no divisions.

When the show moved uptown, there was a split between the camaraderie of the understudies and those on the stage. There was one rehearsal, shortly before the Tony® Awards, when things had got-

ten unpretty. We were there for notes, sitting in the house of the Shubert. Michael was addressing the issue of the stress and tension between some of the understudies and some of the people on the line. He said, "Just look at you, look at how you're sitting"; the understudies sat on one side of the aisle and the people on the line sat on the other. He said, "Just let me walk this line, let me walk this true chorus line," and he did a grand parade up and down the aisle with his arms completely outstretched from his body. He chewed on everyone about that. Yet so much of what he and the new management did fed that conflict. I think Michael wanted a quick fix to a problem that was upsetting the apple cart. I personally felt there was more tension and more strife between the people on the line amongst themselves after moving uptown than there was between the understudies and the line.

TRISH GARLAND [Original Judy]: It was harder on the Original Understudies than it ever was for us. Personally, I was oblivious to a lot of the pain they went through because I was young and not really compassionate. They have a different story than we do. A lot of people got hurt, but I don't think any of it was intentional. It was just our youth.

LAURIE GAMACHE: You made a little bit more each week for every role you covered. If you went on, you made an eighth of your salary on top. Just being a Cassie cover, I made an extra $33 a week. But if I went on as Cassie, I would make an eighth of my salary. If I did a whole week, I'd make a double salary. Sometimes an understudy would make more than the actors they covered. You could be a Judy or Kristine making minimum, but if I was the understudy covering Judy, Bebe, Kristine, Sheila, and Cassie, then I'm making an extra $150 per week, a considerably larger salary than the girls I was covering. That also made it financially difficult if you were an understudy and they offered you a small role. It didn't always behoove you to take a line job when it was offered.

ROBIN LYON: They offered me Maggie and Bebe frequently, but I never took either one. I made too much money as an understudy and I enjoyed playing different roles.

MICHAEL SERRECCHIA: All the Original Understudies aspired to be on the line. We were actually told, "As soon as this gets off the ground and we do companies, then you're going to hit the line." Well, most of us never did. We were just too valuable as

Original Judy, Trish Garland

Photo by Cliff Lipson

understudies. It was so much easier to find three carbon copies of one original for the new companies being mounted than it was to find a carbon copy of someone like me who would have to cover three roles. It was disappointing, of course, and there was resentment because we felt slighted. But it was always, "You're wonderful, you're valuable."

DIANE FRATANTONI: That "valuable stuff" is true to a certain point, but what I ultimately felt was if they really, really wanted you to do a role, they put you in a role.

FRASER ELLIS: There were unofficial "first covers" for certain roles. Tom Porter would always tell you the week before if someone was going on vacation, so you could prepare for it. But sometimes you

never knew. I was never out, mainly because I was always terrified of calling in. I could just hear Tom asking, "What seems to be the problem?" and having to explain. It was just easier to go to work.

KAREN ZIEMBA [Bebe; Understudy]: When I stood by early on, it was usually for Cassie or Diana for a few days or a week at a time. I really take my hat off to swings; it's a lot of frustrating work. When you do go on, you don't have a chance to be confident because you're so busy not running into somebody. It's nerve-wracking, and probably the most difficult job in the theatre.

CYNTHIA ONRUBIA: Everyone should be an understudy or swing just once because it teaches you something about observation and about people around you.

There's nothing worse than doing a show and thinking, "Oh, you're behind me, I never knew that." When you understudy or cover, you have to know; it's very good training.

MICHAEL SERRECCHIA: In retrospect, I would not have exchanged my position in that piece of history for anything because I felt, as an actor, I had the best of all worlds. I got to give the audition as one character, win the audition as another character, and lose the audition as yet another character and each character was very different than the others.

ANTHONY INNEO: On Broadway, I absolutely refused to cover anyone but Zach. I said, "I'm not going on in the opening number, I don't do any of that." Michael was the only one that okayed the

A rare photograph of all the Original Understudies on the line, from left: John Mineo, Donna Drake, Carolyn Kirsch, Michael Serrecchia, Crissy Wilzak, Scott Allen, Brandt Edwards, Chuck Cissel, and Carole Schweid

Photo courtesy Scott Allen

Understudy John Mineo played Al opposite Deborah Geffner's Kristine for almost a year. "He wouldn't accept the part because he made twice the bucks as an understudy." — Deborah Geffner (Karen Jablons and Paul Charles in background)

Photo by Sunny Bak

Zachs and Cassies. Anyone else could get hired and fired by the dance captain, stage manager, or Bob Avian. So when I played Zach, I knew it was Michael who said yes.

Unfortunately, the way they conducted themselves wasn't pleasant. Kurt Johnson, who had been playing the role, went on vacation, and they asked me if I would like to take over the role. I said to Bob Kamlot, "Why, is Kurt leaving?" "No, we're going to let him go." I looked at Bob, and said, "You're going to call him and say don't come back when he's on vacation? This is cruel. I don't know if I can answer you now." I had to tell myself this is none of my business, if the job is open and it's offered, it's what I want. So I said yes.

DEBORAH GEFFNER: There were all these standbys just dying to get on the line. I wasn't even in the show yet as a standby, and they offered me Kristine. It was fun and you got free Vidal Sassoon haircuts.

VICKI FREDERICK: I was Lois Dilettante. I just absolutely gritted my teeth every time I put on those goddamn pink tights, with that goddamn little scarf and ballet slippers.

CYNTHIA ONRUBIA: As Tricia, I always had my Connie leotard and shoes and Bebe, Diana, and Maggie tops in my dance bag, so if I had to go on I could change in the wings.

BILL JONES [Dresser]: One night, we had two or three people on vacation, and a flu epidemic hit the company. All the understudies were on as line characters and there was no one to cut in the opening. Troy Garza, the dance captain, went on as "headband." Zach read off the numbers of the characters to stay, and everyone got in line, except Troy. It made no sense whatsoever. No girls were cut; they were all on the line.

BETTY LYND [Understudy]: Once in London, I was Maggie and Connie combined in one performance. Back then, the understudy coverage wasn't as doubled as it eventually got to be. If Connie and Maggie were both out, management had to choose where to put that one understudy. I didn't play Connie. I came out as Maggie but said Connie's lines of doing KING AND I when I was five and wanting to be a prima ballerina.

ROBIN LYON: I had just joined the company and learned Maggie and Diana when the company manager said, "You're going on for Bebe tonight." I hadn't even done a performance yet and I said, "I don't know the role, the blocking." I panicked but did the show and kept running into people. In the "bah dahs" of the *Montage*, when everyone is facing upstage, I faced downstage. People were pushing me, pulling me, throwing me, kicking me. This was my professional debut.

Photos by Herb Migdoll

"In the 'bah dahs' of the Montage, *when everyone is facing upstage, I faced downstage. People were pushing me, pulling me, throwing me, kicking me. This was my professional debut."*

— *ROBIN LYON*

Photo by Cliff Lipson

Karen Ziemba

RON STAFFORD: Most shows have non-performing Assistant Stage Managers (ASM's) because they have gotten so big, like CATS and LES MIZ. But back then you usually had an ASM who was also an understudy in the show, like me. I found it very difficult being ASM, because at a quarter to eight they would say So-And-So is sick, we need you to go on. You had to mentally think at any moment you were on.

DONN SIMIONE: Understudies made a fortune when they went on, but at that time I wanted to dance. I wanted to do the show. To be an understudy was nothing but a frustration for me all the time. I hated being in the booth. Who wants to sing backstage in a booth? Let's face it, nobody. They always had to go find me. Most people just made it in the nick of time. After I went on though, as a character on the line, I realized how important the booth people were. How much they needed our voices out there.

BETTY LYND: Many of the understudies had difficulties because they were dying to have a role. The offstage booth only reminded them of the fact they were helping people on stage when they wanted to be on stage themselves. It was demoralizing.

FRASER ELLIS: We were out the door as they were still kicking their legs. We were supposed to use headphones but there usually weren't enough to go around. In the booth, you could open a panel and watch what was happening on stage.

KAREN ZIEMBA: We were situated in a horseshoe around the microphones in this room with a curtain. When you're dancing on stage, it's really hard to project vocally so we would be there to enhance. Always the same number of people in the booth, unless one of us was on stage that night. Everybody had a different part they were suppose to sing.

WANDA RICHERT: I'd be schlepping with my big pink fuzzy slippers and nail file to the offstage booth, and I would drive everybody crazy. In New York, everybody did their job, nobody screwed around. We had fun in there, but it was much more professional than the road.

VICKI FREDERICK: When Gerald Ford came to see the show, all these Secret Service men were around with their freeze-dried hair. They were in the booth and all over the theatre. We'd only have on our robes, which would be open a little bit too much, trying to crack up the "Buckingham Palace" guys, these guards.

ROBIN LYON: There was always so much talking and laughing in the booth, it was a wonder everything worked.

RON STAFFORD: The booth singers were basically on their own. They had to be scolded quite a few times because they would run in at the last minute. When I was an offstage singer in London, before they had an onslaught of swings, whoever was cut from the opening sang, that was it. If somebody was sick, there was a blank spot.

Gordon Owens and company

The Drug Scene

DONN SIMIONE: It was definitely there. You had more understudies on as a result and there were probably more injuries. There wasn't nearly as much in the New York Company as the road, but it was very much the times. Michael was tolerant to the extent that he didn't care what anybody did outside, but if it affected their performance, he was no longer tolerant.

PAM SOUSA: When I came back to the show the first time, drugs had come into play, which really threw me tremendously. I was a very straight person. The stage was what I lived for and the fact that people brought an element to it that didn't belong bothered me. It didn't affect me directly as Cassie; it affected the show. If somebody is having a breakdown on stage because they're high and have to leave, it does affect the show. Those times are over; that was the early eighties.

SCOTT PEARSON: The show was based so much upon our lives, it was us. If you were honest to yourself, drugs did not affect the show. Michael loved us to experiment within a certain framework and it was a strict framework. "This must be about you, this must be real." So changes in cast, somebody with a hangover, somebody with a drug problem, it all worked for the character. It became the character was hung over, the character was on drugs. It worked for the show as long as it was real.

JANET WONG: It was pretty open. People who were very young, making a lot of money, having a lot of free time, looked for ways to spend their money and they felt nothing was going to happen.

CHERYL CLARK: One day a representative from Equity came and talked to us. WEST SIDE STORY was playing across the alley from us, and rumor was half of their company had missed the matinee because of bad quaaludes that had been at a party the night before. There really was a drug crisis on Broadway at that time. I had to make a decision, because it was all around me. I was going to do a good job in a difficult role and keep my vocal ability up to par. I stayed drug-free. There wasn't that consciousness back then that we have now. It was a big social thing. It was sort of new and glamorous, and there wasn't that much education. At the Equity meeting, someone was kidding around that ludes were being handed out during the Cassie dance, and there was snickering and I got very vocal, saying that's definitely not something to laugh about. I saw a couple of colleagues fired because of it, which was a real shame.

BRADLEY JONES: I was with the Bus & Truck Company nine months, and by that time we were all really wasted. We had partied really hard on that tour; there was a lot of drug use. We were pushed, ninety-three cities in nine months; it was our way of getting through. We were young kids who were in a lot of pain. Management was working with people who had great hopes, and I believe some people under

"Michael was tolerant to the extent that he didn't care what anybody did outside, but if it affected their performance, he was no longer tolerant." — DONN SIMIONE

Michael misused their power in that they could manipulate us sexually and through drugs. Games were played and we are responsible for allowing this to happen. When I came to Broadway, it was different. There wasn't that going on; it was healthier.

ROBIN LYON: On the road, people were going into their dance bags on stage, doing lines. I didn't get caught up in it. Not to say I never did it, but certainly not on stage.

LOIS ENGLUND: The Original Cast used to make a circle before the show and hold hands, changing attitude and passing love. That continued in the road companies, but not in the Broadway Company. We used to say in the Broadway Company, you should sign in, snort a line, and go up to your dressing room. But cocaine was much more rampant backstage at DANCIN' than at A CHORUS LINE. You could go into the various dressing rooms in DANCIN' and get a snort if you wanted to.

KEVIN McCREADY: I heard that on the road, it was announced that police were about to check the theatre for drugs. "If you have any drugs here, go get rid of it." The company was in the middle of rehearsal. Maybe three people were left on stage; everybody else left.

A CHORUS LINE … The Movie

JUSTIN ROSS: When I went back to the show as Greg in 1983, it was a mixed blessing. Sir Richard Attenborough saw the show a lot and got to see me do it. I was so into the rhythm of Greg, all his dialogue in the monologue is metered, the exact opposite of what they want from a film performance. It was very difficult to lose it. I had one screen test, and waited a long time. One by one people were finding out they were cast. I was one of the last people to find out.

VICKI FREDERICK: When I met Sir Richard Attenborough and read the part, he said "My darling, you are Sheila." I said "Yes, I am." He flew me to New York for a screen test. It was a different script, but Sheila was pretty much the same character as on the stage. I had to fight to keep her the same. I went into the film much more seasoned. But when I first went into the show for Michael, I wasn't. I was a nervous wreck, a little girl as far as experience was concerned.

PAM SOUSA: I was doing the show on Broadway and Sir Richard Attenborough would often come and watch the show. We all thought we were in.

DeLEE LIVELY [Val]: My ex-husband, Eddie Mekka, and I were up for up for Kristine and Al, but were cut during the auditions. I kept telling my agent, "Let me go in for Val," and a short time later, they still hadn't found a Val, so they put me on tape. One month after, I was off to New York for a screen test. Sir Richard said, "Darling, you're lovely, wonderful — go on inside and start rehearsing." I was taken into the room and shown the first dance combination and I heard, "Darling, I think you're fabulous, but there's one more girl I want to see. Can you stay in New York for the weekend?" As I walked out, I saw Audrey Landers on the phone, and knew they were going to give it to her. I didn't stay the weekend and when I got back to L.A., they called to see if I would dub in her dancing. I refused.

MCA
and
Universal Pictures
proudly announce that
MICHAEL BENNETT
will produce and direct
for the screen
A CHORUS LINE

Announcement that appeared in the New York Times *on February 29, 1976*

Cast member George Rios drew this "celebrity line" circa 1979, based on suggestions from Original Company members as to favorite choices for a film version

VICKI FREDERICK: Everybody in Hollywood assumed Bob Fosse wouldn't want it. I asked him once if he would have wanted to choreograph the film of A CHORUS LINE, and he said, "I would have done it. Nobody asked me."

BERNIE JACOBS [President, Shubert Organization]: Michael always believed he was the only person who could properly do a film of A CHORUS LINE. When he made the deal for the movie, he also made a multiple picture deal with MCA, and they set him set him up in an office on Park Avenue. But they treated Michael like a young boy just learning the ropes. He got very unhappy there, and eventually told his agent to get him out: "I don't want anything to do with these people, I don't want to make a movie for them." Michael took the position for a long time that he would do anything to prevent MCA from making a successful movie version. He always believed the movie should be what the show was. It should not be about the making of the show, but about the making of the movie; it should go through the same procedures.

SCOTT PEARSON: Michael was staying with me in Hollywood the day he dropped the negotiations with Universal for the film. He said, "Fuck it, I can't do it. I won't do it on their terms." He left a note saying "Gone fishing" on his desk at Universal and walked out of the whole thing. Apparently, when it came to the film, he had to answer to all these subservients and he couldn't deal with that.

CYNTHIA ONRUBIA: When we were rehearsing SCANDAL, Michael once said, "Okay, everybody who's doing the A CHORUS LINE movie, show me the film's opening combination," which they did.

Clint Eastwood as Don   Olivia Newton-John as Maggie   Sylvester Stallone as Mike   Diana Ross as Connie   David Bowie as Greg   Barbra Streisand as Cassie   Ann-Margret as Sheila   Steve Martin as Bobby

Then he said, "Okay, now let's see mine," and those of us from the stage version complied. I remember Michael said to us, "Why fuck with it?"

THEONI ALDREDGE [Costume Designer]: I've never understood Sir Richard Attenborough. He's wonderful shooting elephants, but not at shooting a dancer. Anyway, comes the Finale, and I get this phone call from Alyce Gilbert, the wardrobe supervisor. "Theoni, there are two people here with cameras ..." "Throw them out." "They want to photograph the Finale costumes." "Throw them out,

Alyce," and she did. Next phone call is from Cy Feuer, the film's producer, whom I've worked with. "I talked to Joe Papp and he said we could use the Finale costumes." I said, "Joe Papp is called a producer and I am called a designer, and I say no." "Why not? You'll get full screen credit." "No. This is a continuity thing. You don't all of a sudden bring in Theoni Aldredge costumes at the end." I went to Michael, he said, "It's up to you, they're your clothes. I wouldn't do it, unless you need the money." When Cy called back with the offer of giving me anything I want, I asked for half a million dollars. He

said, "But Theoni, you're my friend." "'You're my friend?' You walk into my theatre of the last ten years and you don't call me to say that you're going to photograph these clothes? 'You're my friend?' You didn't know I had done these clothes, it was a surprise?" They did not use my designs. What makes me angry is young people will hear this show broke every record on Broadway and the only point of reference they will have is the film. And they'll wonder why.

| Carol Burnett
as Bebe | Cher
as Judy | Stevie Wonder
as Richie | Steve Lawrence
as Al | Eydie Gormé
as Kristine | Bette Midler
as Val | Shaun Cassidy
as Mark | Woody Allen
as Paul | Liza Minnelli
as Diana |

Dressing Rooms

LAURIE GAMACHE: For the most part, dressing rooms were assigned by character, but things got shifted around a little bit. Cassie was the only one who had her own room, which probably didn't make the Zachs very happy. The Cassie room was on the second floor, right up from the stage door. Next to it was a room for three girls who shifted around according to personalities. The others were downstairs behind Alyce and the under-

study girls were in the Bungalow. The guys were on the third and fourth floors, three rooms on each floor — except for the understudies, who were downstairs.

SCOTT ALLEN: The five original understudy men moved into a dressing room together downstairs. We painted, carpeted, put in telephones and plants, and made it almost like an apartment. It was just wonderful. We became known as "The West Side Five" because we were on the west side and there were five of us. We would do what we called "attitude check." Before Donna did her number and most of the cast came underneath the stage to go up to their own dressing rooms, we would open our dressing room door, sit on the floor, and watch the company's attitudes as they walked by.

MICHAEL SERRECCHIA: The "West Side Five" terminology remained for the duration of the run. It was the largest dressing room, and the women would frequently come over and we'd talk, play guitar, and sing. It

was very unexpected. It was a whole completely different world.

PATTI D'BECK [Understudy]: At one point, a group of us called ourselves the "Subterraneans." We were the understudy girls, downstairs in the basement behind Alyce's wardrobe room. It was great, we loved being there. I remember it being highly important to us who came in our dressing room.

KATE WRIGHT: There were six of us in that laundry room. It was close to the phone, the rehearsal floor, wardrobe, and Alyce. When I got the part of Sheila, they offered me a room upstairs but I was just loving my girls in the basement, so I opted to stay and never moved.

JANE SUMMERHAYS: We called ourselves the "Underground Women." There was a shelf we lined with the liquor bottles we had consumed during the twenty minute "Cassie break," during *The Music and the Mirror*. We would all take a swig and go back up for the end of the show.

MURPHY CROSS: Being in that room was like being backstage in a 1940's musical.

PETER VON MAYRHAUSER: That dressing room used to crack me up. It was

Deborah Geffner putting on her lashes for a performance

Love to eat them mousies,
Mousies what I love to eat,
Bite they little heads off,
Nibble on they tiny feet.

Photo courtesy Deborah Geffner

like those old movies of chorus girl dressing rooms. That was it, they were living it. They were always in the middle of having affairs and dramas, very entertaining.

MICHAEL SERRECCHIA: Some of the girls were in the "Bungalow." References to grandeur, a Hollywood Bungalow.

ROBIN LYON: I was in the Bungalow. It went from the best of friends to hatred. When I first came in we were a very close group, like sisters. Then we dealt with horrible personality conflicts.

CYNTHIA ONRUBIA: I remember changing places in the Bungalow every time somebody left because there was one particular spot I wanted. I got it when one of the girls left; it was nice finally having my own space.

CLIVE WILSON: My dressing room-mate was Thommie Walsh. I was working Thommie's nerves for some reason down at the Newman. Michael figured out all the people who weren't getting along and put them together at the Shubert. The company went ballistic when we got uptown and saw the dressing room assignments. Part of Michael's genius is that he put these people together, because we ended up best of friends. So we just had a ball, painted and decorated. We figured, "We're here for a while, let's make it comfortable."

KAY COLE: I shared with Nancy Lane. Our dressing room was very plain and dull when we arrived at the Shubert, and we thought, "Wouldn't it be fun to paint it like the subways — graffiti decor." Everyone contributed, nothing dirty or nasty, just a very eclectic room. We tried to make it slick, hip, and cool, but the cleaning people came in the day after we finished and thought someone had broken into the dressing room. So they painted it over! We were totally disappointed.

JUSTIN ROSS: Thommie and Clive had the best dressing room. They installed grey industrial carpeting to go with a black enamel make-up mirror that was already there. They painted the walls grey, and put a purplish-blue gel over the light and a plant in the corner. They created this soothing, serene, cool environment. When they left the show, I got their dressing room. Of course, I kept all of the motifs.

DEBORAH GEFFNER: There were three of us: Karen Jablons, Rebecca York, and myself, but Rebecca was fired about two weeks into her run. Then Loida Santos

came in and redecorated for us. She brought in matching cushions, her television set, radio, and a big fish tank.

Pam Sousa clowning in the dressing room

LOIDA SANTOS: My baby was in the dressing room with me for over two years. The dressers would watch him during the show.

WANDA RICHERT: I put Christmas lights up all year round in my room. It was a home away from home, even though I lived only five blocks away.

Originals Returning to the Line

FRAN LIEBERGALL: If Original Company members saw that something was happening that wasn't what they remembered as the original intention, they would say something, but usually to management. When Kelly Bishop came back, people were just in awe of her. I remember she was so scared. She had a mental block about one section of the Tap Combination, and for her first few performances, Troy Garza didn't make her do it. It was funny to see her be that vulnerable, so freaked by something in the show.

FRASER ELLIS: One of the most exciting times for me was right after the Gala when Jane Summerhays went on vacation for two weeks; Kelly Bishop came in, and I got to be Bobby and stand next to her. That was a thrill. Sammy Williams came back too, he was really sweet, and Nancy Lane came back. Many of these people came back right after the Gala.

KAY COLE: I guess I was the only Original to come back in a different role. I played Diana at the Shubert for about three months. It was actually a wonderful experience. I heard they needed a Diana and called Michael and asked him if I could do it. He was surprised and he said, "I think of you as Maggie. I don't know, come in and read." So I did and I audi-tioned with Debbie Allen. Michael said, "Okay," gave me the role and I had a wonderful time. Sharing a dressing room with five girls, including the current Maggie, Pam Klinger, I heard stories about what was connecting to them. In some ways, I was seeing myself when I was first doing it. In learning Diana, obviously I knew things by instinct, but I had to learn it like a new part. Especially viewing everything from the other end of the line, which totally changed the perspective and the focus for me, because we start the show on stage right and it dominoes from that viewpoint down the line to the left. It was a totally different feeling on the other end of the stage.

Michael called sometime later and asked if I would come back again as Maggie. I just couldn't do that. It's hard to go backwards when you're starting to move forward in your life.

BOB MacDONALD [Company and General Manager]: I think the thought of Donna McKechnie coming back to play Cassie scared the hell out of the company. We heard all these terrible rumors — arthritis, overweight. But she was wonderful and probably could do it again.

BOB REILLY [Company Manager]: The first week Donna came back to the show in September of 1986 was the first week in many years with perfect cast attendance. Tom Porter laminated the sign-in sheet and had it backstage over his desk.

WAYNE MELEDANDRI: When Donna came back to Broadway, I remember turning to Ron Kurowski, who was playing Bobby, during her first performance, saying, "How am I going to follow Donna McKechnie?" You just felt that energy; it was absolutely thrilling. I performed differently when Donna was in the show. That generation danced because they absolutely loved to and it was expressed in their dancing; it's how they performed. She gave her heart every night.

RON STAFFORD: I couldn't wait to come to work and watch Donna do this again. Her attitude was so uplifting, so positive. She made the show soar.

BOB REILLY: We needed a change, some new energy. We allowed Bob LuPone to come and go. One of the things that used to drive me crazy was his physical fitness regimen. At the back of the house he would say his Zach lines. Then he'd hit the floor, do some push-ups, and the audience could hear him grunting, then he'd get up in time for his next cue. He would come to the theatre five minutes before

curtain. Of course, he would call earlier, "I'm on my way."

TROY GARZA: Bob LuPone had begun to take little liberties, and Bob Avian said to Tom Porter, "Just let him do what he wants, it's not that bad, it gets the cast stimulated." But it became like improv theatre.

WAYNE MELEDANDRI: Bob LuPone challenged a lot of people. He wanted those who were set in doing the show exactly a certain way to look at it differently. And when people are asked to change and they don't want to, you're going to get conflict. From my point of view, what Bob was doing was refreshing. Whether the company liked it or not, they were listening. We didn't know who he was going to call next.

KAREN ZIEMBA: Bob played with a lot of people and many didn't like it. He would pick one of us out and say something like, "Bebe, how old did you say you were?" And I'd jump! I didn't get mad because it made me listen to him; it made me feel as if I were in a real audi-

tion, he was into such realism. Some of the kids couldn't deal with that spontaneity and weren't used to it. It's not so much that it was right for him to do it but it was taking a chance. He was just trying to keep himself fresh and I thought he was excellent. It gave me something to look forward to every night.

KEITH BERNARDO: I think I handled myself incredibly well with Bob but you never knew what was going to happen. Some people got ticked, but it kept the show on its toes. Once he pulled me out of the line at a time when I wasn't supposed to be. I knew it wasn't a mistake, and I thought, do I step forward or not? What should I do? What the hell is he going to ask me? And he did ask me something, and right before I was going to answer, he said, "Back in line." I never got angry about it, but some people did.

ROBIN LYON: Bob LuPone and I had a fun time together until he started to manipulate and control. He would cut off laughs, give me notes. I was probably one of the few people who told him never to give me a note again — that's not his job

in this company, he's an actor just like me, and it's not his place. What he tried to do was very destructive. He was great for the show because of his knowledge of the role. He was a very commanding Zach, which is what we needed, and you need to be a little afraid, and in that respect, it was fine. But he kept changing things in the show. That was the scariest thing of all, and it wasn't funny. Everybody complained about it, but nobody said anything to him.

KEVIN McCREADY: It was like when someone else messes around, they're fucking around, but when Bob LuPone does it, it's acting.

"The thought of Donna McKechnie coming back to play Cassie scared the hell out of the company." — BOB MACDONALD

The Show and Their Careers

WANDA RICHERT: A CHORUS LINE finally made people realize I could act, I wasn't just a dancer from Chicago. Gower Champion said if he had seen me play Cassie, he would have never even considered hiring me as Peggy Sawyer in 42ND STREET, because I was so much a woman as Cassie. It gave me that maturity. I was twenty and playing a thirty-two-year-old.

JANE SUMMERHAYS: It helped me enormously as an actress. Sheila is a role that everybody takes to. I adored playing her and never got tired of doing those scenes. I loved playing comedy, hearing people laugh.

BRADLEY JONES: We were all chorus people with chorus people mentalities. We weren't artists. We needed direction and training. There were a few of us who went on and developed. My regret is I didn't use those years to work on my talent. I couldn't see beyond A CHORUS LINE. It was the pinnacle to me. I didn't use the time to grow.

MURPHY CROSS: I had been doing the show for almost a year on Broadway when a woman came to see it from CBS and wound up giving me a holding contract to do a pilot and two TV films. All because somebody saw me in A CHORUS LINE! Playing Judy, she is such a loveable character that it didn't do anything but help.

PAM SOUSA: It didn't do a damn thing. I don't think the show affected my career. As a performer, I grew a lot. But going into auditions, I almost think it was a black mark. Everyone had done it so much, and I carried Cassie with me so long, that I couldn't get in on straight plays or television. "She's Cassie, she's a dancer." I'm very proud of that credential, but when you try to break into the next thing, it's difficult.

CYNTHIA ONRUBIA: It was my first Broadway show and I got a lot of publicity. I was in every teenage magazine because of the show. They would say, "Fifteen-year-old Cynthia Onrubia uses Johnson's to take off her stage make-up." I was on TO TELL THE TRUTH — who was the youngest member of A CHORUS LINE? That was all press from the show, I didn't hire a publicist or anything.

STEVE BOOCKVOR [Zach]: I am so grateful to the show for giving me a year and a half of a good-paying, joyful job. I didn't change the history of A CHORUS LINE, except in giving Michael some ideas in terms of who Denise Pence, my wife, and I were that he picked up on. At least eighty percent of the Al & Kristine characters are based on us.

JACK NOSEWORTHY [Mark]: The whole experience, including the interviews and publicity of being the final cast member hired, really was a catalyst for the film and television work I'm doing now. It sent my life into another direction.

LYNNE TAYLOR-CORBETT: As young kids then, we weren't as aggressive or in as much control of our destiny as kids are now. We were much more approval-oriented. We didn't "shape" our careers. I don't think any of us did. We were "just get out there and do it" kids and hoped somebody liked us.

KAY COLE: People feel they know a little bit of very personal information about me. To everyone I have ever met, *At the Ballet* has meant something very special. And they all have some kind of wonderful reaction to the song and to me. I'm very proud to have given them that feeling, and to be that person.

RON DENNIS: It gave me my fifteen minutes of fame.

TRISH GARLAND: To make history in the American musical theatre is something that you hope for or dream about or can't even dream about. You have this aspiration to be a dancer, and suddenly you get this huge offering and accept it and then find out that it's even larger than it is. It's a treasure that allowed me to do many things in my life that I'm sure I wouldn't have had the opportunity to do, like directing and choreographing. That wouldn't have happened without Michael. Women weren't getting the work. I am forever grateful.

Photos by Herb Migdoll

"As young kids then, we weren't as aggressive or in as much control of our destiny as kids are now. We didn't 'shape' our careers. We were 'just get out there and do it' kids and hoped somebody liked us." — *LYNNE TAYLOR-CORBETT*

Photo by Martha Swope

*Vicki Frederick:
"Michael came back
at the end of the show
and said, 'You did a
nice job, Vicki.'
I finally got the
Cassie contract
shortly after."*

CHAPTER 2

CASSIE

"Every time a Cassie was changed, it was always a BIG DEAL! It sent tremors through the entire area." — PETER VON MAYRHAUSER

Everybody Wanted to be Cassie

PATTI D'BECK [Cassie Understudy]: Everybody in the show wanted to be Cassie. Girls, boys, we were always doing the number in the basement. That was the dancer's dream — to do that dance on stage.

PETER VON MAYRHAUSER [Stage Manager]: Every time a Cassie was changed, it was always a BIG DEAL! It sent tremors through the entire area.

VICKI FREDERICK: Ann Reinking stayed in the Broadway company while I went to Los Angeles to replace Donna McKechnie. When I came back to New York two months later, Annie went out to L.A. About this time, December of 1976, Michael and Donna left to get married and I went in to the role with the understanding it would be just until Donna got back from her honeymoon.

PETER VON MAYRHAUSER: Vicki was never "officially" given the role; she was the understudy, but actually did it for

months. You can't do that now; Equity would never allow it. When Donna did come back to the New York Company, it was only for a short time, maybe even one night. Oh, we were told constantly that she was going to return and finish out her contract, but she never did.

VICKI FREDERICK: Michael wanted Donna for the Actors' Fund benefit in April of 1977, but Donna did not want to go back into the show.

I was told I was going to be given the part, but Michael refused to rehearse me. It had nothing to do with me personally. It had to do with Michael wanting Donna. In a way, it was Donna who put me in the show.

The hardest performance I have ever done in my entire career was that Actors' Fund. It was so difficult because I knew Michael didn't want me; he wanted Donna to do it. And it wasn't just Michael — everyone in that audience wanted to see Donna McKechnie do that role one more time. I psyched myself into the show

Ann Reinking:
"For about a week, we tried it without the skirt."

Laurie Gamache:
"I was the Cassie Michael never knew."

Cheryl Clark:
"Michael loved my extension."

Photo by Peter Stanford

Photo courtesy Cheryl Clark

Photos by Herb Migdoll

This page:
Deborah Henry

Opposite: Pam Sousa

with Zach's fateful line, "Cassie, stay on stage, please." I thought to myself, "Okay, I will." When I finished the number, I got a standing ovation. Michael came back at the end of the show and said, "You did a nice job, Vicki." I finally got the Cassie contract shortly after.

CYNTHIA ONRUBIA [Connie; Understudy]: I cut school early one day because I knew Michael was auditioning Cassie replacements at the theatre and I wanted to watch. I stood in the back of the orchestra and saw Vicki, Sandahl Bergman, and Rene Ceballos do the Cassie scene, song, and dance, one right after the other. Not even a ten-minute break; the other girls were just standing there in the wings.

Vicki was doing the role at that point but she still had to audition. It was very intense for me. This is about the time they brought in Pam Sousa.

VICKI FREDERICK: Michael called me one night after the show, "Pam Sousa is on the road, and she really wants to come to New York. I just had this great idea that you and Pam share the New York Company." I said, "That is a great idea, but not with me. I can't do that, Michael, I worked really hard to get the role and I'm not going to share it with anybody. If you feel you need to bring Pam in, go right ahead and I'll leave." I hung up the phone and auditioned for DANCIN' and got it.

PETER VON MAYRHAUSER: Pam had been terrific out on the road, so the decision was made to bring her in.

PAM SOUSA: Sharing the role was never presented to me; I wouldn't have done it. Michael made a place for me on Broadway. My six months were up on the road and I wanted to come home to New York and he said, "Open D.C. for me and I'll bring you to Broadway because I want you there."

When I first came into A CHORUS LINE, I was told by some of the Originals, "Cassie knows this character, she doesn't know this one." I knew they were right. Some actors would get pissed, though. I as an actor, never went in with set things. Several of the Gregory Gardners, for instance, didn't like

working with me because I didn't hold conversations with them on stage.

I always thought Cassie was very uncomfortable, and, being uncomfortable, she was afraid to say much. She came from the school where you weren't supposed to talk at auditions. That was my interpretation. Bobby and Sheila kibbitz, because they feel more comfortable. They've worked with Zach. Cassie hasn't been on Broadway in a very long time. Either she talks out of nerves, or she doesn't talk. Sometimes I chose not to respond, or to respond very sparsely. I was told Cassie and Don Kerr had worked together; she knows Connie, Greg, and Bobby and is old friends with Sheila. Cassie knows Al and Kristine, a little. But she didn't have a relationship with anyone else stage left. That's the way I played it.

ANN REINKING: I had asked Michael if

we could make a couple of changes in the dance, because Donna dances primarily from the waist up. She's got a great torso and body work, but for me, it's legs; I'm very short-waisted. We put in jetés for me, quite a few. Michael was really good about it, and I think that's why it worked for so many different Cassies. He said, "This is the foundation and you must stay within this sphere, but within this sphere, you must be yourself and find your way."

Michael really let me be me, within the confines of the part. "If you don't want to do the ending the way it is, you can do your own ending." Donna ends almost in a fourth position, and I was uncomfortable with it. Michael said, "Go where you want to go. If it's not right, I'll tell you." For a while, I was ending the dance with a variety of poses, but Michael ultimately liked where I just turned my head over my shoulder and looked at Zach. He thought

it had a realistic feeling to it. I think that ending was very appropriate, because the character got so involved with her own love of dance, that she just all of a sudden remembered, "Wait a minute, he's watching me." It had kind of a cinematic real thing that Michael enjoyed.

PAM SOUSA: I had been taught the show early on by Clive (Clerk) Wilson, the dance captain on Broadway. This was before it had gotten so cut and dried. When Michael worked with me, we'd play. He allowed me certain liberties that came from me, because he trusted me. My Cassie was based, of course, on Donna, but had my "isms" in it, which I laugh at, because later on some of my work became the "set stuff." The dance was the dance. I would never deviate from the steps, but I did add certain attitude turns. Donna and I have different strengths. As time went

on, Michael couldn't do that with all the girls taking over, so he set the tone of the show after the "ol' girls" left.

CHERYL CLARK: Donna coached me. None of the women could ever duplicate her back and her arms. I truly listened to her about what the drama of the dance meant. And I have to give a lot of credit to Baayork Lee for my understanding and interpretation, because she was right there with Michael and Donna.

Michael loved my extension, it was probably the highest of any of the women that played the role and we incorporated it into the dance. I did the role longer than any other Cassie, between Broadway and the road, and I always religiously stuck to what Donna and Michael wanted.

DEBORAH HENRY: When Michael and I would do the dance, he always thought

he could wear me out. But I tried to match him at his game. He would say, "Do the dance." "Sure," and I'd do it. Then he'd say, "Do it again." "Oh, I'd love to." I'd even have to do it a third time. I wasn't intimidated. I was elated when he was there and I loved dancing with him. He used to get behind me and say, "Outdance me, outdance me."

ANGELIQUE ILO: Much of that dance was hard for me to articulate in my feet. It was easier for short-legged people. I'm long-legged, and Michael, being so small, made little patter. For me, it was almost as if I couldn't make my feet move fast enough.

BOB REILLY [Company Manager]: Donna McKechnie grew up in Michael Bennett's choreographic vocabulary. They witnessed the same things physically. She always

said she could do the choreography because she danced more like a man than a woman. And that's why she said the best person for this dance would be Michael.

KAREN ZIEMBA [Cassie Understudy]: Michael's choreography was very masculine and close to the ground. For a woman with long legs who is wearing heels, it is very difficult. To watch a man do the Cassie dance is incredible — in flats, shuffling along the floor, doing those long strides. Donna had that movement down so beautifully, it was also a part of her. But for somebody else to put that choreography into her body takes time.

FRAN LIEBERGALL [Original Pianist; Vocal Supervisor]: To me, the most inspirational person who ever danced the Cassie choreography was Michael Bennett. A class by himself.

Vicki Frederick

Photo courtesy Wanda Richert

Wanda Richert

KAREN ZIEMBA: You need to do it every night for stamina purposes. You can't not do the show for three weeks and just go on. And you've got to have the skirt — something about the ambiance of the red skirt!

ANGELIQUE ILO: Stamina, stamina, stamina. I would do that darn dance hundreds of times in a row, and still not have the stamina to get through. You had to find your own way of acting and thinking your way through the dance. If it was really slow, it was harder to do, but if that turn section was too fast, you couldn't nail it either. It had to be just right.

CHERYL CLARK: I love teamwork, and to dance to those marvelous musicians, no matter how tired you are — you dance! One conductor conducted the number so fast one Saturday night, I told him it was impossible to dance to that tempo. He said, "Well, we have to get to the country, don't we?" That's unacceptable. First of all, it's cheating the audience; secondly, one can get injured.

PAM SOUSA: I never dictated the tempo, I did what they wanted.

DEBORAH HENRY: I would never bother with tempos, I never talked to anybody, "Could you do this, could you do that?" I danced to what they gave me and I think a great dancer can dance to any tempo.

LYNNE TAYLOR-CORBETT [Cassie]: Nowadays, the "Play me the music ..." reprise in the number would be on tape. If you really go full out with that first dance section, it is so strenuous to come back and sing.

RON STAFFORD [Assistant Stage Manager]: I loved spotting the Cassies in the wings with the flashlight. It was a feeling that even though I am only holding a flashlight, I'm a part of an unbelievable dance number. I was helping them spot and turn. We would drape a towel over our chests and hold the flashlights; we realized that gave the most light for the girls to look at. We were tucked far enough in the back in the wings that audiences never saw us.

WANDA RICHERT: I had given notice in L.A. that I was leaving the show right after the next city stop, which was San Francisco. When I got there, Michael called me into the office and said, "I will give you a raise, I want you to stay." That night he saw the show and told the company, "I have been watching Wanda since she was eighteen, and you, darling, are an actress, you can act your ass off and I want everybody to applaud her." It was incredible.

But after that, management started picking on me. I don't know what it was, but I couldn't handle it. Marty Gold, the stage manager at the time, started giving me problems with my scenes. Tom Hancock,

as much as I loved Tom, started giving me a real hassle with tempos. He wanted it too slow, and I was the only one who danced it as fast as I did. I told him, "I dance it this way because that's how I dance best." Michael never had a problem with it, but they wanted to put me into a mold of what everybody else had done.

There was one day when Tom played my number so slowly, I almost started crying during the song. I wound up pulling the rib muscles on top of my diaphragm on stage. I was in and out of the show and started feeling emotionally crazed because of what they were putting me through. I called Michael at home, "I need a couple days off, I'm just not doing well," and he said to take five days. The injury didn't get better, so I told management I was going to be out another night, that I was going to the doctor for x-rays.

When I came back the following night for the show, I was told to call Michael Bennett. "Darling as of this day, you are fired." Just like that, not a last show, not anything. I said, "Michael, I'm hurt." He said, "Yes, darling, so am I." "You don't understand, I have an injury." "When you get your head together, call me." That's when I went back to Chicago to recuperate with my family and found out about the 42ND STREET auditions. On my opening night in 42ND STREET, Michael sent me a beautiful telegram which said, "Art doesn't imitate life ... I always knew you'd be a big star. Love, Michael."

When I was doing NINE on Broadway, Michael took me to dinner and said, "You need to be on Broadway doing Cassie. What could be better?" When Cheryl Clark leaves, you're coming in." I told him I would love to, I hadn't done A CHORUS LINE in New York. I stayed for a little over two years and was pregnant during my last three months. I was so sick all the time, I kept crackers in the wings and would feel like I was going to faint. I could have lain down on the line and gone to sleep right there in the middle of the show. There was one Saturday night I was feeling so lethargic — it was the end of the Cassie dance and I started crying doing those last turns. I thought to myself, "This is my last night," and I walked up to Tom Porter afterwards and quit.

ANGELIQUE ILO: They asked me to come back for a couple of months between Wanda and Donna McKechnie's return in 1986.

MITCHELL WEISS [Company Manager]: Laurie Gamache had a special place in our hearts because, being the understudy, she somehow wanted Cassie so bad she was willing to stick around if it took forever. And quite honestly, as managers no one believed in their right mind she was ever going to get the chance because they were always going with an outside person. Laurie was kept an understudy because she could do so much and was consistent

and reliable. One tends not to promote people like that. They leave them there.

LAURIE GAMACHE [Final Broadway Cassie]: Everybody knew Donna was leaving, because other Cassies were hanging around. Girls who had done the role would stop by the theatre to say hello to Tom Porter. We started guessing as to who might be coming back to the show. Tom called me in the office and said, "We want to try you." I was shocked. Tom thought I could do it, but since Michael and Bob Avian had never seen me as Cassie, he said, "We'll sign you for three months and then Bob will come in and see you. If he likes you, you'll continue."

Lynne Taylor-Corbett

Photo by Troy Garza

53

FRASER ELLIS [Assistant Stage Manager]: It was Donna who said, "Use Laurie as Cassie, she's great!" I don't know who finally decided, but Donna was behind it.

TROY GARZA [Dance Captain]: She got it because Bob Avian saw her dance one night. Tom Porter and I agreed it was Laurie's turn, she's kicking butt; and Bob came to the show and said she was fantastic.

BOB REILLY: By the end, Laurie acted the shit out of that dance. When she turned her head and stared at Zach at the back of the house, it was really chilling. And it wasn't just Saturday night when we were sold out; it was Tuesday night when we had one hundred people in the audience in February. She knew she had to act it, and that informed the rest of her body. It was remarkable to watch the transformation.

LAURIE GAMACHE: The biggest difference in my work came when I got to a point in my life that paralleled Cassie. When I reached that point, it was as if I used the show for therapy reasons. I just grew into that person and the show was just the right script and the right vehicle for me.

KAREN ZIEMBA: The more you've been in the business and the more you know about yourself as a woman, the more Cassie becomes clear to you because she's like "Everywoman." Just survival, wanting to keep working in the business and get on with your life and not live in the past, is really what that part is all about.

WANDA RICHERT: Cassie was fulfilling to me as an actress, a woman, and a sexual being, because it was so sensual. Our sexual energy is really our creative energy, and when you can put that all together in one number and then sing and act, it's really incredible. I don't think there will ever be a role like that again for a woman.

Photo by Jack Hoffman

Photo by Herb Migdoll

54

Photo by Herb Migdoll

CHAPTER 3

DESIGNING THE LINE

COSTUMES
LIGHTING
SOUND

> *"Michael wanted red costumes for the Finale.*
> *He had just opened FOLLIES, which had*
> *a huge red number. Well, I thought red would be*
> *a big fiasco."* — THEONI ALDREDGE

Costumes

THEONI ALDREDGE [Costume Designer]: The sketches are all gone. Somebody took the entire lot very shortly after we opened on Broadway. I wanted to dress the kids the way they came to rehearsals. I drew tiny little roughs of the kids with Michael sitting next to me. I used to bring a camera to rehearsals and Michael would say, "I've never seen a designer with a pencil and a camera." Color gave us enormous struggles. Michael, for example, wanted the girls that did *At The Ballet* to have a little touch of pink on them. Tharon Musser's lighting designs went from stage lights to color lights, and the cast, of course, was wearing the same clothes throughout. Well, all of a sudden something that was green turned brown. We had no scenery to deal with, so Robin Wagner, the set designer, was never going to be a problem for us. It was between Tharon and myself because lighting colors changed so brilliantly.

ALYCE GILBERT [Wardrobe Supervisor]: I had never done a Broadway show before and I really didn't think I had a chance of moving to the Shubert. But the kids whined to Michael and he went along. Nonetheless, I would not agree to be the assistant on the show. Either I was going as the supervisor, or somebody else was going to take over.

THEONI ALDREDGE: Michael wanted red costumes for the Finale. He had just opened FOLLIES, which had a huge red number. Well, I thought red would be a big fiasco. And we had our first disagreement. I kept wondering, is this real? Are these kids really dancing at the end, or is this being played out in their imaginations? To me, it was fantasy. I wanted a color that wasn't real, not definite like blue or red or green. Then Michael had another idea: "What if they enter with part of their costume, then go off and re-enter with more of their costume, and at

the very end, the last curtain call, it's the full costume." I told him, "Michael, we don't have enough time for the change as it is." At the dress rehearsal, the Finale music started, the first boy came out in the costume, and there was dead silence. I thought Michael hated it. I sat there very quietly, then I felt a tap on my shoulder, and Michael whispered into my ear, "I was wrong."

ALYCE GILBERT: Michael allowed me an hour to stage the quick change at the Public. There were wigs involved at that point, too.

THEONI ALDREDGE: Barbara Matera executed the Finale costumes; the NYSF shop made the rehearsal clothes. We spent all sorts of money on the Finale costumes because they were all beaded.

BARBARA MATERA [Finale Costume Executor]: Michael was in my shop all the

time — he was very interested in costumes. I think Donna McKechnie was our model for the girls because she had quite a lot of say about everything. Theoni instigated the color of the Finale costume; Michael wanted something else. They went round and round in circles until they came up with this sparkling color that everyone thinks is gold, but isn't really.

ALYCE GILBERT: There were problems with the original set of Finale costumes; the zippers, for instance, weren't heavy enough. On Broadway we made a second set for the Original Cast so they could alternate them, which was wonderful for the clothes. Then we made a set for the understudies, who hadn't had them earlier. When the replacements and road people came in, the principals got two Finale costumes and the understudies got one. Eventually we made a third set for the Original Cast who went to Los Angeles.

BARBARA MATERA: By the time we made the patterns, it took a week to complete one costume. We had a lot of beaders. There was a lot involved with all the stripes and the beading. We didn't make replacements very often because they held up so well; they're made of a very sturdy fabric.

ALYCE GILBERT: The problem with dry cleaning any beaded costume is that the beads come off. We always used R&S Cleaners on 2nd Avenue and 13th Street. Since the satin is dyed, it reacts to sweat and to being pressed. But they were remarkably substantial. The girls' Finale leotards were washed and the vests went to the cleaners. Since the armhole in the vest was cut very wide, they didn't have to be cleaned that often, and consequently held up for a long time.

WOODY SHELP [Finale Hat Maker]: We were working on CHICAGO in Philadelphia. I came back to New York on a Sunday night, went right to the shop, and started on A CHORUS LINE. Their first dress rehearsal was the following Sunday. I went to rehearsal with unfinished hats; there was no way the beading could have been finished. All the girls wore blonde wigs. The minute they came on stage, Michael cut them. The girls' hats were now too big because they had been sized for wigs. So I had to resize them all. I also hadn't realized how much the hats were going to be handled — they had to be built a lot stronger than I originally planned. Rose Gambino did all the beading until the show closed. After the first nineteen hats were made, another set was ordered for the principals and one set for the understudies. There was a third set made for the Original Company. When they sent out three companies, I made 116; that's two hats apiece. The girls' hats were pink and the boys' coffee-colored. It took about two days to build one Finale hat because of all the steps involved, at a cost, originally, of $125. I have now made 706 Finale hats.

ALYCE GILBERT: There are certain things in the logo shot that were never seen at the Shubert because the photo call was the day of the first dress rehearsal downtown. A number of things were eliminated by the end of the first week that are in that photograph. Mike was originally in a long-sleeved beige tee-shirt with a printed motif around the front — a very seventies sort of thing, which lasted about two weeks. Maggie is wearing this crocheted knit top; and the pants she wore came off within two days. She wore the crocheted top through the whole run downtown; it happened to be in stock at the Festival costume shop.

KAY COLE [Original Maggie]: I went through the most costume changes. I had about five different costumes and it took forever to find the right one. The first outfit they had for me was too boyish, which is the one that they actually used in the logo — pants and a shirt. Michael didn't think it was feminine enough. They tried a weird crocheted wraparound top that was so uncomfortable and hard to dance in. I was thrilled when they got rid of it!

ALYCE GILBERT: The biggest changes came in the people who were eliminated in the opening; they went through a major

"The black top lasted only three performances. It ultimately became a yellow terry sweatshirt."
—*Justin Ross (top)*
Danny Weathers (below)

transition. Donna was always in the skirt. The TKTS booth had just opened, and Bill Kellerd, Theoni's assistant, had a friend who worked there. We got the green-and-pink tee-shirts from them for Al to wear. Now the TKTS tee-shirts are red-and-white, but for the run of A CHORUS LINE, they were green-and-pink. This was also a very transitional period for dance wear in general. Matte finishes were still on the leotards, except for Sheila. Hers was the first milliskin leotard available commercially; it had just come into Capezio. Michael originally did not like it, so we tried dying it, and he didn't like that either. We went back to the shiny one, which always worked for the Sheila character.

BILL JONES [Dresser]: Sheila's costume looks a little bit like a suit of armor — very hard and metallic. It's perfect for her.

THEONI ALDREDGE: When it came time for duplicate line costumes, we custom-made them. Originally half were bought, and half were made. The dance pants were all made by us.

JUSTIN ROSS [Greg]: As the first replacement cast, they tried very hard to accommodate us. There were a few changes that went in for our cast. Connie, played by Lauren Kayahara, was put in a very pretty

pink low-cut leotard. She was a little bit taller and daintier than Baayork, with long legs. Michel Stuart as Greg originally wore those long black velvet pants with wrestling shoes, which have no heel support. The pants ballooned over the shoe, so it looked like big bell bottoms over sneakers. I like to have a little bit of a heel, and playing a character who has an attitude, the heel gave me a bit of stature. So when Theoni came around to each of us and asked if we were comfortable with the original costume, I mentioned the shoe element, and she said, "Well, what would you like?" "How about boots? Something Cossacky." "Okay, we'll give you boots." And that's how those boots were born. My opening night, I had the black knee high boots, black velour cossack pants and a black, white, and gray velour top. Kelly Bishop looked at me and said, "My, aren't we going to a formal audition." That top lasted only three performances, however, because I got lost against all the black on stage. It ultimately became a yellow terry sweatshirt.

ALYCE GILBERT: Gregory Gardner underwent a radical change when Michel Stuart left. The two boys who were coming in whined and whined at Michael that they didn't want to wear those "clown" pants. Connie's costume also changed. Michael said, "Oh, they have pretty bodies, let's put a leotard on them." It worked for some roles, it didn't work for others.

ANN REINKING [Cassie]: My Cassie leotard didn't have a scoop neck. I always wore things to elongate that which was short and make longer that what was long. I asked if I could shear the neck down and make it a V, and Theoni agreed. In the beginning, I didn't want to use a skirt at all, it just cut me all wrong — I didn't look good. So for about a week, we tried it without the skirt. Michael missed the skirt. If you're doing SWEET CHARITY, you have to wear a little black dress, and if you're doing SWAN LAKE, you should wear feathers. The red skirt is a Cassie signature that shouldn't be missed. I was primarily doing the same choreography, but without the skirt, the look changed. I asked if we could drop the waist, "It will look like it's on my waist, but it's really on my hips." Theoni put snaps all around so the skirt would stay in place. Donna's skirt always opened on the right. Doing the bourrés at the end of the Cassie dance, her skirt would flow out. I thought it would be beautiful if it were on the other side. You could see the leg working and the skirt would flow more gracefully — fanning out one way as the legs were going the other way. All the subsequent Cassies decided they liked that. Donna always wore it on the right; I wore it on the left, and from then on all the girls followed suit.

ALYCE GILBERT: Annie has a completely different body than Donna. The one thing you never want to put on Ann Reinking is

a leotard and a skirt. She has a very short torso, which is why she has legs that are a mile long. It looked odd on her because it snapped around her hip and it was so long, but it looked even odder when it was around her waist. Michael did try the dance without the skirt, but it just didn't work. The dance needs a skirt; she needs to be covered. You need that movement.

WANDA RICHERT [Cassie]: I finally got the Cassie turtleneck, which looked quite stunning. But it never felt like what Cassie is supposed to look like, so I didn't want to get too comfortable with it. It was the same cut as the standard Cassie leotard, only it was a turtleneck, and dyed to match the skirts.

DEBORAH HENRY [Cassie; Val]: I didn't wear the winter turtleneck very often. I could adapt to any temperature, so I wore the costume as it was and put golf socks in my shoes. As long as I had cushy warm feet, I was fine.

ALYCE GILBERT: There was this radical switch in London when they brought in Petra Siniawski, who had red hair. Michael remembered the image of Donna on stage at the Newman in a blue rehearsal leotard. Tharon had been sitting in the house that day and mumbled about doing something very interesting with the lighting. Suddenly Michael had this girl who was red-headed, freckled, and frail

who, when put into the red leotard, looked red-headed, freckled, and really, really frail! Theoni was trying to explain to Bill Kellerd over the phone what kind of blue this ought to be if Michael wanted a blue Cassie costume. A steel-blue was selected and she wore it all the way through. But she was the only person who ever wore blue, and it was an aberration. The understudy who replaced her and everybody else wore the classic Cassie red, as it should be.

CHERYL CLARK [Cassie]: Because my passés are so high, we had to make sure my skirt was shorter. I got my heel caught in the skirt once, and I was hurt quite badly. The length of the skirt is important when you have a high extension.

ALYCE GILBERT: The original Cassie leotards were actually bought; subsequent ones were dyed to match. We'd send the leotard and the fabric for the skirt to the dyer. They'd come back the same or they'd come back different; you'd either use them or throw them out, depending on how the Festival budget was at the time. The real Cassie color is very bright red, but we were at the mercy of the dyer. It was never a leotard that you could buy retail. You'd have to call Bal Toggery and order six dozen in white with red thread so that when you're dyeing, the thread would be the same color. The skirt is made of Alix Jersey, a nylon jersey.

Photo by Herb Migdoll

Ann Reinking in Finale garb

GAY MARSHALL [Diana]: It's funny how much the costume starts to drive you mad. Suddenly they changed it so Diana could take off the lavender turtleneck underneath the tee-shirt. Your big freedom was to wear just the little tee-shirt with the

green leotard, which was heaven. Little things like that made such a difference. The socks were so important! They had to be really thick wool socks, the kind that you would go skiing in, for warmth and comfort. I felt they made me springy. Alyce let me wear high-top Reeboks. She knew I had a rough time with my ankles.

DEBORAH HENRY: I had the original Valerie Clark costume. It was made with lace, and hung like a midriff. If you felt cold, you could wear a turtleneck underneath. Alyce made me a special bra with padding inside to make me look like a natural 34. But one time when I went to start the Val monologue, my padding dropped. One of the falsies was down in front of my stomach and the other was where it was supposed to be — so I had one breast and one nothing.

ALYCE GILBERT: A number of women playing Val on the road had small bosoms, and they started padding and padding and padding, to the point where it was in relation to the Sheilas — and then the Sheilas got bigger! It turned into competitive padding for a long time. The person who was maintaining the acting on the road seemed to need the visual reinforcement in a big way.

WANDA RICHERT: I had about three falsies in each side of my bra at one point, and I was wearing a front hook bra. As I went into the position where you lean over forward with your arms clasped in front of you in *The Music and the Mirror,* I felt my bra unhook in the front. These three falsies that were folded up in all different ways were moving slowing under my armpits, and I hadn't even done the slow section of the dance yet. It was so cold on stage, my nipples were sticking out through the leotard. I monitored everything I was doing in my upper body and danced the hell out of my lower body, because I thought everybody would see that I have no tits — and the ones that I had when I started the number were now on my back! I figured if I worked my way into the wings at some point, I could throw them out onto the floor but I couldn't maneuver it and had to finish the number. I hit the last lunge, and thought, "Now what the hell am I going to do?" I just stood up and crossed my arms in front of me.

ALYCE GILBERT: Hair was always a problem because no one was ever employed to be in charge of it. A couple of the tours carried someone once in a while to maintain it. There were agreements with Vidal Sassoon studios in various cities to cut hair. The kids were mostly left to wear their own hairstyles. The problem was when we got into the big crunchy hairstyles later on. No one had the authority to make them stop. The girls would get perms and absolutely every woman who ever stood up there with crunchy hair looked like a no-neck monster.

KAY COLE: I had come from doing SGT. PEPPER, so I had major rock 'n'roll hair — frizzed and permed. During the course of A CHORUS LINE rehearsals, we kept cutting it because Michael wanted it shorter. The goal was for all of us to be able to dance in hair that suited the character but was good for dancing. You're up there all the time, so you need to look somewhat presentable.

TRISH GARLAND [Original Judy]: Michael hated my hair, which was really long. "Get that hair out of your face!" he would always scream at me. So my hairdresser created that pageboy cut for me.

KATE WRIGHT [Sheila]: When I started, I had very long hair. Thommie Walsh told me in no uncertain terms, "It's got to go." So we cut it to the shoulder. I had never put a hot roller in my hair and had to learn how to do it, which was not easy. Then my hair started to get fried from the rollers. So I started going once a week to have this treatment to keep the body and prevent it from being so fried. I went to the company manager and said, "This is costing me a bundle." They picked up the expense and every week I would get these wonderful treatments. As Sheila, since my hair is in the script, they paid for haircuts, too. But then I made a big mistake. My hair gets flat in the middle of the show and I liked to reset it, so now I'm doing the hot rollers twice a show and the ends

are brutal. I went and got a perm — the perm of the decade. It took so long to take on my hair that I missed the performance. I called the theatre, "I'm not calling in sick, I'm calling in permed." That perm came out so terrible, my hair shot straight out from my head. I couldn't get the Finale hat on!

KERRY CASSERLY [Kristine]: There was a time when they were dyeing your hair to look like the original. And if there were too many blondes, you were changed.

KATE WRIGHT: Kelly had a little pony tail at the back of her neck and she would flip the elastic off and put it around her wrist. Then she would run her fingers through the back of her hair and say "… Better?" Mine was up in a little ballet bun. I would start the show with about fifty pins in it to get through the opening and then sneak the pins out of my hair when I wasn't dancing. By the time Zach said to let my hair down, I just took out the last two pins. I would shake my hair and it would cascade beautifully.

LAURIE GAMACHE [Final Cassie]: There was a rider in the contract that said they could have your hair be whatever they wanted, but they had to pay for any changes. After you finished, they had to pay to have it restored to the way it was before.

Photo by Sunny Bak

VICKI FREDERICK [Cassie]: I always wore it straight back in a pony tail for the whole show except when I did the Cassie dance. My hair was so heavy that there was no way I could do the head whips without it coming out of the pony tail, and Michael loved it.

ALYCE GILBERT: Vicki has Walt Disney hair. When it came out in the dance, there was this great curtain of hair, it was lovely. Ann Reinking's hair was a real problem. When it hangs, it's not a good look, especially for dancing and standing. That was always the problem with A CHORUS LINE, because you dance and you stand and you dance and you stand. It's difficult to cover and to stay warm. You can't fix your hair during the show. In most shows, you dance and leave the stage. In A CHORUS LINE, you stand there and your hair gets worse and worse.

Wearing the winter layers are Rene Ceballos as Bebe, Edward Love as Richie, and Mitzi Hamilton as Val

61

THEONI ALDREDGE: Shoes are something the kids have a lot to say about. Michael once put Donna in a t-strap, and then everybody asked for t-straps and started with the "I can't dance in the shoes I'm wearing" routine. Michael said, "That's right, you can't dance." They complained about sneakers and Michael said, "An entire brilliant show was danced in sneakers called WEST SIDE STORY. They had no trouble dancing. Now, who can't dance in sneakers?"

KAREN ZIEMBA [Bebe; Understudy]: We each got hand-made custom shoes.

ALYCE GILBERT: The really radical change happened when Michael wanted the Bus & Truck more contemporary. There was all this milliskin all of a sudden and it was absolutely scary. The Connie had this little camisole with a belt and leg warmers. Bell bottoms went out of the pants, which came after flares had disappeared in contemporary life although they hung on in dance wear a lot longer. There was always the feeling that the wide bottom of the pants made your leg look longer. Thommie Walsh was always the cutting edge of flares; his flares were bigger than anybody's. The Bobby costume changed, but not drastically. It was always pants and a sweater. There were boys whose necks weren't as long as Thommie's and didn't wear the scarf. The original sweater, an Indian fabric that was

made in Chile, was originally bought at Unique and we eventually found more in SoHo. We had just enough to cover New York, but not enough to send out on tour. So we re-shopped, and changed the color of the shirt and the sweater.

BRADLEY JONES [Greg]: For the Bus & Truck tour, they brought in the whole design team. Michael wanted to update the look. Theoni told everybody she would work with whatever they wanted to wear.

LAURIE GAMACHE: Certain characters were so connected to a specific look that you couldn't take it away. Diana got brighter trunks, but it wouldn't be Diana anymore if she wasn't wearing that velour shirt. Sheila couldn't change. The colors of the Don tee-shirt changed from blue to hot pink stripes, and it was cut without sleeves. The Bebe costume changed to a maroon one-piece leotard with black tights; Maggie to a pink short-sleeve leotard with beige tights, and the shirt was gone for a while. Judy's costume was higher cut and brighter purple; Val's costume became a brighter purple. I had that old brown Kristine suit, which is very narrow with low legs. I looped the ties through to cinch the legs up and pulled the top out and tucked it under my bra, so I had a much wider line on my shoulders and more leg. I walked in to Theoni and said, "This is how I want to wear it. May I wear it like this?" She looked and said,

"Yes, you may." So when anybody gave me shit about hiking my legs up, I said, "Theoni Aldredge said I could do it."

KERRY CASSERLY: My dresser, Diana Warner, sewed my leotards just how I wanted so I could tie them at my hips. Alyce kept her eye on us, saying the girls' leg lines were getting way too high. I wore the black tights on the road, but when I got to Broadway, I switched to beige.

ALYCE GILBERT: The milliskin pants became such an issue on tour and so offensive to audiences that we just kept pulling them out.

BILL JONES: When costumes first started coming back to New York from the road, they were stored in a space area above the proscenium at the Shubert. That got filled to the ceiling real fast. It also violated some fire laws. We found another space under the orchestra pit, only the doorway was blocked by an air conditioning duct. You had to crawl under it to enter the room. We lasted there about six months until we discovered that it was also a fire trap. Next we found this horrible space under Shubert Alley. It was dark and filthy, and grease and fumes would come in from the alley above. The first few years we used it, the last twelve feet or so of the floor wasn't even paved. It was dirt! Whenever it rained or snowed, the water just poured into this room, which was

packed solid with clothes, so all the costumes had to be in double plastic bags. At one end were bookcases that were just stacked with shoes, going up to the ceiling, and huge bags of hats. Then along another wall were long shelves with laundry baskets filled with line costumes. The rest of the room had at least seven racks packed solid with Finale costumes, each one in a plastic bag and labeled with the name of its occupant and measurements. We nicknamed this underground storage area the "Chorus Line Boutique."

ALYCE GILBERT The men's Finale costumes were beaded with #2 copper bugle bead outlining the stripes. It's basic menswear trimming. There are two bands around the sleeves of Austrian crystals in a circular path defined by double rows of bronze bugle beads around each sleeve. The same kind of detailing happened on the lapel. The three seams in the back of the jacket are defined with that same pattern of lockrose, and the edges are defined by the bronze coppery bugles. The vest has stripes of alternating copper bugle and rose. Originally they were a light rose, which is a paler pink. About five years into the run, they stopped making the light rose, and Barbara Matera replaced it with regular rose. On the old costumes we had to intermingle the two colors. From a distance, they blended, but up close, they were really quite different. Those stripes are also outlined with crystal. The edges of the vest are defined with a row of bugles. There are large crystal buttons, two on each cuff, and six big ones pretending to button the jacket. There is a mirror in the center of the bow tie and small crystal pieces that act as if they were studs in the shirt fronts for the guys. The girls have the same treatment on their vests as the boys, except it goes all the way around. The bodices themselves are sequins in various hues of peach, copper, and pink. It changed a fair amount over the years as different people were beading them. But it's basically a big paisley design, with lots of copper bugles and clear opalescent sequins. There's a good deal on the front that you don't see because it's under the vest. They also had mirrors in their bow ties. The Finale costumes are really one of the brilliant pieces of twentieth-century costume design. They worked in a very definitive, glamorous way. The fact that Theoni designed those jackets to be short made all the difference in maintaining the line over the years. When you have tails, you have to even them along the whole

"The Bobby costume changed but not drastically. There were boys whose necks weren't as long as Thommie's and didn't wear the scarf."
— Alyce Gilbert

"Sheila's costume looks a little bit like a suit of armor — very hard and metallic." — Bill Jones

(Thommie Walsh and Kelly Bishop pictured)

line. Every time you bring somebody in, the length of the tail is yet another problem to be dealt with. The same thing with the fact that girls don't have jackets, they have vests — it made an enormous difference in the number of girls that were able to wear those costumes. With this "hat" choreography, where one arm is raised for practically the whole number, the shoulder padding on a jacket is very unattractive on a woman. It makes them look clunkier, clumsier, much less glamorous. The vest line is much more flattering, and with the sleeves all beaded, it's really much more glamorous than wearing a jacket. The Finale is based on reflection. With the mirrors turning, all the fabrics are reflective: the satin vests, the jackets, the trousers. Even the girls' satin shoes and boys' patent leather shoes all reflect the light. It's why audiences never know what color they are. In the early days, we routinely made new Finale costumes for each new hire. I knew there would come a time when they wouldn't spend the money to make new costumes, and we'd have to pass down the costumes and squeeze the actors into them. We wound up having to use Finale costumes that had originally been made for dancers of a very different shape because the bodies had changed so much over the years, especially with the "pumped up" rage of the eighties. The very first set of Finale costumes at the Public were done inexpensively as a favor to the Festival. When the new ones came

in, the girls' were $950 and the boys' were $1,050 each. That was without the hats, just the costume. Hat and shoes were always separate items. That was a lot of money in those days. It would be several thousand now.

BILL JONES: There were five dressers working on the Broadway show. Once the performance began it was very easy, but it took about three hours to set up. Since the actors sweat so much on stage, everything except for the gold was washed and ironed for every performance. Alyce would get there as the sun was coming up and start the laundry — about four or five loads per show. Then two people, depending on whose turn it was to set up, arrived at 2:00 p.m. One person would iron everything, the shirts, pants, gold costumes, and another person would go through all the beading. They're very heavily beaded, and you have to keep up or you'd never catch up. Then the clothes had to be sorted and distributed to all the dressing rooms and the Finale costumes had to be preset for the quick change, stage right. That change at the end was very fast. As soon as Paul and Larry leave the stage after the accident scene, they go right down to wardrobe and change because they weren't on again until the Finale. Zach's last line from the back of the house is, "But if today were the day you had to stop dancing." Then he runs to wardrobe, and says his last line, "I'm very

glad we're going to be working together," from a mike offstage right, in Finale costume. The line onstage is looking at him in the back of the house, but in actuality he's standing in the wings just offstage. The people who don't get the job run offstage and they're the first ones on for the Finale. The guys underdress their socks, and the women underdress their mesh tights. Just as the dresser is finishing the first group, the others come offstage. Basically they did all the undressing themselves. The guys that were really good were half naked by the time they got to where the change was. They took everything off, and the dresser held the jumpsuit so they could step into it and pull their shoes on. Then the dresser suited them up while they zippered up and went on to the next person. The men's jumpsuit is all one piece — pants, vest, and sleeveless shirt all together, and there's one zipper that runs from the crotch all the way up. No one had shoe strings, they all had gold elastic so it would just pull open.

ALYCE GILBERT: Not all of the 378 Finale costumes made survived to the end. The line costumes? There is no way at all of ever figuring out how many. The Finale shoes came from Capezio and the rest of the shoes came from G. Banks Custom Shoes.

Alyce Gilbert

MICHAEL BENNETT, *acknowledging the creative team and key staff members to the audience, following the Gala 3389th Performance:* There is a mother of A CHORUS LINE and her name is Alyce Gilbert.

THEONI ALDREDGE: Alyce always made new kids feel welcome, there was always a gift waiting for them. She never forgot birthdays or holidays. Mother Hen … Alyce *was* A CHORUS LINE.

MITCHELL WEISS [Company Manager]: If I could move that woman into my apartment as my best-friend-aunt, I would do it in a second. She is beyond talented. I don't know how she ever kept her temper sometimes; she just never seemed to lose it. I guess that is why Michael liked her so much.

RON STAFFORD [Assistant Stage Manager]: Alyce was amazing. To go down to that room was like being in a department store. It was so well organized — a drawer for every character.

JUSTIN ROSS: Alyce was always calm, prepared, and she made you feel totally safe and taken care of. And that was such an enormous gift to everyone who ever passed through that basement because there was never a time, regardless of what

kind of catastrophe was happening, when Alyce wasn't on top of it.

KATE WRIGHT: I adored Alyce. She was so good to me and good to her girls. She saw us through all our nervous breakdowns, our broken love affairs. We went through tons with six single girls sharing the dressing room behind her. Could you imagine?

PATTI D'BECK [Assistant Dance Captain; Understudy]: Alyce was always trying to fix me because I was constantly going on stage with my costumes inside out.

WAYNE MELEDANDRI [Paul]: You knew that Alyce would always be available and there for you. She was the anchor.

KAREN ZIEMBA: She was the most organized woman and she just lived at that theater, it meant so much to her. She ran it so smoothly, every bead on every costume was put back on when it would come off.

FRASER ELLIS [Assistant Stage Manager; Understudy]: She always knew all the dish.

WANDA RICHERT: Alyce was my pal. I would be amazed just watching her walk

around that wardrobe room. She was wonderful.

DEBORAH HENRY: She was maternal with me, always making sure my skirt had not one wrinkle in it. Alyce extended herself and you could see it through her work.

MICHAEL GRUBER [Final Mike]: She was the best. She kept every thing impeccable. If the shoes started to go, we had new shoes. Not even a question.

LOIDA SANTOS [Diana]: She was a wonderful, gentle soul. There was this warmth and sincerity about her, she accommodated you as much as she possibly could.

KEVIN McCREADY [Final Larry]: Alyce is the most extraordinary, wonderful woman. I think everyone feels the same way.

The *"mother"* of
A CHORUS LINE,
Alyce Gilbert

The Lights Were Cued to the Music

THARON MUSSER [Lighting Designer]: I went to thousands of rehearsals down on 19th Street, where we went through many stages. At one point the line was going to be a light box in the floor. At another point, for what we know about snow in Puerto Rico, we were going to have all the kids in a sled in the background during *Nothing*. One day Michael leaned over and said, "You know, we have to do something to help the audience know when the characters are expressing internal thoughts." And I said, "Well, the light won't be blue." It was a very gradual process. Just watching it and watching the nature of the show organically emerge.

I wanted to have a lot of lines on the stage. I brought Michael a picture out of David Duncan's photography book. A cue in the show became a reproduction of that picture — magenta and green on a line of people.

One day I said to Michael, "I'm not going to use specials on this show, I want to do a Mondrian. I don't mean palette, I mean patterns on the floor. We'll use whatever is in that place when we need a spe-cial." He said, "What do you mean, Mondrian?" "Come over to the house," I said. So he came over, I got down my art books and showed him a typical Mondrian. Michael and I always worked from art books. Lighting is such an intangible thing, you can't do sketches. Art books are a great way to demonstrate to a director the kind of color or texture you're thinking about.

Michael and I had an unspoken agreement. We just sensed. There were times when I would get a picture on the stage but it didn't work for the scene; but if Michael liked it, he'd change the blocking. We had a relationship that I've never had with anybody else and don't imagine I ever will again. It was very, very special.

All 128 light cues in the show were on dance counts. We spent quite a bit of time with our original production stage manager, Jeff Hamlin, teaching him to count because it had to be that precise. He cued off score. I had cued opera off score so there was no reason a musical couldn't be cued off score. And it's the only thing Michael understood. It had to be on the music. The dancers were, so why couldn't we? And Jeff did a fantastic job.

JEFF HAMLIN [Original Production Stage Manager]: I had to interpret the information Michael and Tharon were giving me about the rhythm of the show from a lighting standpoint, and then get that information out to the follow-spot operators, and call the show. When we were down at the Public, we actually had two lighting positions for control. We had the booth with a preset board and an electrician, but we also had a whole other system upstage right. I think I kept the job of stage manager for Michael because of the way I worked on that with Tharon. That's where he really gained confidence in me.

Michael was one of the few directors who not only understood the technical aspects of the theatre, but actually loved it, loved working on lights and figuring out the cues. He wanted the lights to be in synch with the bursts of music. Everything was on musical counts. That was both its challenge and its great joy.

THARON MUSSER: The challenge was making it right. And right was making Michael happy, and making Michael happy was doing what's right for the work.

"I picked Joan up on my motorcycle and we came tearing down Shubert Alley, and there's the sheriff." — *BOB KAMLOT*

The computerized lighting board was a first on Broadway, but it evolved because of the Public Theatre. They had what we never had on Broadway — a preset board. I only brought in a special board because I needed a little more than they had, but otherwise that was how we did the show. So when the Shuberts said we could have anything we wanted, I said, "Okay, Broadway missed one whole era of preset boards, which even colleges have. Let's skip to the next generation. We want to go to memory."

Well, believe it or not, there were none invented at the time. We told Frank DeVerna, who runs Four Star — where we rent equipment — about the board we wanted. When they decided to move A CHORUS LINE uptown early, he couldn't produce it in time, and I said, "Frank, if we miss this chance, it will be another ten years before Broadway catches up to snuff." So Frank called me and said "Get packing! We're leaving tomorrow for Hillsboro, Oregon." I said, "What in the hell for?" "They've got a switchboard I want you to see and they can deliver by our date." We flew out to Oregon, looked at this board, and I said, "Eeech! However, I don't think we have a choice. It's now or never." Their proto-type, which we named Sam, was brought in on the show and made history. We had Sam up until two or three years before we closed on Broadway.

BOB KAMLOT [Original General Manager]: We were the first show to have a computerized board, the likes of which today would be laughable. Computerization in those days was unheard of because it was too expensive. Tharon Musser made it happen.

RON STAFFORD : You didn't just push a button, like you do in most companies nowadays. True, the board was all pro-grammed, but you still had to manually bring the fading up and down. You gave the "go" to the electrician sitting beside you, because tempos changed from night to night. The way it was designed was exact — when the music ended, the lights went out. Making it all work was like painting. The design of the show is so integral that you were helping to create the whole picture.

BOB KAMLOT: On the first day of the take-in at the Shubert, David Merrick came with the sheriff and stopped the move because he claimed that our lighting equip-ment belonged to him. Now, we purchased that lighting equipment from Four Star Stage Lighting because we knew the show was going to run so there was no sense renting it. I got a panicky call from Jeff Hamlin around 1:00 p.m. I called our attor-ney and the Shubert Organization and we all came rushing down to the theatre. Joan Daily was the attorney who handled most of the Festival activities. I picked up Joan

on my motorcycle and we came tearing down Shubert Alley, and there's the sheriff. So we went upstairs and collected Gerry Schoenfeld for the showdown.

GERALD SCHOENFELD [Chairman, Shubert Organization]: David Merrick's lawyer came in with the sheriff and was

Tharon Musser and Michael Bennett

Assistant Stage Manager Ron Stafford at the lighting board

going to seize the lights. I told the sheriff, "If anybody touches those lights, and the show doesn't open, there will be a major lawsuit." We had quite a testy argument there for a good half hour. He backed off and the lights weren't touched.

BOB KAMLOT: Frank DeVerna, who owned Four Star, later sued David Merrick. It went on for years and years. David Merrick had acquired a lot of lighting equipment over the course of his theatrical career. He had an arrangement with Four Star to store it at their facility. In return, Frank DeVerna would have the right to rent it until such time as David Merrick needed it. But this particular equipment was not David Merrick's. It was all brand new because we had just bought it. But Merrick, being who he was, just went right in. Needless to say, Frank won.

THARON MUSSER: Michael and I didn't want to see shadows on the back wall of the stage. The Shuberts said again, "All right, what do you want to do?" and I said, "I want to sling a bridge from the ceiling up there."

PHIL SMITH [Vice President, Shubert Organization]: A CHORUS LINE didn't make very many demands on the theatre except the lighting bridge, which was a big effort. The chandeliers had to come down. Pete Sumerall engineered the whole thing. He punched right into the Shubert offices. The big problem was whether Bernie and Gerry would object to these huge things coming up into the middle of their office space.

GERRY SCHOENFELD: That lighting bridge was some headache. It went right up into our offices. The spot crew had to go into the offices, then down a ladder to the bridge. The lighting angle had to be 45 degrees so it would not reflect in the mirrors and bounce back into the eyes of the audience. We cut holes in the ceiling, hung the bridge — and wouldn't you know, the beams were not long enough, which meant the angles were not right! We then had to take it down and put in new beams to correct the angle.

PHIL SMITH: Tharon said she needed to get that exact bounce of light. She was concerned with the patterns she created on the stage, which were beautiful if you were upstairs and looked down. But if the aim of the light didn't hit the stage properly, it would bounce, hit the mylar, and create shadows and confusion. Tharon wanted to get the cleanest look possible and it had to be this exact angle. She had to get out and over the people in the balcony, because otherwise the angle of the spots would hit their heads. So we agreed to allow a lighting bridge to be installed.

BERNARD JACOBS [President, Shubert Organization]: We tried to talk Michael out of it. We tried to convince him that the lights wouldn't have been much different off either the first or second balcony rail, or a combination of both balcony rails. But Tharon Musser was insistent that it come in at a 45 degree angle, and both balconies deviated from that. Michael

eventually said the show would not work without the lighting bridge, so we built the lighting bridge.

GERRY SCHOENFELD: We did alterations for other shows, such as enlarging orchestra pits and dressing room areas, but the lighting bridge was the first one of its kind. Of course, the classic alteration is CATS. The CHORUS LINE alteration was minor compared to that, but it was revolutionary at the time.

FRED OLSSON [Shubert Organization Facilities Director]: Some people had ideas of steel going across the whole theatre. Peter Feller, the famous theatre technician, also got involved with the layout of the light bridge. One of us came up with the idea of taking the chandeliers out. The Shuberts then provided supplemental lighting to give a little more light so people could read their programs and so forth. Taking the chandeliers down made it much easier to construct the bridge because the holes were already in the ceiling. You did less damage. There was also

a mural on the ceiling, a painting, which we peeled off. Where there had been attachment points for the chandeliers, we hung steel members to support this huge catwalk on which the people would light the show. This was going to be much more than your average lighting bridge, which more or less goes up and down on cables. This came up right through the floor of the Shubert offices and had steel girders, maybe a foot thick, across the floor to hold it.

PHIL SMITH: We installed the gondola, and put the follow-spot guys up there. We were obviously nervous that the thing wouldn't be strong enough. The idea of somebody going down into it, especially without a cage around this open ladder!

TONY D'AIUTO [Spotlight Operator]: When the show first opened, the guys were frightened to work up there because it wasn't closed in. Later on they put a wall up and they made it a little safer. But once you were up there, you were locked in. You couldn't leave the platform; you

would shake the lamps, the spotlights. So you had to sit still and be very quiet during the show. You couldn't talk because you were out in the audience, only about ten feet from the balcony.

GERRY SCHOENFELD: One day I went down the ladder to the bridge myself, and, to tell you the truth, I wasn't very happy on that bridge. You're way up there! I held onto that ladder with a death grip. Although the offices here are theoretically on the second floor, it's the equivalent of the fifth floor, and the bridge was just a little bit, eighteen feet, twelve feet, whatever it was, down from the office floor to the bridge. But after a while, the guys were scrambling up and down like monkeys.

KEITH MARSTON [Shubert Organization Projects Coordinator]: Because of the access from the second floor, there was no need to have the bridge go up and down. It wasn't on winches, it was fixed positioning. You could walk along the whole thing.

"We have to do something to help the audience know when the characters are expressing internal thoughts." — *THARON MUSSER*

*One of the many creative lighting
designs used in A CHORUS LINE*

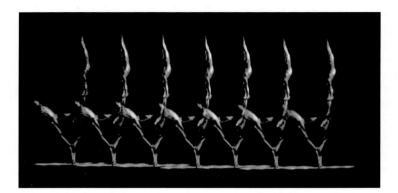

Trois Acrobates: Folies-Bergère *by David Douglas Duncan was Tharon Musser's inspiration for a lighting design*

FRED OLSSON: And, of course, they had to have a man there to operate the spots. If it were a fixed light, we wouldn't have built a bridge, we would have just had a truss.

KEITH MARSTON: A metal plate trap door closed and then opened when the ladder was in use. Nobody could fall in when it was not in use.

JEFF HAMLIN: Tharon and Michael insisted that the stage manager call the show from the front of the house as opposed to in the wings. That had never happened before. See, at the Newman we had a modern theatre with a control booth at the back of the auditorium. Michael and Tharon finally had a stage manager who could actually see what he was doing and could call the show with sensitivity and physicality. They would accept no less at the Shubert.

FRASER ELLIS: You take the elevator to the Shubert offices, and walk down a

flight to the balcony level. At the rear of the balcony is the stage manager's booth where the stage manager called the show and the computer for the lights was housed.

THARON MUSSER: There were basically no other changes from the Newman to the Shubert. We even reproduced where the follow spots were in the Shubert to get the angle we wanted.

Our next problem was that the Shubert orchestra didn't rake as steeply as the Newman. The footlights in A CHORUS LINE are used decoratively. They are not really used to light, but I certainly didn't want to lose them. At the same time, if you had those footlights on the stage of the Shubert Theatre, the first few rows of the orchestra would not see the feet of the dancers. Joe Papp came up with the perfect idea of putting them on a little elevator and just having them come up when you need them. We did that through all the runs, except in London. Robin Wagner and I had gone over for pre-production, and told them what we needed. When I went back for tech rehearsals, there in the orchestra pit were these huge hydraulic tubes to raise the footlights. They could have leveled the Drury Lane stage with those things! Finally, on tour we simply laid the footlights flat facing right up to the ceiling and had a little piece of mylar that just flipped up and reflected them back in our mirrors. That's all there was to it.

The road companies were reproduced right down to the Bus & Truck. We were getting the same look. We reproduced the New York thing. The traveling companies were put together, production-wise, in New York. Robin, myself, and Michael would figure out ways to cut down time. That's the main thing — the time in and out of the theatres. On the first date wherever a tour opened, we were all there to be sure it worked. If necessary, we'd go to a second date to clean up this or that, but most of the time one date did it. We had good crews.

PETER VON MAYRHAUSER [Stage Manager]: When we were on the road, they would literally take out a tape measure and measure the Mondrian patterns. If a pattern had to be 6½ inches by 12 inches, it would be checked. They were that thorough about it. It was amazing.

JEFF HAMLIN: There were great advantages of working down at the Public. Youth. Energy. They were all kids. One of the great disappointments was that we could not take our follow-spot operators up to the Shubert because they weren't members of Local 1. There were two women, which was unheard of in 1975. Going to the Shubert meant leaving a lot of things behind — but we were also coming into the kind of environment that really was the show.

THARON MUSSER: In New York, I had one assistant — Richard Winkler, who's now done the show all over the world for me. And we had the crew: one board operator, and three follow-spot people. They changed throughout the years, but one guy was on the follow spot for almost the entire run.

TONY D'AIUTO: I was supposed to open the show on Broadway, but I was working on another show and couldn't leave. I finally came in at the beginning of 1978 when a job opened up. They had held the job for me for three weeks until I could get there. It wasn't the lead operator, but the front light man on the right side, house right.

The challenge was to do pickups in the dark. Head shots in the dark. That was the big challenge. To do all these in succession. You had to look at the show, learn it before you even ran the spot, and then try to get up there and work it. You were cued all through the show, except for the head shots. The head shot couldn't be cued, it was too quick. When Mike Linn, the lead operator, left, I moved over into his spot, then I became the head front

light man where I did all the cueing. You cue, you count, everything. All three lights are worked in unison. You go so many counts on, so many counts off, you're cueing all during the show.

This is what made A CHORUS LINE so beautiful. Everything worked together, you never stopped cueing from beginning to end. We worked by the light cues, not music cues. I would have a headset on all during the show, and on specific light cues, I would cue the front lights. I never in all the years I was in the business, starting with the original DAMN YANKEES in the fifties had to wear a headset during a show. Front lights had their cues and they just did it.

A CHORUS LINE was the first show where the front-light man had to wear a headset and listen to the lighting cues during the whole show. I was completely fascinated all thirteen years with how the front lights work. It was very difficult for most people to learn. They were intimidated. Even I was intimidated at first. The bounce, the *Montage*, where the lights come up on characters in the dark, was the hardest. Front lights did the whole *At the Ballet*. We did it all. There wasn't any

other lighting there, just us. When we finished, the stage lights would come up; the line was in logo formation.

THARON MUSSER: When we did *At the Ballet* for the first time, I had the follow-spots right from the beginning. During one sequence, I just had them do a very slow color shift to lavender, and Michael said "My God, she's just put on a tutu. I don't have to redo this number and I thought I did." It's the way one feels music for one thing.

TONY D'AIUTO: The whole basis of front-light work is to be there without the audience knowing you're there. If you can accomplish that, you've accomplished the epitome of front-light work. Except, of course, in the bounce sequence, where you're consciously doing that kind of thing. But basically, you're supposed to be blending in with the show, not being obvious.

We were constantly training release men our way, so that A CHORUS LINE never varied. It always looked the same. We had an ongoing training program, and it never stopped. These people worked for no pay, just to be able to go up there and

"Pickups in the dark. Head shots in the dark. All these in succession. You had to look at the show, learn it before you even ran the spot, and then try to get up there and work it." — TONY D'AIUTO

work on A CHORUS LINE.

Since there was no curtain, we had to be at the theatre about an hour earlier to do all the light checks. We got paid extra to be there early and take care of all the lighting. Make sure everything was working properly, do a complete run-through, lighting-wise, of the whole show. Every performance. It was a short show for us. One guy left the theatre around 9:20 p.m., after the Cassie dance. They used to alternate, one left at 9:20 and one left around 10:10. They were finished with their cues. My last cue was after the Paul monologue. Then one man had to stay for *What I Did For Love*. Nothing during the Alternatives scene. We were out by the Finale.

But I used to stay to see the end of the show. On matinee days, I used to deliberately take the last cue and stay to see the end of it. I loved the end of the show. I loved that finale. I've retired since the show closed and I hold a record. No one else has ever run a front light as long as I have in one show. I did thirteen years. Since the beginning of 1978. No breaks, a continuous run.

THARON MUSSER: When you get to the tech rehearsal you're really scared shitless. You can talk color but you can't really show anybody color except on the stage, even if you show them swatches. That first tech is the scariest time in your life, because for the first time, you're baring

your soul. No matter how much you talk and how much you're in synch with each other, the nitty-gritty is when you turn those lights on for the first time. And A CHORUS LINE worked. I don't think we changed anything from what I had pre-planned and brought in. It was all used.

I loved the final dialogue scene and the look we got there. When Priscilla went into *What I Did for Love* and starts down from upstage center, Michael asked, "Aren't you going to give her a spot?" and I said, "She's walking through the woods. Be sure she phrases so that she's singing the lyrics when she's in the light, not when she's walking through the darkness." We gave her the spot when she got down stage. That whole thing was, to me, as if they were sitting out at a lake or a park saying what are you going to do when you grow up.

I'd check on the show through the years if we had a change of stage management, change of electrician. Every so often we had a cleanup of the show. Checking the focus to be sure it was all still up to snuff, but the electricians were very good about that. The thing they had to be most careful about were the side lights because I had them in such strict paths. If a shudder tipped or anything, it was terrible. Then we got to the point two to three years into the run when we had run long enough that we had to start changing our units — we had 312 lighting units and footlights in A CHORUS LINE.

RON STAFFORD: A CHORUS LINE was very specific. It was black and white. Every night when the show started, if that opening light cue was wrong, Tom Porter, our stage manager, would beep you on the phone asking, "What is going on up there?" Even if it was a split second off. Because it had to be right with the first down beat of the music and Zach's line.

FRASER ELLIS: Ron Stafford taught me how to call the show, and Morris Freed helped a lot, too. The first thing you do is write down all the cues, the warnings, and then you'd sit in the booth and watch. Next, you would tap the stage manager on the leg on the cues, on the "go"s. And he would say, too fast, too slow, whatever. Once you were okay with that, he'd let you call small sections of the show, until you'd finally called a whole show with the stage manager there with you. Then they'd let you do it by yourself. It was a gradual thing. It wasn't BAM — you're on, because it was just too much. Especially with the Cassie dance and the Finale — there were a million cues, the foot light cues, the mirrors, the follow spots — lots of lights.

Sound

ABE JACOB [Sound Designer]: Michael Bennett wanted to do a musical that was as simple as possible: a black box, some mirrors and rehearsal clothes. He didn't want a lot of microphones. He wanted area miking.

The innovation of A CHORUS LINE was just being real. We'd come from the times of HAIR and JESUS CHRIST SUPERSTAR, which brought sound to the forefront. A CHORUS LINE went back to being sort of a very natural, realistic show that had moments of exaggeration. There were no sound effects, no pre-recorded effects. Just singers in a booth. At the Shubert, the booth was just offstage left. No elaborate television monitor; they could just see the stage. They had earphones.

OTTS MUNDERLOH [Original Sound Mixer]: The sound that Abe and Michael were going for was the most *real* sound they could get.

ABE JACOB: Michael wanted it to be a rehearsal piano, and I wanted it to be an MGM movie.

Down at the Public we came up with the shotgun mikes across the front of the stage. He liked them as part of the look of the set, and he used that look when he blocked people. The actors stood right in front of a microphone to deliver important lines. Later at the Shubert we had five floor mikes, five hanging mikes, and two in the offstage singers' booth.

There was very little communication at the Newman between the conductor and the cast or vice versa. There was no orchestra pit; the orchestra was backstage. One of the NYSF apprentices sat on a little catwalk on the side of the Newman to mix the sound of the orchestra. And that was the extent of sound for the show at the Newman.

Michael wanted to maintain the illusion of an offstage orchestra, or no orchestra at all, until the mirrors turned. At the Public it was easy to achieve because there was no pit; since the orchestra was in the load-

Abe Jacob's sound design shop order for the move to the Shubert

The sound console was situated next to Zach's station in the last row

ing dock, all we had to do was treat it for sound. Michael wanted to keep that feeling at the Shubert. Tharon loved the idea of not having orchestra pit lights.

The original reasoning for covering the orchestra pit, more than strictly for sound purposes, was Tharon and Michael wanted total black. The pit was always covered from the beginning. It was acoustically transparent.

OTTS MUNDERLOH: But it was only a visual. The pit at the Shubert is small, and deeply under the stage, which doesn't help the pit sound live at all.

ABE JACOB: If Michael liked what we did, he didn't say anything; if he didn't like it, he let us know about it.

There were a lot of cues for stage monitor loudspeakers to go up or down, depending on whether it was underscoring and dialogue, or music and a single vocal, or a dance number. Woe be the operator if he did not bring the monitor back up for the dance section!

Sound wasn't thought about much on the move. It was there, it worked, and there wasn't a problem with it. It never received any of the notoriety that Tharon, for example, brought to the show. When new people came into the show, I would stop in and listen. But at the end of the run, in the last four years, no matter what you wanted to do, it was never done — that was simply the way it was.

The only thing that changed when we moved to the Shubert was a very specialized reverb unit that we came up with for the internal *Montages.* It was a large EMT Stereo reverb chamber with an electronic

plate, in a box eight feet long, four feet high, two feet wide. It was hung from the ceiling of the basement. A dressing room was built around it. When it finally started to wear out over the years, we literally couldn't get it out of the basement.

The show was going to be such a great hit that we couldn't take out any seats for sound. The equipment had to fit into just one row of seats, up against the standing room wall. Fortunately, at the Shubert there is a large column that supports the first mezzanine, so we had the space of the column to stash a little equipment in, plus five seats — and, of course, the two seats on the end that later became Zach's table.

OTTS MUNDERLOH: It was a challenge to keep the actor playing Zach to pay attention to the show, and not reach over and play with the knobs. In the beginning there were two seats, which were always sold and occupied, on the aisle and then the sound console further in the row. The Zach and Larry characters would have to excuse themselves to get by, then come sit in by the sound console. But they were forever getting up. Larry only stays for a little while, but Zach comes and goes for most of the show. We had a great time in the back of the theatre.

GERALD SCHOENFELD: We all have the same purpose, which is not to remove too many seats, but seats always have to be taken out in the back of the orchestra for

the sound board. Each seat, depending on what the price scale is, is worth a lot of money. Today, one seat is worth is about $19,000 if you sell that seat every performance for the year. So you try to remove as few as eight and not more than twelve seats. But all of the boards are custommade and of varying sizes. It's also a question of where they should be located. Some, like in the Imperial Theatre with DREAMGIRLS, were located outside of the seating area, along the back wall of the auditorium, which is ideal. Nowadays, in redoing the theatres, we put in cable runs under the floor so that there is no wiring going back to the sound consoles.

ABE JACOB: Then it was a matter of trying to make Zach sound as if he's coming from the back of the theatre. We ended up with loudspeakers at the rear of the house. The Shubert was a little difficult because it has two balconies, so we needed speakers in the back of every location.

OTTS MUNDERLOH: We started off with two speakers on the proscenium arch for the front of the orchestra, two on the sides in the rear of the orchestra, two in the boxes for the first mezzanine, and two hung on the light bridge that Tharon had built for the follow spots, to cover the upper balcony. And then there were three on the rear of each level for the Zach system. The speakers on the proscenium arch and the ones on the boxes never changed.

But as speakers got smaller, and the quality came up, you could hang a row of speakers along the balcony rail for the orchestra without obstructing any sight lines.

ABE JACOB: We also added a set of speakers under the balcony for the rear of the mezzanine floor, which we dug into the wall. Our original mixing console stayed until the last two years. We finally had to change it, because we literally couldn't get any parts for it. Surprisingly enough, that console stayed there; its replacement sat right on top of it.

OTTS MUNDERLOH: We didn't want to take out any more seats for the replacement. The new console was larger and deeper, so they put it on top of the standing room wall. Instead of physically being able to sit *in back* of the console, we now were in the *standing room position* mixing the sound.

ABE JACOB: The backstage intercom system was by far the most difficult part of the show and a critical element to keep stage management, cast, and crew happy. The follow spots had to hear one thing, the stage manager up in the lighting booth had to hear the entire show, plus the Zach system and the music. We changed intercoms three or four times. There were also a couple of amplifier substitutions. The sound equipment was probably worth $35,000 to $50,000 at

most. We rented everything.

OTTS MUNDERLOH: During Paul's monologue, the air conditioning, which was controlled from the Booth Theatre, had to be shut off every night.

ABE JACOB: It was a very quiet moment, and Michael wanted everything to be really focused on Paul as the lights came up on him. We just couldn't get it loud enough without it sounding very artificial. Remember, it was summer when we moved to the Shubert. The air conditioning noise was so loud, I suggested that during the applause for the Cassie dance, we shut the air off, and nobody would notice. When the cast comes back in for the beginning of the *Rehearsal Ones*, we could turn the air back on. And it worked. They had a guy who was cued to go over

The covered orchestra pit and shotgun mikes

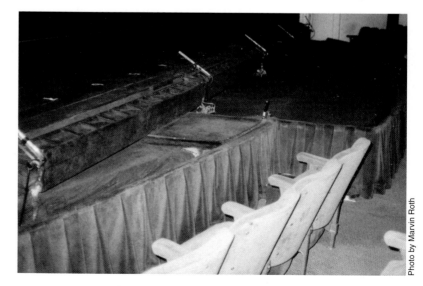

*Otts Munderloh
and Abe Jacob*

sound systems came out at the same time. I went out to operate and mix the show in San Francisco, Otts did Toronto, and we met in London. Steve Terry was doing the new company in New York.

OTTS MUNDERLOH: The only thing that really changes as you take the show around on the road is the theatre itself; how big it is, and the acoustical problems that you encounter in each theatre. Another factor is how loud each person is in the role. Sound also changes depending on whether there are substitute musicians playing that night, or cast changes.

ABE JACOB: We were just going to recreate what was in New York, including the Zach system in the rear of the house. We also instituted a microphone called "Zach's step," which remained all the way through the end of the tours, even though in some cities he didn't exit through the orchestra. He went off the side and came around, but there was always a Zach step mike, halfway up the steps. Then we actually put a wireless on Zach. He was the first person to get a wireless so he could have the freedom of movement. Then we

to the Booth Theatre and shut the air conditioning off. Although the controls for each of the five theatres along 44th and 45th Streets were at the Booth, it didn't affect any other show. It was similar to having all the exit lights turned off in the beginning before the mirrors did the first turn. The work on A CHORUS LINE was different than what you normally think of as sound and lighting design.

The Original, National, and International Companies all rehearsed together and the

had to do it for everybody. But those first tours were all without wireless mikes.

OTTS MUNDERLOH: The funniest part about going to London was that we were the *loud* show at the Drury Lane. We got them started being loud. They had never used this much equipment before.

ABE JACOB: The best thing about London was Autograph Sound. They willingly cooperated in all the crazy things that we Americans came over to tell them how to do. We had asked them for Altech Loudspeakers, not a name well-known in the UK. The distributors in the UK were a competing sound rental company that was bidding with Autograph for A CHORUS LINE, but Autograph worked out an arrangement, got the show and it started their company. Now Autograph is probably the largest supplier of sound equipment in Europe.

A CHORUS LINE was a training ground for everybody doing sound design today in the theatre. They came, in one way or another, from A CHORUS LINE.

*"A CHORUS LINE was a training ground for everybody
doing sound design today in the theatre.
They came, in one way or another, from A CHORUS LINE. "* — ABE JACOB

• • • • • • • • • • • • • •

CHAPTER 4

MUSIC
AND THE
MUSICIANS

• • • • • • • • • • • • • •

Priscilla Lopez and company recording
What I Did For Love *for the cast album.*

"As I waited, I saw the dance captain giving the cast all kinds of problems, screaming at them. Eventually I said to Herb, 'When are they going to do the run-through?' He said, 'You just saw it!'" — LARRY ABEL

Developing and Orchestrating the Score

DON PIPPIN [Original Musical Director; Vocal Arranger]: Michael called me and said, "We're doing this little workshop thing. It's only paying $100 a week, but come down, a lot of people think it's interesting." So I went and there were all these people rehearsing to a drum beat. There seemed to be no score; no songs; it was like they were improvising everything. Michael saw me at the door and motioned me over — he was standing up on a little riser. I sat by him watching the dancers do this routine. And I said to Michael, "I thought you were choreographing this? Are you just directing it?" I saw Barry Bostwick on the floor, but I didn't *recognize* him as Bostwick, or I would have known he was a character in the play. But I thought *he* was the choreographer.

I was taken in by what eventually would become the opening number. It was so real I felt it was being created for the first time and just being learned by them at that moment. Of course, Michael was so excited that I thought this was real that he wanted to keep that feeling. Out of that impulse would come all the changes and the structural organization of Kleban and Hamlisch under Michael's guidance. It was interesting how he guided and molded them. Michael didn't write the music but the mold was set.

The tempo was there; they were already working to a drumbeat with an improv going on. That whole tempo of the opening number never changed. There was the waltz and the 6/4 jazz combination; and they were improvising about "I hope I get this job."

Watching bits and pieces I remember thinking there's *something* there. I couldn't claim what it was, but I felt we were inside the guts of show business. It was something I had never experienced before, and I had done a lot of work at that point. So I said, "Okay Michael, I'm aboard."

LARRY ABEL [Chief Music Copyist]: I had been Herb Harris' chief copyist for all of his projects. In the very beginning Herb asked me to come to the American Theater Lab where they were doing a run-through of A CHORUS LINE. He wanted to introduce me to Michael, Marvin, and some of the others. As I waited, wandering around the theatre, I saw the dance captain giving the cast all kinds of problems, screaming at them, throwing people out of the rehearsal for chewing gum and carrying on about not doing their steps properly. Eventually I said to Herb, "When are they going to do the run-through?" He said, "You just saw it!" They all got such a kick out of that.

FRAN LIEBERGALL [Original Pianist; Vocal Supervisor]: Two weeks before the workshop started, we all met at City Center: Michael Bennett, Bob Avian, Donna, Baayork, Bobby Thomas (the drummer), and Jeff Hamlin, our stage manager. I sat down at the piano and there was no music in front of me. This was what this workshop was for — to create the choreography.

The first thing Michael said was, "Give me a rock feel in 6/4." Whoever heard of a rock feel in 6/4? I let Bobby Thomas start the rhythm. I took it from there, playing some kind of minor chords, just improvisation, jazzy kind of stuff. Later in rehearsal, Marvin came in and put a melody over it that became the opening of *I Hope I Get It.* We also did the ballet combination and a little of *Tap.* Thank God for Bobby Thomas, he was the inspiration. He knew what Michael Bennett needed in order to dance.

BOBBY THOMAS [Music Coordinator]: I had worked with Michael since he was eighteen when he first came to New York at the June Taylor Studios. Through the years I was his musical confidante. We had a lot of great creative moments together. I'm a jazz musician and Michael was my alter-ego. We had a connection. We could look at each other and tell when things were working and when they weren't. And when they weren't, we had signals. I would pull my ear or scratch my nose or rub my eyes, so no one else in the room would know it. That way it wouldn't spoil the flow of the rehearsal.

FRAN LIEBERGALL: They had already done the first workshop. There was some choreography in place, some sense of a book. I was going on from City Center to actual rehearsals for the second workshop.

There had been another pianist, Miles Chase, who played the first workshop. I can see where he was not suited to Michael Bennett and Marvin Hamlisch. Miles is not the kind of person who gets it the first time. He needs to study it and there was no time for that. I was too young and too stupid to know I couldn't do it. It was a matter of patching together pieces of music they had from the first workshop: "Take this and cut this and go back to that." You had to be that fast.

BOBBY THOMAS: Michael was very rhythm oriented. He knew rhythm very well. He could dance to and hear music from rhythm, which is something a lot of people can't do. I would play rhythms and hit accents — and he would just move. We had warm-ups every day for the dancers. The rhythm would get more and more boisterous and punctuated, which is what the body does. But while all that is happening, Michael and I are thinking, "What are we going to do today to start a production number?"

One thing you have to realize about choreographers is that when they talk to

Michael Bennett
and music
coordinator
Bobby Thomas

Original orchestra members Jerry Goldberg (Assistant Conductor, later Conductor), Fran Liebergall (pianist / vocal coach), Ben Herman (percussionist), and Bob Milliken (trumpet) stayed with the show until it closed

you, you pay attention, but you don't actually try to understand what they're saying. It's totally impossible. I learned that from my first job out of college working with Jerome Robbins. Robbins told me about an idea for a ballet, and went on and on, and I thought, "Oh, God, I'm fired. There is no way in the world I can understand what this man is talking about." While he was walking away, I checked out the tempo that he was walking in and his attitude, and he turned

around, and said, "Are you ready to start?" I told him I was, and started playing to his walking tempo and that attitude. He stopped me and said, "How did you know that?" I've used that trick with every choreographer since.

I could sense what Michael wanted. I would hum things for Fran to play on the piano, and before you knew it, it was like a production number. It wasn't the actual music that you heard, but it was enough of something for Marvin to build on. Like

the opening of the jazz combination — those beats are an exercise that we used in dance class, something that was in 6/4 and 4/4, combination of 10. I taught Michael how to count like a musician.

DON PIPPIN: I pitched in right away, because music was being written and I was doing a lot of vocal arrangements. One of the things I loved about Michael was that he responded theatrically, not just musically. He was very appreciative to any kind of little nuance that I would come up with. He either liked it or he didn't, and my batting average was very good. He would always say, "That's great, can you make it twice as long?" I always seemed to be right on target.

FRAN LIEBERGALL: We were having trouble with Donna's number. It had gone through a myriad of changes and names and different melodies, lyrics, and dances. We just couldn't come up with the right kind of arrangement for the dance. This was before it became the number as we know it today. Michael called a meeting at his apartment to figure it out. At the meeting were Bobby Thomas, Bob Avian, Donna, Michael, Marvin, and Harold Wheeler. We had the first dance break already; it was the second one that was the problem.

Michael said, "Now I really want to bring this down and sexy." Bobby Thomas started playing his thighs, since

there were no drums, and Michael started singing this strain of a melody that he wanted to hear. It came from another song that Donna used to sing in the show called *Inside the Music*. It's where that saxophone solo comes from, in the slow section of the Cassie dance. Michael accentuated where he wanted the accents and we all started playing it. I was playing a little, Harold Wheeler played a little, and before you knew it, we had this arrangement. We put it down on tape and Harold wrote it out and orchestrated it, which he is not given credit for in the show.

BOBBY THOMAS: I killed my thighs that night. I counted thirty-one renditions of that song. Every one we tried was too frantic. It was more like WEST SIDE STORY music. It wasn't working. It had to have this undercurrent going on, but with this wonderful flow of music on top. I was beating my thighs, Marvin would play something, and it wouldn't be right. I was sitting off to the side and started moving in closer slapping out rhythms on my thigh, saying "Here you go, Marvin, you hear that rhythm? I want a long melody over it." He would start playing something, and I would stop him. "Too busy," I would say. Marvin wanted to put as many notes in as possible.

I started the rhythm again; he played, but he kept wanting to put Leonard Bernstein in there. "No Leonard Bernstein!" I said. Finally, he put the right melody over it. "Cool; wonderful," I urged him to continue. It kept going in the right direction, and then we had it. It took us about an hour. It was me doing it on my thigh, then Fran got it. And then we *all* realized it was working. I thought it was very generous of Marvin to allow me so much input, although Michael was insisting on it anyhow.

HAROLD WHEELER [Orchestrator]: I had started working with Michael Bennett on PROMISES, PROMISES. We came to a parting of the ways during COMPANY. I wanted a percentage royalty, versus the fixed royalties they offered. So I opted not to work on the show. Michael and I didn't speak until a few years later when I got a call about A CHORUS LINE. They were having problems with *The Music and the Mirror* and Bobby Thomas said, "We need Harold."

Michael was stubborn and I was stubborn. But Bobby pulled a trick. He called and asked if I would get together with him for a drink. We set a meeting for 2:00 in some tacky bar on 8th Avenue in the Broadway district. We sat down, had a drink, just talking over old times, and unbeknownst to me, he had also asked Michael to meet him at 2:15. So Michael walked in at 2:15, as Bobby and I are sitting there having a drink. He sat down and Bobby got up and said, "I've got to leave — you guys work this out." And

that was the beginning of our getting back together.

There was a big number called *Turkey Lurkey* in PROMISES. *Turkey Lurkey* became our private guideline for what worked. We always tried to outdo ourselves. The *Turkey Lurkey* number in A CHORUS LINE would have been *The Music and the Mirror*, but it wasn't happening. I went to the theatre, looked at what they had, and then spent four or five days in rehearsal re-working it with Michael, Bobby, and Donna. The result we came up with is in the show now.

Working with Michael always stretched you beyond your normal capacity. When we worked out the number and choreography, it all started to fall in line. But we kept thinking in the back of our heads that we had to top *Turkey Lurkey*. There is a point as a dance arranger where you try to derive your dance music from the song, and that may have been what was wrong with the Cassie dance before. You really had to deviate from the song and go into original dance music, and then bring it back to the song at the end.

With the Cassie dance, I had the freedom to go wherever the feeling started to go. Michael created the mood first, because he knew what he wanted and Bobby and I would sit and improvise around that. Then I would fine-tune, come back in with what we did the day before taking us to a new level. But Michael had it worked out. It wasn't a

Marvin Hamlisch,
Pamela Blair,
Ed Kleban —
Dance: 10, Looks: 3

case of creating a piece of music that Michael then choreographed. We never worked that way; it was always a combined effort. Even after we did the first performances at the Public, there were minor changes, additional accents that were put in. It then translated itself right uptown.

DON PIPPIN: The original melody and song to *Hello Twelve* was a ragtime, almost a Charleston beat. It went into rehearsal that way. Michael, brilliant as he was, decided the pulse and style of the number just wasn't these kids. They wouldn't do something to that period sound; they would do something more contemporary. About two days later the whole thing changed into what we now know as that number. *Joanne* was replaced by *I Can Do That. Joanne* had too much of a romantic overtone for the character. It wasn't spunky enough for Mike. Nothing was wrong with the song; it was well-crafted, but it just wasn't right for the character. *Sing* was not originally a duet for Al and Kristine. The entire line backed her up.

RON DENNIS [Original Richie]: Michael had taken out a number called *Confidence* that Baayork Lee and I had opened the show with in early rehearsals. She was on one end of the line and I was in my spot. It was about the kind of show we both could do as ethnics. At different points, we would stick our heads out and look down the line at each other. It was another one of those internals. It was a cute little ditty, but they felt it was too light and too musical comedy.

DON PIPPIN: Arrangements were a daily thing. You'd be amazed at how much of the music in A CHORUS LINE is so intertwined in arrangements. In the *Montage* sections, for example, you are not aware of the complexity because it flows so easily. *What I Did For Love* was one of the tougher songs because it was a strange number to have in the show; suddenly there was a pop tune. I don't think Michael ever really liked the song that much. It was there because nobody could come up with a better idea. When I first heard it, I thought, "Oh, God, I can't believe this. Marvin's sticking a pop tune in here, at the end of the show. Can this work?" But it was so brilliant the way it was framed. That's what saved it; it's the setup that made it work. It was that brilliant scene in front of it, "What do you do when you can't dance anymore?"

MARVIN HAMLISCH [Composer (from his book, *The Way I Was*)]: The show needs some sort of summing up. Michael and I feel it must come in a slow, haunting song. So I stroll through Central Park. Where else can you find inspiration in this town? But it's freezing out there. So I hopped on the crosstown bus. And wouldn't you know, a melody slipped into my head on 79th Street between Fifth and Madison. It stayed with me for hours. I played it for Ed. He thinks it's right. I'm working on the melody. Maybe I should get back on the bus. The tune can't be overly sentimental. Yet it must answer the paramount question of the evening: If these dancers had to stop dancing forever, would they still think it had all been worth it? The answer is an emphatic yes. What these kids had done, they had done for love. And that was the lyric Ed came up with. It's masterful and emotional and, in its own way, heartbreaking.

LARRY ABEL: Marvin gave me a lift after rehearsal one day. He said that *What I Did For Love* was going to be the smash of the show before it even opened. Marvin knew

what he had written. He said, "That's a great piece of music."

FRAN LIEBERGALL: Originally Michael wanted a light musical motif for each character, their own little theme, but it wasn't able to be that progressive. In the alternatives scene, you had little musical glimpses of the characters, a little flavor when each spoke, and that was their underscoring. Kelly's boom-chick-a-boom, "Can I sit on your lap?" underscore was Bobby Thomas and Michael saying, "Sexy." Bobby would play that beat and Marvin would come in and say, "This is the kind of melody I want."

BOBBY THOMAS: *At the Ballet* is fantastic, a gem of the show. Part of it is in 3/4, but when you hear it, you don't realize there is a South American rhythm under a 3/4 Viennese Waltz. When Michael heard anything Latin, he went wild!

I did the arrangement on *Shit Richie*. It was there, but not really happening, so Michael said "Why don't you do it, BT." And I did. When the kids heard it, they went crazy. The band loved it. Frank

Perowsky actually did the orchestration for it, but I did the arrangement.

RON DENNIS: The "Gimme the ball" lyrics were based on Candy Brown's story. She had been in the second workshop, but by the time the third one came around, she decided to do CHICAGO instead, because that definitely was going to Broadway. When I got involved, in that third and last workshop, Michael thought my own story wasn't juicy enough, so he used Candy Brown's. She was one of a few African-American people who went to an all white school. She was in everything — choir, newspaper, sports. She was always trying to play everything, saying, "Gimme the ball, gimme the ball." Nobody would give it to her.

Two weeks before we opened at the Newman, Michael gave me a tape of the lyrics with Bobby Thomas playing percussion. "Go home and make something out of it." Just like that. I figured Michael knew deep down that I could do something or he wouldn't have given it to me at the last minute. I tried my best to make it as close to what Aretha Franklin would sing. That's how *Gimme the Ball* came

about. It was all my vocal melody. The "go to it" sections were added. Everyone else created the steps to put into that number, resulting in this backup chorus of sixteen people and me.

DON PIPPIN: What turned out to be the famous bows, the Finale, was only temporary. It was never to be the end of the show. It was just thrown together to end the show until we could get the Finale done — which we never did. There was to be a very Las Vegas finale, for which I did all the vocal arrangements. They were going to have the spotlight, the "star," and do this whole "Red Shoes" routine with the light on the stage and the company around it. They learned the whole vocal arrangement in a very Kay Thompson sort of style. But it never got staged; there was never time to develop the idea. We had to open and Michael literally threw the Finale together. That became the end of the show. The rest is history.

BOBBY THOMAS: Michael amazed me, the way he worked for clarity. When something wasn't right, he knew how to take out the "garbage" so it would be

"One thing you have to realize about choreographers is that when they talk to you, you pay attention, but you don't actually try to understand what they're saying." — BOBBY THOMAS

crystal clear. No one knew what was going on until it all came together. It was just piece by piece, and all of a sudden, it happened. Every day you would go to rehearsal and there would be another pleasant surprise. Another piece of the puzzle was being put together. I used to call Michael "Michelangelo."

FRAN LIEBERGALL: Because of the pulse that Michael had wanted for the Cassie dance, the sexiness, the funkiness, Harold Wheeler was brought in to orchestrate the number. Jonathan Tunick orchestrated *At the Ballet* and *Nothing*. He had the nuances that Michael needed for those numbers. Billy Byers was mostly *Montage* and *I Can Do That*. Hershey Kay, the *One* internal sections. Phil Lang orchestrated *Dance: 10, Looks: 3* and Ralph Burns did the last chorus of the *One* finale, the big finish. Michael's intention was to get the best of everybody.

DON PIPPIN: With *I Hope I Get It*, the beginning forty bars are Larry Wilcox and the rest are Billy Byers. *And* was Tunick. The *Montage* was more than one person, but Byers did more than anybody else. When we heard these orchestrations, there was nothing bad, nothing was weak.

LARRY ABEL: Marvin was in charge of everything. He would call and tell me when I would get my assignments and from whom. There were numerous

arrangers, including several freelance people who really didn't get the credit but worked on the show: Jonathan Tunick, Harold Wheeler, Larry Wilcox, Phil Lang, Ralph Burns, Billy Byers, Hershey Kay, even Bobby Thomas, who supplied something in one of the *Montage*s. So I had music from all different sources. That is Marvin's way of working. He will seek out the best person available. He didn't let one day go by without calling me and saying, "Today you'll get this, tomorrow you'll get this; if you don't get it, call me right away." He was fantastic.

Marvin would assign the same orchestration to two different people and he'd want them both by the end of the day. Then he would present both versions to Michael and ask which one he liked. Michael would say, "I like this part of this version and that part of that version and this part and this part." Then Marvin would tell Michael, "No problem. Larry, do it." And I was ready with several copyists, scissors in hand, cutting and pasting.

BERNARD FOX [Music Copyist]: There must have been twelve to fourteen copyists who worked on A CHORUS LINE. We put the orchestra parts onto paper so the musicians could read them during performance on their music stands. We would extract each part from the score. If there had to be any changes thereafter, if they needed a little more music, change of key, etc., we would have to have them ready

for the next day. Always deadlines.

The vocal parts went on forever, because there were so many counterparts, maybe six or seven different voices going on in one section, which meant you could only get approximately four bars or so per page. And for such a long number as the *Montage* section, it was quite lucrative because we get paid by the page. Finally toward the end, when they set the show, we would clean up the parts because changes were marked in pencil. Marvin always liked a clean book.

JONATHAN TUNICK [Orchestrator]: The first I ever heard of A CHORUS LINE was in a phone call from Ed Kleban. I had gone to high school with Ed; he was a very good modern jazz pianist and we played in bands together when we were kids. Ed wanted my advice. He had been approached about writing the lyrics for a show that Michael was going to direct and Marvin was going to do the music for.

Ed didn't just want to be a lyricist, he wanted to be a composer/lyricist. Should he take this job strictly as a lyricist? My advice to him was to take it. He needed the exposure. He needed the experience of working with a first class director and certainly Marvin was a very respectable composer. I told him to do it and then move on immediately to his next project which

Michael Bennett and Don Pippin in the studio
for the Original Cast recording

he could write by himself. As it turns out — which I didn't know at the time — this was precisely the advice that Oscar Hammerstein gave to Stephen Sondheim when he was offered WEST SIDE STORY.

Ironically, Ed really didn't go on to much else. All of his future projects were one way or the other aborted. He sort of made a career of having been the lyricist of A CHORUS LINE, which is rather sad because he was a wonderfully talented composer as well as lyricist and musical dramatist.

A little time went by and I heard from Michael Bennett that he wanted me to orchestrate the show. I didn't want to do it. I had just finished orchestrating GOOD-TIME CHARLIE which I liked very much, but it had been very difficult. It was not successful, and I was very tired and didn't want to sit down and write another score. I went up to Michael's apartment and he played me demos of several songs which were very good. But I said, "I'm just not up to it. I don't want to do a show now. I will be of no help to you. Get somebody else." I recommended somebody who ultimately didn't work out.

As it turned out, *nobody* was available to do this show. Michael wound up spending his days on the telephone calling arrangers saying, "Please come down and do a number." I did a few, but not having been a supervisor orchestrator (there wasn't one), I couldn't tell you exactly what ended up in the book. I did

an orchestration of *What I Did For Love*, as did Ralph Burns. I have been told what's in the book is sort of half and half.

A CHORUS LINE was a hodgepodge. An arranger would come down, watch a number, take it away, turn it in, and have no further contact with the show. There was so little contact, because there was no central orchestrator. It ended up being a grab bag of arrangers.

The extent of my involvement was *my* choice. Michael said I could have anything I want. "Take the show, have a royalty, conduct the show." Who knew that this would move uptown and become the greatest hit ever on Broadway? There wasn't the slightest hint that would happen at the time. On the other hand, I was glad to help my friends. I really didn't want to work hard at that point and Ed and Marvin needed some help. I was happy to pitch in, which I did. I did *At the Ballet* and Priscilla's number, *Nothing.* They never did get my sports car effect right, which was supposed to be the sound of a hot engine going by fast — vrrroom. It was interpreted as a car horn. It never came off. And I did *I Hope I Get It* with all the combinations.

BILLY BYERS [Orchestrator]: I was working with Marvin in California. We had done a couple of movies, THE WAY WE WERE and THE STING. When Marvin did A CHORUS LINE, he got together a crew of his favorite arrangers. Marvin

role-casted. He said, "That's So-and-So's kind of number." He brought me to New York, I did my numbers and went back to California. In the middle of doing my taxes, I got a frantic call from Marvin who asked me to come back and make fixes. He didn't like what he had been getting. Jonathan Tunick did *At the Ballet* and it was a masterpiece; I never touched it.

Aside from about thirty-two bars that Ralph Burns wrote of the Finale, *One* (for which he is not credited in the program), I rewrote everything else the other guys had done. When I first came in I was supposed to do one or two numbers, which I did, but I also did Larry Wilcox' work. He had gotten sick at the time and wasn't able to finish. I rewrote the Hershey Kay and Phil Lang numbers. I wound up rewriting *Tits & Ass* and *The Music and the Mirror*. I did the song and the dance. Marvin didn't like twelve bars I had written in the Cassie dance so he brought in Harold Wheeler for the twelve bars, where you hear the saxophone, near the end. The *Montage* was originally done by Hershey Kay and I wound up rewriting that too. I also did the underscoring. It was fun! The whole process was done over a period of two months, maybe two and a half. It is very difficult to assign credit, number by number, as to whose orchestrations were used in the show.

When the show was a big success, they wanted to open up numerous companies to play around the world. The people who were in the Original Company had very

> *"A CHORUS LINE was a hodgepodge. An arranger would come down, watch a number, take it away, turn it in and have no further contact with the show."* — JONATHAN TUNICK

personalized voices, not like routine Broadway voices. But when the show became mainstream, new actors sang in different registers, and Marvin brought me back to do transpositions of the solo numbers into keys which would be more accessible to a larger group of performers.

RALPH BURNS [Orchestrator]: I was in Philadelphia working on the musical CHICAGO when Marvin called me. He has certain favorite arrangers and luckily I was one of them. I told him I couldn't do A CHORUS LINE because of my commitment to CHICAGO. I would never leave Bob Fosse. But Marvin never gives up. He likes to have several arrangers work on something. He said, "You have to do this for me. You are my good luck charm and this is the end of the show." So I said, "Sure, Marvin, but you come to Philadelphia, I can't get up to New York." Marvin took the train down and brought the whole Finale, a complete sketch of the vocal routine, and played it for me, made a tape and said, "This is it, Ralph."

Hershey had done the start of it, as *One* is used a lot through the show before it becomes the Finale. But Marvin needed me for the big finish. He wanted the piece to start out small and build and build and build. He sketched out every note. It's weird, because I never saw the number. It was the only dance routine I worked on that I had never seen. I sat down, wrote the orchestration and then sent it back up to New York. I never heard it but Marvin and Michael both called from New York and they were very happy.

They paid nothing. It was the smallest amount of money that I had ever received in my life because it was Off-Broadway scale, but that was all right. They called me again when I came back to New York, still busy with CHICAGO. Marvin said, "We have a number that needs to go into the show tomorrow." I think I did it overnight, a rush deal. It was a number for Wayne Cilento called *Joanne*, which didn't last.

Because I was working on CHICAGO during the day, I had to keep my work for A CHORUS LINE a big secret. I was signed to CHICAGO and the producers couldn't know about this. I loved Michael, but I loved Fosse more than anybody and he would have been terribly hurt. Besides, I was supposed to be working night and day on CHICAGO. That's why my name was never listed in the credits for A CHORUS LINE. I insisted upon it.

JONATHAN TUNICK: As far as I know, everybody was asked and only three of us wanted billing. Why one would *not* want to be billed, I don't know. Perhaps, and this is total speculation, one might not want to be perceived as doing piece work or doing odd jobs, as it were. I had no problem with it; it wasn't an issue with me.

HAROLD WHEELER: At that point if I did a show on Broadway, I did a show. I wasn't sharing. So I asked not to be credited. It was my choice. They offered me billing and I said I didn't want to be listed with all the other orchestrators.

JONATHAN TUNICK: I don't think it was an advantage using all these orchestrators. It could have been otherwise and I have to take the blame for it. There should be one hand on the show, just as there is one set designer. Imagine every number being choreographed by a different choreographer or designed by a different costume designer, without any central authority. I don't think A CHORUS LINE got the best of all these people because they weren't committed.

The Musicians

HERB HARRIS [Music Contractor]: As music administrator for the Festival, I've always gone for the best orchestra. I had heard enough about A CHORUS LINE to know the needs of this show and the kind of varied musical fare we were going to have. It was very difficult to get the kind of orchestra I wanted because it was Off-Broadway where the pay scales are considerably lower. Exacerbating that problem was the declaration I heard when I finally gathered my orchestra: "You can't hire until you get an okay," and that okay was to come from Billy Byers. So I had to submit a list of names of potential orchestra members. I was not in the habit of that protocol and it took them weeks to give me the go-ahead. By the time I got an okay to hire, it was just about two weeks before our first rehearsal. I lost some good people. A number of the guys had already taken other gigs, so I had to find replacements. I didn't appreciate the situation. The sooner you can get going, the sooner you can get the best people.

VINCENT FANUELE [Musician; Assistant Conductor]: Tommy Mitchell was the original bass trombone player, but he left the show before previews ever started for religious reasons; he was offended by the cursing in the show. He left and Blaise Turi took over. A lot of us were offered the show.

JONATHAN TUNICK: There was trouble getting an orchestra. It was a busy season, there were a lot of shows. I had wanted to bring over a bunch of players from GOOD-TIME CHARLIE, but the conductor wouldn't let them go, even though the show was closing in a few weeks. I was mostly responsible for setting the instrumentation. I felt that with the limited number of players, the most important thing was to get a big sound on the dance numbers.

DON PIPPIN: We had a very good trumpet section. Trombones were good and we had an excellent percussionist. We didn't have a strong drumming situation until some years later. That was constantly the big thorn in my side. Michael had this loyalty to people he worked with. Bobby Thomas was just a rehearsal drummer for Michael, but there was a very close bond there. Bobby recruited the first drummer, Allen Herman, who would not have been my choice. But Allen didn't last very long. I bet to this day, Fran doesn't realize she caused him to get fired. She didn't do it maliciously; it was out of her youthful naiveté. He missed a performance, and we covered for him, but it was Fran who went to somebody in management and told them and he got canned. Allen is on the recording, though.

HERB HARRIS: That was the only train wreck in terms of personnel. Everybody else turned out to be okay.

AL MATTALIANO [Musician]: Herb called and asked if I wanted to play trumpet and, of course, I accepted. I was one of the "fringe" musicians. I wasn't as much a part of the Broadway scene as those "first call" guys. I didn't have the Broadway connections. Later on I found out that almost every musician in town had been called for A CHORUS LINE and a lot of them refused because of the pay scale Off-Broadway.

MARVIN ROTH [Musician]: I got the call first from Herb Harris, who told me Don

The first page of Marvin Roth's score

Pippin, the show's conductor, was asking for me. When I hesitated, Don then called himself saying, "This is going to be a great show." Now, I'd heard that particular expression before, having done twenty-four other shows before A CHORUS LINE. I accepted, even though it was going to be very little money.

There I was, schlepping a baritone saxophone, a contrabass clarinet, regular clarinet, a bassoon, and a flute — all on the subway. I'm what is known as a doubler, and over the years, doubling became somewhat of a monster. If theatre producers had to hire a bassoon player, a baritone sax player, and a flute player, and so on, it would cost them a fortune. So doubling became a standard practice for Broadway.

In addition to all my other instruments, they told me to bring a contrabass clarinet to the first rehearsal. I went to a music dealer on 48th Street, told him what I needed and he took me down to the basement where he dug one out of a box. It was a monster made of metal, looked like a still, with pipes coming up, doubled up on themselves. It was huge. He put it together, got an old reed somewhere, played a few rotten notes — it sounded awful, it was so low. I dragged that thing downtown to be used in one of Billy Byers' orchestrations.

I started to play what I saw on the music, and Billy Byers stopped the rehearsal. "Hold it fellas, there's something wrong back there." And he singled me out. "What are you playing?" "What it says here, contrabass." He came close and said, "That's the wrong instrument. You have a B flat contrabass clarinet. You were told to bring an E flat contrabass clarinet." I didn't know there were two different kinds, I had never played a contrabass clarinet before. I obviously made a mistake when I picked it up from the music dealer in not specifying which one. But Billy transposed it temporarily for me so we could get through the rehearsal. That was my first embarrassment ever, sitting there playing wrong notes on the wrong instrument. We straightened it out, and they rented the E flat instrument for months until they finally bought one, which I ended up playing for fifteen years.

AL MATTALIANO: There weren't too many challenges as far as playing the score. But the music was different than the ordinary, run-of-the-mill, musical comedy type scores. In the very beginning, each arranger would be at rehearsal and more or less mold the music into shape, depending on what he wanted it to sound like. The arrangers would rehearse the orchestra.

MARVIN ROTH: We were enjoying the arrangements and playing without any people singing. When they brought in the cast, and those kids heard something other than a piano, they went wild. Then we, in turn, started to appreciate what was happening. When the kids came in to do their thing, everything just seemed to fit right in its slot.

FRAN LIEBERGALL: A lot of the dance music in the show is me because I created it in rehearsal. But that was just part of my job which started to change in the middle of rehearsals. One day Michael and Marvin were walking out of the room and Marvin said, "Oh Frannie, just teach them the parts. Just divide it up and give it to them." And then he gave me this other responsibility. Up until then Don Pippin had been in charge of all the vocal arrangements and I was just the pianist. I guess Michael was aware I knew my stuff just because I was there all the time. During previews when things would change in rehearsal during the day and Don wasn't around — he had other obligations, and couldn't be there every single second of the day — I would say, "Don, here are the list of changes for tonight."

This was the first time I had to play a political game. I was doing what Michael and Marvin told me to do. I learned to be careful about walking on toes at that point. Don is a renowned conductor; I had to give him his due. But I was disappointed when they brought Jerry Goldberg in Off-Broadway because I thought I was going to be assistant conductor, even though I didn't have one ounce of conducting experience. I just assumed that it would be mine. That was little bit of a jar.

JERRY GOLDBERG [Original Assistant Conductor]: When I found out what was involved, I said frankly, "I don't know whether I could do that, Marvin. I have a family." And I had other work that I was doing. So that's where we left it. Several months later, after I had heard all these rumblings about what was happening downtown, I got a call from Don Pippin. They were ready to go into previews and Don didn't have an assistant who could take over if need be. He said, "Marvin would like you to come downtown and if you like what's going on, we want you to join us." What I saw was incredible. They were already in previews, their first weekend. Immediately I said, "Sign me on." I started that next week and sat through every performance. They wanted me to be ready to conduct in two weeks, if need be.

JONATHAN TUNICK: The only regrets, if you want to call them that, I had about *At the Ballet* or the show in general was that the orchestra wasn't big enough. It really wasn't adequate for the task. It was fine for downtown with sixteen musicians but I would have liked strings. I certainly suggested it. When the show was moving uptown, they needed ten more players to fill the union's minimum. I said to Michael, "Let me write in some strings and then the ballads will sound great." But Michael was superstitious about it. He didn't want to wake a sleeping dog; he was afraid. I would have loved to have added strings

particularly to the ballads. They really sound rather stark without them. We lacked not only warmth, but size, meaning a largeness rather than a loudness.

DON PIPPIN: I was the big fighter against adding strings. I really fought steadily, but Michael made the final decision. I heard all this talk about adding strings and said, "Marvin, you're out of your mind. You have a unique sound, why do you want it to sound like everybody else?" I was really very upset about it, and spoke to Michael and he listened. Years later at a seminar with Jonathan Tunick, I was talking about how opposed I was to strings and why, and Jonathan said, "Oh, *you* were the one! I'm the one who wanted strings!"

FRAN LIEBERGALL: They didn't want this sweet string kind of sound, but more of a brassy sound, a band sound. The entire orchestra moved from the Newman to Broadway, but there we added Jaime Austria. We split the bass chair because our bass player downtown, Roland Wilson, could not play upright; electric was his forté. They brought in Jaime for the record album to play a string bass part; and when we moved into the pit at the Shubert, he was hired.

There were two bass players in the pit on Broadway; one played the electric parts, and the other played the string bass. In the original orchestration, there were three

trumpets, three trombones, four reeds, harp, guitar, bass, keyboards, and one each on percussion and drums. Sixteen people. The Shubert had a twenty-six-man minimum. So they had to add ten more people to the payroll because they didn't want to re-orchestrate to accommodate more musicians. The other bass player on Broadway brought that total down to nine slots which had to be filled by what is known as "walkers." At that time, there were no rules on who those people could be. Historically, there were people who couldn't even read music who were put on the musician's payroll. Not, however, on A CHORUS LINE.

JERRY GOLDBERG: We never had anybody who was not a musician as a walker on payroll. They were all musicians, but they weren't all there specifically to come in and play the show eight times a week. The walker could be hired as a replacement if he were somebody who could take over that chair, but then you'd have to hire somebody else to be the walker because you always had to be paying twenty-six musicians. They got paid base union salary and made that money for fifteen years. We had some superb musicians on payroll as walkers. I would have loved to have heard them play more than they did.

HERB HARRIS: I hired a trumpet walker purposely because it was a rough trumpet book; I hired different players with different agreements. With the trumpet walker, I

said, "Look, there are three guys blowing, but it's a rough book and if one of them has to take off, or wants to do only six shows, I'll need you in there." So that worked out. The drum situation worked out because Hank Jaramillo was a fine drummer, and they actually preferred his playing to most of our regular guys. The only walkers were drums, trumpet, and wind.

AL MATTALIANO: There never should have been any walkers. There should have been parts written for all those people, and they should have utilized them in the pit. Some of the musicians were resentful. In the very beginning, when Bob Milliken found out that there were going to be walkers, he felt we should have a trumpet walker so we could utilize a player for when guys took off. As a result of his opening his mouth, we got a trumpet walker. He would play two shows for each trumpet player, so we each would have two shows off. Our steady guys played six shows instead of eight. That started right from the beginning at the Shubert. That whole situation, the determination of who became walkers was political. I'm sure Herb Harris had something to do with that. He was a walker. There was no rhyme or reason.

DON PIPPIN: Our walkers were superior, the best in the business. I would have liked to have them in the pit. But the others had already been hired.

Photos by Marvin Roth

Upper left: Andy Sterman and Vinny Della Rocca at the musicians' lockers
Upper right: Ken Dybisz, Marvin Roth, Andy Sterman, and Vinny Della Rocca
Lower left: Joe Maggio, reeds, stayed with the show all fifteen years
Lower right: Bernice Horowitz played harp for the entire run

Life in the Pit

HERB HARRIS: When we were at the Newman, I had to go down and work out the seating arrangement off stage left. There was no pit, and there wasn't any room on stage right. I set up the orchestra so that we could fit in, and then worked out miking and all that. In the early days, people didn't actually know there was an orchestra. They thought it was on tape, as they did when we got to the Broadway pit.

MARVIN ROTH: Somebody along the way wrote a question to one of the columnists asking if there was live music at A CHORUS LINE. The columnist explained that it was live, but that the pit was covered. That's why our names went into the programs. We were a nonentity. People thought it was a recording. I did twenty-four Broadway shows and had never seen my name in print in a program until A CHORUS LINE. It was compensation for being in a covered pit.

Don Pippin's custom-made baton

HERB HARRIS: We were the first orchestra to be covered up. Michael wanted no indication that there was an orchestra. He didn't want any warming up in the pit. That was a problem — they would have to warm up with the door closed.

DON PIPPIN: With a covered pit, you felt denied the very organic impact of the show. You could feel it but you couldn't experience it. The whole show for me was a little black and white five-inch monitor and earphones.

FRAN LIEBERGALL: Don had a head set and video monitor in the pit and coordinated everything. Not only did he have to listen and adapt to a certain extent, but the cast also had to be trained to know what the cut-off counts were, because they had nobody to watch. They had to work together to make it happen.

BOB ROGERS [Conductor]: You can't

conduct to a monitor. Other shows, like CATS, have the conductor on a monitor, so at least the cast can see what the conductor is doing, just for coordination purposes, before the actual music is made. But when you're looking the other way, and you're trying to conduct a little figure on a monitor, it just seems so unreal. At times, the monitor used to blank out. But it didn't matter, it had no real effect. Most of it was based on trust.

JONATHAN TUNICK: Covering the pit is a destructive thing to do to an orchestra from two points of view. First of all, it cuts off all the live sound. Not only does the audience not hear the orchestra but it requires that every instrument be miked and sent into a mixing board, thereby neutralizing the blend that the musicians create themselves. The other negative effect is that the players in the orchestra are cut off from the performers on the stage. They had absolutely no connection with one another.

JERRY GOLDBERG: We spent a week putting the show into the Shubert. Don would sit out front because he wanted to get a balance. They had to make a decision on how they were going to set the pit up. Strangely enough, the rhythm section took up half the pit and the Shubert

A CHORUS LINE

OCT 1975

doesn't have a large space. Marvin, Don, Herb Harris, and the sound man all had suggestions. There were pros and cons to all of them. I'm not sure whether we had the ideal setup. We had a brass section in front of the woodwinds, which was a little blarey. The harp was all the way to my left, and the woodwinds were kind of strewn around; they weren't sitting together. Marvin Roth was all the way in the back.

MARVIN ROTH: Where I was sitting was a sorry thing, way in the corner. The top of my bassoon would sometimes hit the roof of the pit. I'd have to be careful. Then they started with all these drapes, fish nets, boards, and cables.

BOB ROGERS: There were complaints for all seven years I was there. We did some fixing. We put in a barrier between the guitarist and the drummer. We put in a plexiglass frame like a vertical divider so that the blast of the drum wasn't going directly to the guitar. Everybody was squeezed in. I probably got hearing loss from just being in that space every night for seven years. There was a lot of sound coming at me in the conductor's stand. It was not an ideal situation.

HERB HARRIS: I made suggestions about the electronic pianos and organs, finding ones that were small enough to fit them in the pit.

DON PIPPIN: You had to be careful about fans in the pit because the sound would pick up on the mikes.

MARVIN ROTH: The heat was brutal down there.

AL MATTALIANO: The scrim they had over us would get full of dirt and dust, and sometimes it wasn't cleaned every day. We would have to shame them into cleaning and vacuuming. The conditions for musicians in the pit were really not very good.

FRAN LIEBERGALL: What was great for the musicians is they didn't have to dress. They could literally come in wearing anything. Guys went in and out of the pit. By the time the show started to run, they were playing cards and taking breaks. The show didn't have an intermission, but the musicians took their own.

VINCENT FANUELE: There were a lot of times we used to take a break. We'd play the opening, and then the brass section would leave the pit because we are not in that whole introduction scene with Zach. Trombones used to have to go back first to play the next number, which was Diana's underscoring in the introduction. Then the trumpets would come back in. The brass section was right by the pit door so we could just run right out.

Photo by Roberta Hershenson

MARVIN ROTH: We all used to leave during Paul's monologue. That break was like a vacation. I wrote the breaks into my score so my subs knew when they could leave the pit. There was a big sign on the metal sliding door to the pit that read WHEN YOU COME BACK INTO THE PIT, PLEASE BE QUIET.

DON PIPPIN: There was no height in the pit, and I don't like to conduct without a baton. So Bernice Horowitz's husband, Dick, who is percussionist at the Met, made me these A CHORUS LINE batons. They were much shorter than regular batons; more like oversized toothpicks. They were beautifully shaped and he only made them for me.

I played the organ and the harpsichord and conducted at the same time. I don't remember playing those downtown. I think these were added as additional colors because we needed something more uptown.

Running through a number before the show: Jerry Goldberg (Conductor), Fran Liebergall at the keyboard, Ben Herman on percussion, and Vincent Forchetti on trombone. The monitor would televise the show for the conductor during performance.

Marvin Roth, fifteen-year veteran of the reed section

HERB HARRIS: The musician's strike in 1975 delayed the opening of A CHORUS LINE, but there was little chance of losing orchestra members, since the show was obviously a huge hit. Nobody knew it was going to run fifteen years, but they certainly weren't going to go out and take another job, either.

JERRY GOLDBERG: I was offered another show during the musician's strike. I turned it down, I just loved doing A CHORUS LINE so much. I never tired of it. We were supposed to open in September; then we opened in October. Three weeks is a long time, but everybody just sat tight because we all knew we were going to come back as strong as ever.

AL MATTALIANO: The cast organized a rally in Shubert Alley against us, putting us down because we were striking. I resented that attitude very much. People on the street came by and literally were spitting on us, because we were stopping them from going to see their favorite shows. As I recall, it was not just the A CHORUS LINE cast, but many shows.

DON PIPPIN: A CHORUS LINE was the first show to have booth singers (not pit singers, PROMISES, PROMISES had done that). The understudies in A CHORUS LINE were in the booth, which was the backup sound. That was my idea. I was aware early on, when we first started working on the floor, that as good as these performers were, they were not going to be able to carry all that heavy vocal stuff on their own. We'd have to back it up, and the understudies were sitting around with nothing to do. And it worked. Originally I was going to have the actors in the pit with us, but there was not physically enough time for them to run downstairs, so this little booth was built. They did not even work with a television monitor. It was the only time that booth singers, rather than watching the conductor, watched the stage. They had a clear view to the stage, which was their guide, and the earphones were to hear the orchestra.

FRAN LIEBERGALL: The first place that the offstage singers were added was in the *Monster Montage*. It started with "My only adolescence …" because the cast is pulsing like crazy on stage. We added the voices to make it more dynamic and when Judy sang, "My only adolescence," her understudy would double that. "Where did it go, it was so" was Diana/Bebe. Whoever was the Diana/Bebe cover would double; we would add voices all the way through the breakout — the "wah wahs" — which were very important because most of the cast used that as a vocal resting place. They had a lot of lay-outs in the choreography, so we helped them offstage, all through the end of the *Monster Montage*, "Go to it." They also sang in *One*, in the "smile and sing" chorus, and in the very last chorus, and finally in *What I Did For Love*, from the point the ensemble comes in all the way through the end. And the entire Finale, through the bows. They did not sing in *I Hope I Get It*, because they were on stage in that number. But they would sing offstage after they were eliminated in the opening. On tour, sometimes there was a microphone where they exit on stage right, and they could sing from there. But at the Shubert, we never had a microphone stage right, and the booth was on stage left. So they sang, "God, I think I've got it" through the end of the opening, right there from the wings, using the overhead mikes.

The Original Cast Recording

DON PIPPIN: A CHORUS LINE never followed a conductor; there was no television monitor for the cast. I took great pride in the fact that the show was rehearsed and drilled. It's what I call muscle memory. You drill it until it's in their muscles, everything about breathing, phrasing, crescendos. Dancers, because of their technique, tend to be able to do that more than singers, because it becomes an overall body experience. The only time we ever had a visual performance of A CHORUS LINE was on the cast album.

I do not think it's one of the most brilliant cast albums because I don't think Goddard Lieberson was really the right producer for it. A CHORUS LINE was a little too contemporary for his understanding. I remember on *Nothing*, Goddy wanted the drummer to use brushes instead of sticks. It was a hard recording, because it was not a well-planned recording session, which I would have to fault Marvin Hamlisch for. It should have been better planned. We were actually making up things in the studio, which I think is ridiculous on a recording. It should all be planned ahead.

FRAN FORCHETTI: Marvin Hamlisch is on the original cast album. He starts playing the very beginning of *What I Did For Love* because we changed it for the recording; it is not what you hear on stage. That's Marvin playing his *The Way We Were* intro, and then he played all the way through Priscilla's second chorus, as I was turning pages for him. On the section right before, "Gone, love is never gone …," he stood up and I moved in and took over from that point on.

A lot of tempos for the recording were slowed down. They wanted to fill an album and I guess Michael wanted things to be more laid out so listeners would understand every single lyric, which was very important to him.

RON DENNIS: When we were recording the cast album, Marvin Hamlisch sidled up to me and said, "Richie (he never called me by my real name, it was always Richie), you know, we can't put *Gimme the Ball* on the album." "Why not?" "Because you say 'shit' a couple of times." That had me fuming, so I high-tailed it over to Michael. "What is this about, *Gimme the Ball* not being on the album because I say 'shit'?" He said, "Who told you that?" "Marvin. If Pam Blair can say 'tits and ass' ninety-nine times, why can't I say 'shit'?" He said, "Ron, don't worry about it." Needless to say, the song is on the album. I finally realized that Marvin wanted sole credit for everything on the album. Since *Gimme the Ball* was the only thing he did not write the music to, he was pissed that it was going to be on it.

Taps were added to Wayne Cilento's solo, I Can Do That, for the recording session

The entire company and musicians, conducted by Don Pippin, recording the Original Cast Album

Left: Kay Cole, Kelly Bishop, and Nancy Lane recording At the Ballet

Below: Marvin Hamlisch, Cindy Garvey, and Don Pippin

Over the Years

FRAN LIEBERGALL: The transition of Original Company to second company wasn't easy because we wanted them to fit in and be a part of what was happening already. At the same time, Michael wanted the replacement cast to feel like they were individually important. We had to use what they had to offer, and transpositions were made. Donna and Ann Reinking did not sing in the same key. It was changed to suit the personality, to suit their bodies, to suit their vocal quality. There was a lot of leeway, notes were changed. We really adapted to new people.

JERRY GOLDBERG: When Ann came in, her voice was lower, so we dropped the key a third. That's when the brass section was rearranged. Some of the woodwinds might have been also, because the range of the instruments didn't work the same when we dropped it a whole third. They had to reshuffle and reorchestrate a little bit because it was a big change. The tempos tended to change in the dance sections, primarily for *The Music and the Mirror*, depending on who was dancing. We adapted depending on how strong the performer would look in a particular section.

FRAN LIEBERGALL: In the ensemble numbers, we found where each singer fit best and put them in that slot. But *Nothing* and *What I Did For Love* had three sets of keys, and *Dance:10, Looks: 3* had at least two keys. In the International Company, *At the Ballet* went up a half step because it was too low for Jane Summerhays. She is the only person I recall who sang it higher. Then the Bebe had to sing it a half step higher, but they modulated back down in the flute solo, during Maggie's speech, so that the Maggie never had to belt higher than an E. When Michael was with us, he had the final say on these kinds of changes. If it didn't sound right in a particular key, I would say so.

MARVIN ROTH: We were very close to the Original Company. Downstairs, outside of the pit, we had old couches. The Original Cast was very friendly and we hung out. As the casts changed, we became estranged from them. They would have their little corner where they did their warm-ups, but never mingled with the musicians. Only the Original Cast did that.

FRAN LIEBERGALL: When I left the pit in 1977, it was really because there was so much happening all over the world in terms of the other companies. I had gone to London for a month when the English cast was rehearsing, came back and did the International Company, then went to California for the National Company. It became difficult when I was in the Shubert pit as a pianist because I had been given this authority by Michael with all the other companies. As supervisor of the show, it was my job to coordinate what was happening on stage with the orchestra, and that was a difficult position for me to be in because I was also giving notes to conductors. I had to learn how to disassociate myself that way, so eventually I left the pit. It was best for the show and for me. It gave the conductor more control. Don Pippin had left by then anyway.

It was difficult on the road, too. You'd have these guys who thought they knew it all, and Baayork, Jeff Hamlin, Otts Munderloh, and I would come into town and say, "No, this is the way Michael Bennett wants it," and they would have to bow to our authority. A letter even went out from Michael to the stage managers, conductors, and heads of all the departments saying, "These four people represent me and whatever they say goes."

JERRY GOLDBERG: I was with the show from the first week of previews to the last performance. I was hired as the associate conductor for the first three years on Broadway, with Don Pippin. I brought Bob Rogers into the show on keyboard when we needed to replace Fran who

moved up to vocal coach. When Don left in 1979, he spoke to me about taking over, but at the time I was busy doing other things. I felt it was unfair to the show, so I stayed where I was and Bob moved up from the piano to take over conducting. I conducted the last three years of the show.

MARVIN ROTH: Jerry knew more about the show than Bob Rogers. Bob ended up taking Fran's place at the piano. That's how he learned the show. Why he was selected to be the conductor, I don't know. We were like a training school for conductors going out on the road.

BOB ROGERS: My job was to maintain the show the way it had been. I had words with some musicians who tried to get a little too contemporary and add too much of their own. My job was to keep the show from changing, to keep it alive, which is hard to do with guys who were sitting in the pit for years. The most fresh shows were the ones where you had three or four really great subs playing, because they would be replacing people who were very tired. You get some new blood in a pit and it affects everybody in a very positive way.

The most exciting shows were the ones where you had a mix of the best regular guys and then some subs from the outside who brought in that enthusiasm; then you would have a crackerjack show. It broke the monotony. We all got bored, the musicians, me, the same thing over and over again for all those years. But ultimately in terms of style, we tried to keep it really where it was, not try to update it, not to get faster or slower, just to maintain it.

FRAN LIEBERGALL: That original orchestra really knew what it was supposed to be. There was a magical thing that would happen in the pit when those original players would get together, as opposed to when subs were in. It would still be great, the orchestrations were phenomenal, but there was a clicking that happened when we got those guys together, especially the trumpets and trombones. There was nothing like it.

AL MATTALIANO: It's not easy to do a show for fifteen years and play the same thing night in and night out, where you can almost tell time by what notes you're playing.

JERRY GOLDBERG: Drummers had a bit of leeway, a flexibility and a spontaneity. The drummer stays in tempo, but he will fill in with a figure, he'll feel the figure from the moment, use his own fill.

MARVIN ROTH: Don Pippin would know what the tempos were supposed to be. It was when we had different conductors coming in that tempos changed. Nobody can conduct at exactly the same tempo as a previous conductor. We only follow the conductor. If he is conducting fast, then the orchestra plays fast.

AL MATTALIANO: There can be a different conductor, but the musicians are going to play the parts the same. Certain conductors can make particular passages sound better by bringing more out of the musicians, but, ultimately, the piece was established by the time replacement conductors came in. Tempos could possibly be different; a conductor might brighten it up. We would recognize a deviation from what a tempo used to be, but it didn't matter to us really. It was the conductor's problem.

"It's not easy to do a show for fifteen years and play the same thing night in and night out, where you can almost tell time by what notes you're playing." — AL MATTALIANO

BOB ROGERS: There was a lot of trust between the leader of the pit and who was up on stage. Everything was done by "we know this is going to happen at this time." Drumming is the pulse of the Cassie number, every moment of it. When a drummer would change, the cast could always tell. You need to have a rapport with the drummer and let him know what you want; he's the one who drives the band.

MARVIN ROTH: The drum and the piano are the two kings of A CHORUS LINE. You can't do without either one of them. One side of the pit looked like a drummer's jungle. I suppose every instrument is important, but it leaned towards the drums and the piano and guitar. The rest of us added some color. There were only four of us in the reed section, and I think there were twenty-one instruments among the four of us — that's a lot for four people to be playing.

ALPHONSE STEPHENSON [Conductor]: In 1980, I contemplated taking a leave of absence from the priesthood. I had been ordained for five years, but I was now forced to choose between my life in the church and my life in music. Michael Bennett and I were friends, and over dinner one evening he said, "Tomorrow I'm interviewing conductors for a national tour of A CHORUS LINE. If you want the job, I'll cancel the interviews. If it turns out you can't do the job, I'll fire you in two weeks."

After Michael had offered me the job, he said, "Herb Harris will call you in the morning." I didn't know who Herb Harris was, and I thought this could be an audition for him. The only thing I had prepared to play was the third act of LA BOHÈME. I was a student of opera, and didn't know Broadway. I went to Herb Harris' house with my score of the opera. I thought he was going to ask me to play the piano, but we just talked, went out to lunch, and that was the end of that.

HERB HARRIS: Michael called and asked me to meet with Alphonse and report back to him. I knew that Michael was very disposed to using Alphonse, so I met with him, and we talked music. I told Michael it would probably work out, but I also told him the reservations I had — his lack of experience in theatre, for example. Alphonse came down and studied the score. After that Michael said, "Let's have him try out, then tell me what you think." And I said I felt he could do it.

ALPHONSE STEPHENSON: I was the third conductor at the Shubert. Jerry had been there the whole time, so that would really make me the fourth conductor, since Jerry was the assistant. Trying to step into the shoes of somebody like Don Pippin, that's a lot. You try to get into the tempo of the company — that's the first thing to do. Then subtly you can move things, but essentially it had to remain

what the company was used to.

It's about chemistry, too; the conductor's chemistry with the drummer. I was received very warmly when I came into the company; I knew none of them. Most of them were the original orchestra members. My style was a little bit more operatic than the Broadway style of Bob Rogers and Don, so at least I got their attention. But of course they were responding to the Broadway style too, so it was a give-and-take situation. The biggest challenge of going into the New York Company every night was this: even though this might be your eighth performance of the week, or your 3000th performance in the run, there were people plunking down $45 that night to see something that they had never experienced before. I had to get myself psyched up for those people, to bring the best thing possible forward.

MARVIN ROTH: Alphonse had a temper, a very explosive response to things that did not go right in the pit. He had a problem with some people who didn't care for his conducting, and got flack from the stage about tempos, I believe. That's probably one of the reasons why he left. They couldn't handle his tempos anymore.

VINCENT FANUELE: When Jerry became the conductor, I was already subbing on bass trombone. In addition to being assistant conductor, I rotated with the three trombone players.

I had been offered the show originally at the same time I was offered PIPPIN. My wife, Priscilla Lopez, was in the original A CHORUS LINE cast. If A CHORUS LINE was a bomb, Priscilla and I didn't both want to be in the same show. So I decided to go with PIPPIN, which was already a big Broadway hit.

JERRY GOLDBERG: In all the fifteen years I worked on A CHORUS LINE, the only time I ever spent outside of the Broadway Company was when I trained a new conductor on the road. I went out to Baltimore for two weeks because they were in between conductors and I played and taught the show at the same time.

FRAN LIEBERGALL: It was tricky, because it was non-stop. But the charts were so great, the guys loved playing the music, and it went quickly — two hours, no intermission, and great music to play. I run into guys today and they say A CHORUS LINE was the greatest gig they ever had. Plus the guys who had walkers, they only had to play six shows a week, and they were out in two hours. They were home by the time most other musicians were just getting out of their shows! But besides that, they really loved the music. The whole scene was just great.

HERB HARRIS: It was a rough fifteen years, but we all got through it.

In the Pit

CONTRACTOR/
PERSONNEL MANAGER
Herbert Harris

CONDUCTOR
Don Pippin*
   Bob Rogers
   Alphonse Stephenson
   Jerry Goldberg

ASST. CONDUCTOR
Jerry Goldberg*
   Vincent Fanuele

KEYBOARDS
Fran Liebergall*
   Bob Rogers
   Mack Schlefer
   Gary Adams
   Jeffrey Saver
   Nick Archer
   Richard Schacher

PERCUSSION
Ben Herman*

DRUMS
Allen Herman*
   Earl Williams
   Dorian McGee
   Hank Jaramillo

ELECTRIC BASS
Roland Wilson*

UPRIGHT BASS
Jaime Austria*

GUITAR
George Davis*
   Joseph Ravo

TRUMPETS
Bob Milliken*
Al Mattaliano*
James Morreale*
   John Frosk

TROMBONES
Vincent Forchetti*
Gordon "Early" Anderson*

BASS TROMBONES
Blaise Turi *
   Brad McDougall
   Vincent Fanuele

REEDS
Joseph Maggio*
Stanley "Buzz" Brauner*
   Lino Gomez
   Andrew Sterman
Norman Wells*
   Ken Dybisz
Marvin Roth*

HARP
Bernice Horowitz*

HOUSE CONTRACTOR
Phil LeBow*
   Vincent Forchetti

Original musician; replacements are listed under the musicians they took over for; original musicians who do not have a replacement stayed the entire fifteen years. Additionally, there were dozens of substitute players through the years.

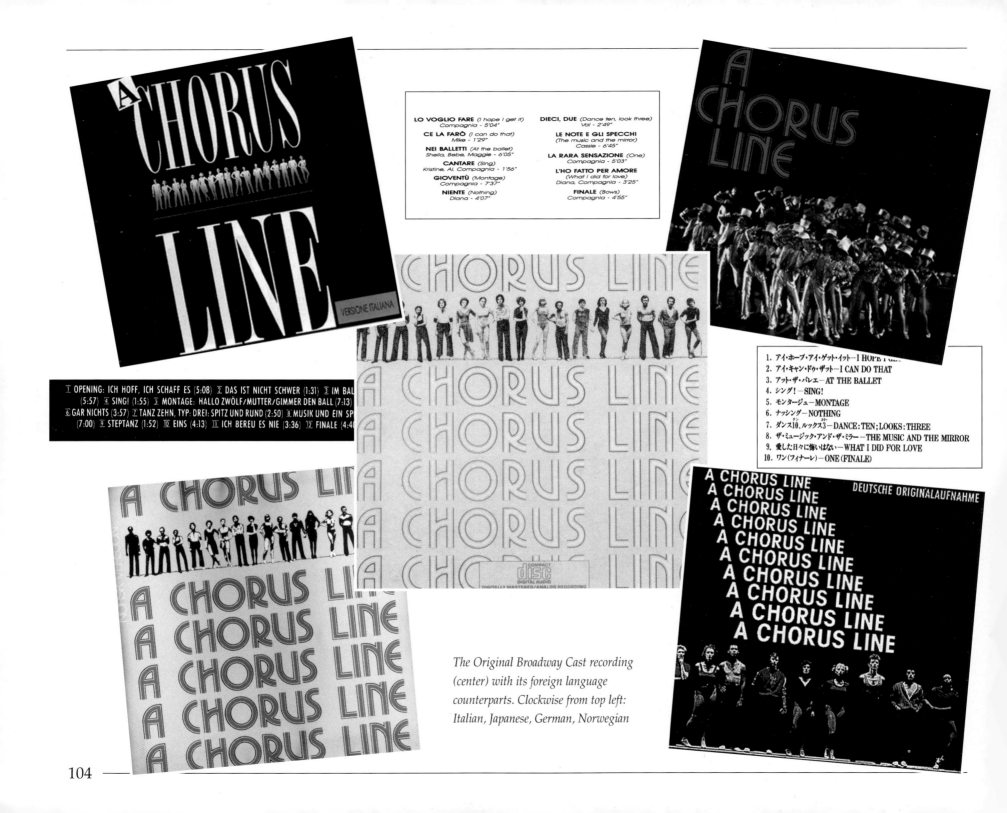

LO VOGLIO FARE *(I hope I get it)*
Compagnia - 5'04"

CE LA FARÒ *(I can do that)*
Mike - 1'29"

NEI BALLETTI *(At the ballet)*
Sheila, Bebe, Maggie - 6'05"

CANTARE *(Sing)*
Kristine, Al, Compagnia - 1'56"

GIOVENTÙ *(Montage)*
Compagnia - 7'37"

NIENTE *(Nothing)*
Diana - 4'07"

DIECI, DUE *(Dance ten, look three)*
Val - 2'49"

LE NOTE E GLI SPECCHI
(The music and the mirror)
Cassie - 6'45"

LA RARA SENSAZIONE *(One)*
Compagnia - 5'03"

L'HO FATTO PER AMORE
(What I did for love)
Diana, Compagnia - 3'25"

FINALE *(Bows)*
Compagnia - 4'55"

Ⅰ OPENING: ICH HOFF, ICH SCHAFF ES (5:08) Ⅱ DAS IST NICHT SCHWER (1:31) Ⅲ IM BALL
(5:57) Ⅳ SING! (1:55) Ⅴ MONTAGE: HALLO ZWÖLF/MUTTER/GIMMER DEN BALL (7:13)
Ⅵ GAR NICHTS (3:57) Ⅶ TANZ ZEHN, TYP: DREI: SPITZ UND RUND (2:50) Ⅷ MUSIK UND EIN SPI
(7:00) Ⅸ STEPTANZ (1:52) Ⅹ EINS (4:13) Ⅺ ICH BEREU ES NIE (3:36) Ⅻ FINALE (4:40

1. アイ・ホープ・アイ・ゲット・イット―I HOPE I GE
2. アイ・キャン・ドゥ・ザット―I CAN DO THAT
3. アット・ザ・バレエ―AT THE BALLET
4. シング！―SING!
5. モンタージュ―MONTAGE
6. ナッシング―NOTHING
7. ダンス10, ルックス3―DANCE: TEN; LOOKS: THREE
8. ザ・ミュージック・アンド・ザ・ミラー―THE MUSIC AND THE MIRROR
9. 愛した日々に悔いはない―WHAT I DID FOR LOVE
10. ワン（フィナーレ）―ONE (FINALE)

*The Original Broadway Cast recording
(center) with its foreign language
counterparts. Clockwise from top left:
Italian, Japanese, German, Norwegian*

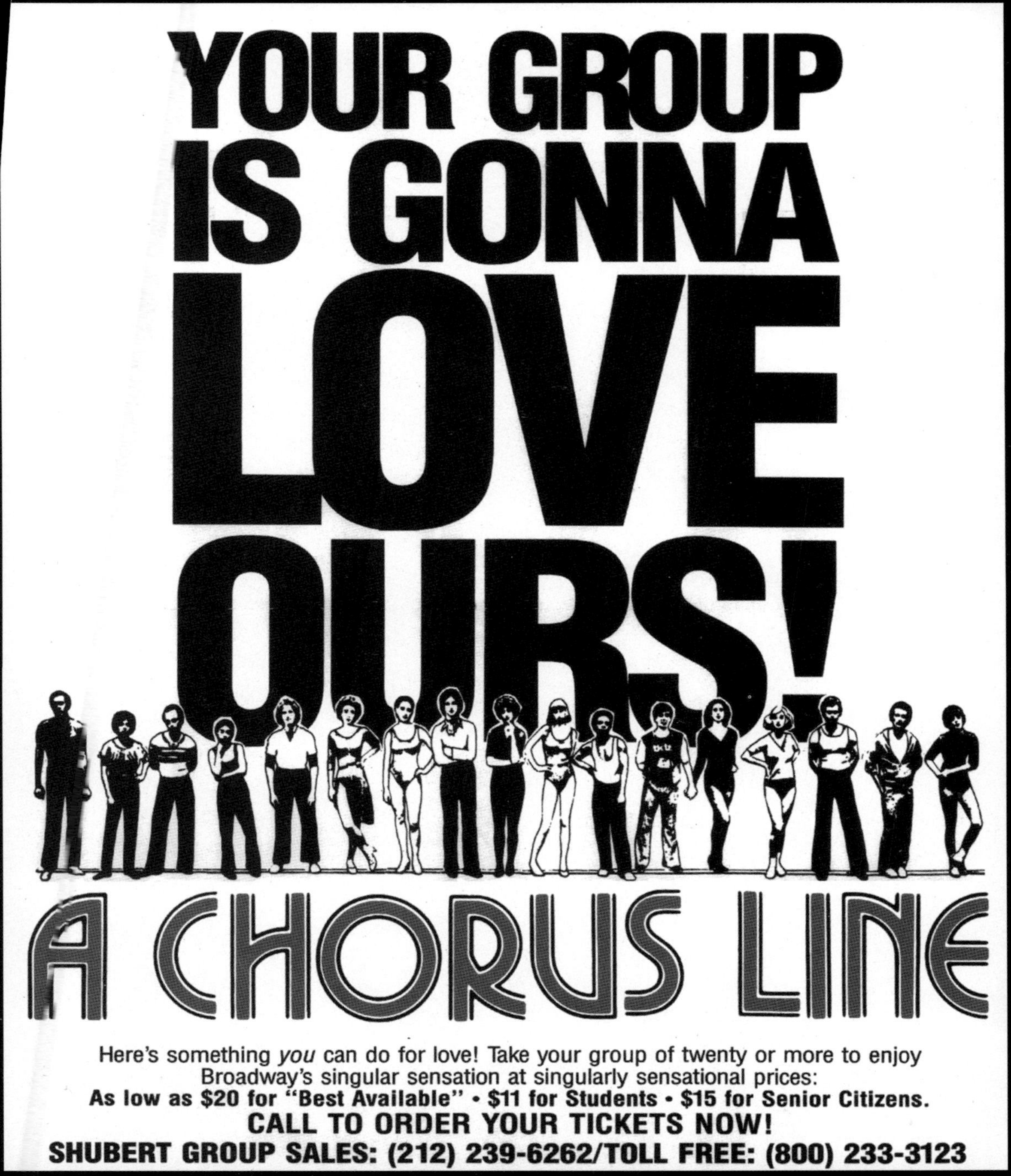

CHAPTER 5

SELLING THE SHOW

GROUPS
SALES
MARKETING

"It was a buzz phenomenon.
We just didn't know what we had. It was different from anything
that had been done before." — ALISON HARPER

New York Shakespeare Festival Subscription Office

ALISON HARPER [NYSF Subscription Director]: Bernie Gersten, Michael Bennett, Marvin Hamlisch, and various others had cooked up this workshop of A CHORUS LINE, which was not at all Mr. Papp's kind of theatre. We were used to doing middle-European dramas. What did we know about musicals? There was a buzz about it from the very start. And the buzz persisted. Suddenly it was the first preview and there were six empty seats. They were the last empty seats of the run.

Within a week, this place was a zoo. The first preview was on Wednesday evening, April 16. Some nights we already had as many as a hundred people sitting on the

steps. It was terribly illegal. Why the fire department never closed us down, I'll never know. There were a dozen limousines outside, night after night after night. Thursday evening, April 17, the second night ever, in the audience were Ruth Mitchell, Don Josephson, Grover Dale, Drew Elliot, Archer King, Ronnie Lee, Al Pacino, Flora Roberts, Neil Simon, and Bobby Van. These people knew to come immediately. By the third night, April 18, Lee Guber, Manny Azenberg, Ken Harper. Saturday matinee the first week, Lucie Arnaz, five house seats. The next week, Garson Kanin, Jules Fisher, Ron Rifkin. It happened incredibly fast.

It was a buzz phenomenon. There

wasn't that much hype; we just didn't know what we had. It was different from anything that had been done before. Tickets for the cast were very hard to arrange because we weren't used to big companies with any major demand from the actors. Each name came up three times a week, eligible for a pair.

On May 22, 1975, the day the reviews came out, the Festival box office opened at 10:00 a.m. instead of 1:00 p.m. There was already a line out the door, and we kept selling all day until 8:00 that night, taking in something like $20,000 that day alone — which was totally unheard of for any Off-Broadway box office. And this, remember, was with a $7.00 ticket, all

cash. When we took in $20,000, we had $20,000 in *cash*. Credit cards didn't come to the Festival until several years later.

It was much too much for us to handle. The box office staff was probably as big as it ever was going to get. Certain people were manipulative about getting tickets and some of the actors became spoiled very fast. I was glad to see the end of it here, if you really want to know.

It just went on and on and on. In the house seat book there are no locations, everything was filled on a best-available basis. There were specific seat assignments on the actual tickets, but everything

that went into the box office was on a best-available. You couldn't do it now at today's prices, but at $7 a ticket in a 299 seat house, you could manage it.

Bob Ullman had his own press allotment and put in his own orders directly for house seats. But once he knew it was going to Broadway, he would just roll his eyes and say, "Oh, darling, they can wait!"

Katharine Hepburn picked up tickets herself in the pouring rain. The box office treasurer was late for some reason and all the petty cash and box office things were kept in one of those little tin coin boxes, for which he had the key. So Ms. Hepburn just took a letter knife off somebody's desk and wrenched the lock open, paid for her tickets, and went away. She came on Tuesday, June 17. Richard Rodgers came that day, as well as Calvin Klein, Peter Allen — you know, just your regular Tuesday night crowd. We were up to 94 house seats in a 299 seat house. Right from the beginning we gave ourselves

extra seats. The Newman is this long space, with these funny little platforms on each side; we put six seats on each of those, adding twelve seats. Then we had all these people on the steps.

The photocopied programs were used only for previews and the paper color changed as they were updated. This would clue the staff as to which program to use. Here's a memo about staff discounts from Mr. Papp:

"There is a great deal of enthusiasm for A CHORUS LINE, which I hope everyone on the staff shares and feels a part of. The unprecedented demand for tickets has created a much needed source of income for the Festival. With other productions we are able to offer discounts because they do not cut into potential revenue. But because A CHORUS LINE has a very high weekly operating cost, as well as the ability to earn back some of these expenses at the box office, I feel it is necessary to discontinue staff discount tickets. Between now and May 18, however, those of you who have not already done so, may obtain one pair of tickets for your personal use at the $3.50 staff rate. Please make reservations through the box office or Alison Harper. So that you can advise your friends to see the show early, you should also be aware that effective May 20, we will raise ticket prices. This increase, even if we play at capacity, will still result in a loss of $3-4,000 per week. I appreciate the work all of you have been doing which has generated such tremendous enthusiasm for A CHORUS LINE."

The minute we knew it was going to Broadway we developed a group sales department at the Festival. It was a totally new experience. But we learned very, very fast. We went into overdrive with our group sales department, and sold A CHORUS LINE for years.

Selling Groups

NANCY HELLER [NYSF Audience Development]: It doesn't pay to have a whole group sales department if you've only got a 300-seat theatre downtown. But we also had Lincoln Center and Broadway shows to develop. It was easy to market because A CHORUS LINE was such a hit. Initially, you just had to keep up with the demand for tickets and decide what kind of group discounts to give. We hired Abbey Tetenbaum, who had done the Mobile Theatre with me in the summer, and he formed "Abbey's Groups." Then we needed more people.

MITCHELL WEISS [NYSF Grouptix]: Across my desk alone, starting in 1978, I took in over a million dollars a year in group sales, and there were three of us there. We had an outreach program for the shows at the Public Theatre, as well as A CHORUS LINE, in which we basically did the marketing. We kept a very detailed record of who ordered tickets, so we had a very large database at our command.

JANET ROBINSON [Group Sales Box Office]: When the determination was made to move to Broadway, we got involved.

RONNIE LEE [Group Sales Box Office]: We took an active part in A CHORUS LINE group sales from the beginning. I don't think Abbey's Groups happened yet. They came after us, really. We had developed our own customer base since 1960 — it's a fairly large, substantial list. There's no denying that the NYSF Grouptix did come up with new customers. But I know that when it moved uptown, we were their group sales source.

CLIFF SCOTT [NYSF Grouptix]: The focus of the Festival was changing. The institution was shifting to a marketing strategy versus an audience development strategy. There was an evolution going on that continued through my tenure. Do we sell the show or do we sell the institution and all of its shows? It also manifested itself in issues concerning the weekly grosses versus concern about who was seeing the shows.

My first job was to sell groups. I didn't have to start a marketing campaign. A CHORUS LINE was

already five or six years in the running; it kind of sold itself. There were demands for groups pretty heavily through the mid-eighties. The record breaking 3389th performance gave it another boost. My sales were primarily educational groups.

I fought hard and vocally at that time to keep the balcony group rate at $9.50. Balcony seats were selling for $21, then raised to $25 and $27. This was at a time when many balcony seats may have been going empty anyway. But I fought and kept the $9.50 group rate as long as there was a minimum of twenty people. If there was a group of fourteen with everybody in a wheelchair, of course you can't put them in the balcony. So we would accommodate them at $9.50 in the orchestra.

RONNIE LEE: There was a program run by the Board of Education that started during the run of A CHORUS LINE. They would buy around $150,000 worth of tickets from us in July for a selection of shows. The prerequisites were that the tickets had to be inexpensive and available in vast quantities. The NYSF, with its very acute positive sense of public awareness, made these tickets available to give students in the seventh to ninth grades added enrichment.

The performances were special matinees of A CHORUS LINE not on sale to the public. They were on either Tuesdays or Thursdays, and were the ninth performance of the week. I don't think they ever cancelled any regular performance. We filled that theatre. It was exhilarating for the cast. They got reactions that they didn't ordinarily get, and in different places. Of

> *"Across my desk alone,*
> *I took in over a million dollars a year*
> *in group sales."* — MITCHELL WEISS

course, they had to adapt to the noise, because kids respond with little care toward the person sitting next to them. We did those performances for about three years. A CHORUS LINE was the start of that program. Unfortunately, it doesn't exist any longer.

CLIFF SCOTT: We wanted to sell tickets. Generally, on the bottom line, it didn't matter *who* sold the tickets. On a more careful examination of the issue, however, if Shubert Group Sales or Ronnie Lee's company sold a ticket, they got a commission, but if the NYSF sold a ticket, we kept the commission. We paid ourselves in a sense. We were running the group sales operation for downtown and the other shows. The cost of running it was pretty minimal in comparison to the return. The department made money for the NYSF.

The other side was an audience development perspective. If someone called for A CHORUS LINE, they got on our mailing list and were told about the other shows we were doing, though only about 25% of these people who called really gave two hoots about anything other than A CHORUS LINE. If four phone calls came

in, three were only interested in A CHORUS LINE and they had no interest in the NYSF or other productions we were doing. They were calling from Michigan, they were coming to New York, they wanted A CHORUS LINE, and that was it.

Groups were not viewed as the main target, though, because you wanted people to call Tele-Charge and spend $35; we didn't want them to call and spend $9.50. This was the conflict between marketing the show and developing an audience.

NANCY HELLER: In its heyday, if you wanted house seats to A CHORUS LINE, you had to make a contribution to the Festival. It was an ongoing fund-raising project.

JACK THOMAS [Shubert Group Sales]: There's a certain demand that exists from the tour and travel market, which has to do with seeing a show that the folks back home will know. When they go back to Oregon or Idaho, they can tell their friends, "I saw that show," and their friends immediately say, "Oh, yes, isn't that a wonderful show, I've always wanted to see that." Those tourists are

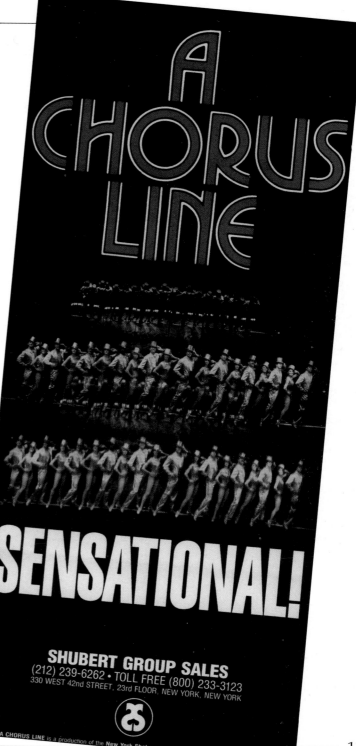

already very interested in seeing a big-name Broadway show. You have to keep yourself in the public eye. Anniversaries are obviously one thing, milestones, passing landmarks, those sorts of things.

We would ask them to consider A CHORUS LINE for a couple of reasons. One, because it is baseline Broadway. It's the show on which all other shows are built, the ultimate Broadway show. Price was obviously another big component. A show that had been running as long as A CHORUS LINE can be very aggressive at pricing strategies in order to pull people in volume. We would take direct mail pieces and use price as one of the principal selling points. Often Shubert Group Sales and the NYSF shared the design of each

other's mailers, and plugged in their own names across the bottom. I always worked directly with the Festival when they were creating a new piece.

Groups were the lion's share of the audience for A CHORUS LINE. If you booked far enough in advance and were buying 20, 40, 60 tickets, you could get good seats. Shubert Group Sales had two or three groups at almost every performance. Certainly in the last few years, there was always inventory available for virtually all regular performances.

The box office crews at the Shubert were terrific. They knew that groups were their bread and butter and they took really good care to make sure the machinery ran smoothly.

"If four phone calls came in, three were only interested in A CHORUS LINE and they had no interest in other productions we were doing. They were coming to New York, they wanted A CHORUS LINE, and that was it." — CLIFF SCOTT

Shubert Theatre Box Office

BILL FRIENDLY [Box Office]: We sold all the Shubert tickets and then had to refund all the tickets because of the three week musicians' strike in September/October 1975. We were allowed to cross the picket line just to come in and do that. We refunded their money because we didn't know when the strike was going to end.

At that time we had hard stock tickets, we weren't computerized yet, so you couldn't sell a year and a half in advance. We sold about six months in advance and every week that would go by, we would add another week.

I had been in the business for five years when I did A CHORUS LINE, and there was never such pressure as there was for that show. The main stress was that we didn't have computers. You should see what it was like to take an order. You've got three million dollars worth of $15 tickets in advance and we had to count it up by hand. That took all day. We'd come in Sunday morning at 10 a.m. and leave maybe 2:00 the next morning. And, naturally, we didn't get paid for that.

We probably had one of the largest box office personnels ever: seven plus the treasurer. We did mail, phones, credit card sales. Two people sat in the back room all day long taking phone orders. Mail orders were all the same, everyone wanted fourth row center, and they were all from diggers and scalpers.

Mary Porter, one of the best people in the business, ran the mail room. She had every single mail order in order of the date it was received, the date they wanted, how many seats. The lady was incredible. She knew who was who; she had a box for people who had already gotten tickets ten times, who were basically scalpers. We had some very good box office people. Most of them became treasurers. I was there just for the first year.

The last seven weeks I was there, I worked seven days a week, forty-nine days straight. Even though we were closed on Sundays, I had to come in and do things upstairs. When I was given my first vacation, I went away, and the day I came back I had no job. The treasurer had retired and no one ever bothered to call me on vacation and tell me. The whole crew had changed, a new treasurer came in and he brought his staff with him.

NOREEN MORGAN [Box Office]: We would get anywhere from 200 to 300 mail orders a day. Sometimes even more. Now you don't see mail orders that much anymore because people either order over the phone or come to the theatre or buy through ticket brokers. It's not the same as it used to be. We had phone-charge, but back in the seventies mail orders were popular because people weren't thinking about picking up the phone as much. Now you use the phone for everything. With hard tickets we had to do audits about every three or four months. At that time, we were closed on Sundays but we would

come in and count up all the tickets, do the paper work and make sure we balanced.

MICHAEL MILIONE [Box Office]: I started on A CHORUS LINE during the New York City transit strike. I remember being interviewed in the lobby by Eyewitness News asking me about how business was affected. As it happened, we sold out all week because people were staying in the city. The strike was a great time for Broadway.

NOREEN MORGAN: The Shubert converted to computers in 1980. The first theatre to be computerized, however, was the Winter Garden, with 42ND STREET.

MICHAEL MILIONE: I was there during the transition of hard stock to computerized tickets. That first day of the transition was chaos. I didn't get to go to school for it but I went over to the Shubert office about two or three times and they trained me. It was easier for me to pick it up than it was for the old timers because they were so used to the hard ticket. For me, everything was new, since I was just get-ting into the business. I helped the others in the box office learn the computer. It was like family.

NOREEN MORGAN: We sold the bal-cony to a lot of kids, school groups. I used to have to fight with the older people who wanted to buy balcony seats, telling them there is no way they could go up there. You would be scared to death that some-thing was going to happen to them climb-ing the steps and on Wednesday after-noons that was a hassle. But after a while, if they insist on the balcony, you have to sell it to them — and then they come back and say you were right.

A CHORUS LINE definitely had more walk-ups than anything else. We had a lot of mail orders from out-of-towners, but people who could get to the box office themselves weren't thinking about calling up. We did a big phone business but noth-ing like walk-ups in those days. I remem-ber at one point we had ten people in the box office. We had an office upstairs where the phone orders were filled and the group tickets were pulled. The box office assigned the locations for groups; they still do. For a while that was my job. I was upstairs all day and would come downstairs to work the show at night. You were never sitting around doing nothing. And we had a pretty good phone staff too. We had maybe eight or ten people answering phones and taking orders.

As soon as people found out that we sent tickets to TKTS, the lines over there were tremendous. It was the biggest show they had for quite a while. We would use TKTS as a last resort. In the early days we would send over balcony seats, but some-times we didn't have those to send because of school groups.

MICHAEL MILIONE: It was still very box office strong, more than phone or mail. I don't think they were even using twofers yet. It was still a walk-up show. Bob MacDonald was one of the greatest managers I ever worked with. We never had any problems with management. Naturally, since the Shubert is the flagship theatre, everything had to be on the up and up all the time. Always jackets and ties. It was hectic, the phones didn't stop. Each person had about three or four phone lines and the lights just kept going all day long. It was one call after the other, and we were accepting charge cards. You had to write the card number, put it on a log sheet and send it down to the box office where they would fill the order with tickets. They would send it back up to us and we either mailed the tickets out or

made it into a HABO [Held At Box Office]. Everything was done by hand.

JOE McLAUGHLIN [Box Office]: The Shubert did a lateral move in 1982 with three treasurers who took over each others' box offices. We were doing JOSEPH and went to the Shubert, the Shubert crew went to the Winter Garden to do CATS and the CATS crew went to the Royale to do JOSEPH. I stayed with A CHORUS LINE until the end in 1990.

The TKTS booth basically carried us over the years. In the morning we'd open up and send them 200 to 250 tickets automatically, then we'd balance the books out, sit there, and sell tickets. Other shows didn't do that, couldn't do that. Because our nut was so low, like $120,000 a week, the wagon, as we called it, could practically make the nut by itself each week. They'd do $60,000 to $70,000. They would usually sell most of the allotment we sent them in the morning and call up for more. So with the wagon, a couple of groups and some sales at the window, we made our nut. We also gave TDF tickets for mailings. We would see three or four months in advance that it was getting a little quiet, so we'd bang out 1,000 tickets for TDF for a particular week and build up our money so it would be closer to the nut. We always looked in advance; it was smart. That's the way we kept the show running.

BOB REILLY [Company Manager]: Harry Pearl was the best box office treasurer in the world. It was amazing how he worked the TKTS booth and the window. On a Saturday, I'd be there for the matinee, and I'd ask Harry how we were for the evening, and he would say, "Well, Bob, I'm going to send a little more to the booth, but the window is doing well." Today the booth is linked electronically, but back in those days, you would have to call the booth and say, "I'm sending you twenty-five more," and they would send a runner to pick them up. Harry would work it so that on a Saturday night, at 8:05 p.m. we would sell our last full price ticket at the window. He got every nickel he could into the show. He was the box office treasurer on GREASE at the Royale, and kept that show running longer than it should have. He was with A CHORUS LINE way before I got there. He could sell a ticket, he was magic that way.

There were bad nights. Tuesday nights in January and February, with papering the house, we'd have 110 people. It was not pretty. Everybody always talked about painting curtains of people's faces and drawing them across the mezzanine, to make it look like they're sitting in a theatre. But to see the house rocking on a Saturday night was something else.

JOE McLAUGHLIN: I remember a couple of hundred seat nights here and there, but it was mainly around the summertime when we switched from a Tuesday

through Sunday schedule back to a Monday through Saturday schedule. That one day would always be bad. And Sundays were not effective for the show. The show was making money on cruise control. There wasn't a lot of competition on Monday nights, but there was a lot more on Sundays. Holiday matinees were pretty good, tourists again.

ED SHERIDAN [Box Office]: I was with the show for the last four years. About two months before it was going to close, we got the definite word. There was a substantial surge of business when they made the announcement.

MICHAEL MILIONE: A CHORUS LINE had class audiences. It was on a slight down-swing when I started, but the people who went to see that show all knew theatre.

Wish
you
were
here.

Ⓢ Shubert Theatre 44th Street, N.Y.C.

Hit Show Club: Discount Coupons

STEVE GARDNER [Hit Show Club]: The show had been floundering for a couple of months by January 1982. I distributed several million discount tickets over a period of six weeks. The campaign brought in enough money to keep them going comfortably and not thinking of when they were going to close. It gathered enough steam to give them confidence to run the big record-breaking Gala in September 1983 — and that was the key. It just took off from there. The show started to do tremendous business, as if it were a new show. In the eight-year period I was associated with A CHORUS LINE, the show took in the neighborhood of $13,000,000 just on Hit Show Club discount tickets alone. And that's a pretty good neighborhood.

We had to find potential audiences fairly close to the center of town without destroying full price tickets. We went to neighborhoods like the Upper West Side, Greenwich Village, and the East Side. There were plenty of people who hadn't seen it plus all those who might see it again at a lower price.

I didn't think nonprofit theatres like NYSF should be charged as much as a regular Broadway show. We charged them about 25% less, about $1000 a week less than we would have ordinarily charged. We did it for practically no profit, but we absorbed it. But figure at $1000 a week for eight years, we happily contributed about $400,000 to the NYSF! I would say an average of 200,000 coupons were printed a week. At ten million a year, that's 80 million coupons printed and distributed throughout its eight years on Hit Show Club coupons. Toward the end, when sales started to weaken, they didn't want to spend that money. Although they were still taking in at least two or three times what they were spending, they just didn't want to put out that much for promotion.

"In the eight year period I was associated with A CHORUS LINE, the show took in the neighborhood of $13,000,000 just on Hit Show Club discount tickets alone. And that's a pretty good neighborhood." — STEVE GARDNER

Direct Mail Pieces

CLIFF SCOTT: Part of the problem with the NYSF was getting approval — which was practically impossible because ultimately Mr. Papp made the decisions. He was a wonderful genius of a man, but access to him was severely restricted by those around him. You could send a memo to Mr. Papp saying you needed something, but you would never hear back. I don't think he saw it as unimportant; he had other priorities. But all of my pieces had to be approved by him, so I figured out fast the best way to get something approved was to submit work that was already approved.

The staff surrounding Mr. Papp tried to make decisions for him, which I guess was their job. But they never would take a risk and go to bat for you. He never actually rejected anything I wanted to do, since he was not involved in the process. That was the big problem in marketing. Everything on the group sales mail pieces were images that had been used before.

I remember looking at the first draft of the long poster with the multiple casts — the one that was used as a group sales direct mailer to celebrate becoming the longest running show on Broadway — and thinking there's a real problem here. Joe Papp's name is not on it. There's no Michael Bennett on it either. What credits do we print? We ultimately used exactly what's on the album, in the same order, except for Robert Rogers, the conductor at the time of the Gala, who is also given credit on the Gala poster. Payton Silver, the head of merchandising, was the inspiration for the piece. He coordinated the printing for the souvenir program book. He used to hang the center spread of the program in his office showing the cast on the line, taped to the wall. Then he would put the next company photo below it. During his tenure, he had about eight or nine on the wall. One day I was walking by Payton's office, thinking about how to celebrate 3389. And I remember looking at his wall of photographs thinking why don't we do that? Why don't we use each photograph of the line, find out who all these people are and list them in alphabetical order. And then we'll put a time line on the other side to tie in historical events related to the show.

SUSAN FRANK [NYSF Freelance Graphic Designer]: I designed the entire poster. We had two versions, one for NYSF in-house group sales, and the other for Ronnie's Group Sales Box Office. I designed it so they could eventually cut the group sales information off the bottom and have a poster. I wanted to make a long, thin poster, a really monumental type poster, because it was a monumental event. It was my idea to insert all the historical things. There were a few errors, but the photos used were the only ones we could locate. The design was never disputed, although originally it had been designed in black, white, and silver. I was a very lucky designer at the Festival; they literally let me do whatever I wanted.

BROADWAY'S ONE SINGULAR SENSATION, A CHORUS LINE, THE LONGEST RUNNING SHOW IN BROADWAY HISTORY, HAS NEVER BEEN BETTER THAN NOW!

WINNER
TEN TONY AWARDS

WINNER
PULITZER PRIZE FOR DRAMA

THE AWARD-WINNING
A CHORUS LINE
THE BEST MUSICAL...EVER!

GROUP SALES BOX OFFICE

The Souvenir Program

A CHORUS LINE

The cover of the first souvenir program

NANCY HELLER: I tried to make the souvenir program different from what was typically done for Broadway shows. This was my opportunity to meet the artists, take a tape recorder around and say, "Tell me about your involvement in the show, what did you do?" I wrote the interviews, which became the substance of the A CHORUS LINE souvenir book. I did all the interviews while we were still at The Public.

There is nothing on Michael Bennett in the souvenir book. Michael didn't like what I had excerpted of his comments — and he didn't like the cast interviews. He felt the interviews portrayed the actors as having contributed more than he really thought they had. First he said, "I don't want this in there and I'm going to rewrite it." But ultimately the souvenir program was a relatively low priority, and he ended up just letting it go as written.

You couldn't change what those people thought about their contribution. He never approved anything with regard to his own interview. And that's why there is nothing about Michael Bennett in the souvenir book of A CHORUS LINE.

HERB MIGDOLL [Freelance Photographer]: They had us photographing an invited rehearsal. I got a lot of photographs between that run-through and the previews from which I put together a dummy souvenir program to show Joe Papp.

Nancy had forewarned me that she had assigned the souvenir program to Susan Frank, whom Nancy had expected to collaborate with on the book. I came in like a bat out of hell. I was not involved in the politics of taking the job away from this other lady. I was determined to do my presentation to Papp and either I was going to get the job or not — and I got it.

The image on the actual cover of the program was the photograph that Joe Papp saw as the cover on my dummy. The first three spreads were exactly as they

appear in the souvenir program. At that presentation, he saw my idea of the strip photos of the individual actors. I had to get everybody in very sharply and clearly in a double spread. If I got them all reasonably vertical and cropped to the head, they'd fit. It's called expedition design. How can you get everybody in a double spread and make it look really unusual and special? I have to get so many photos on this side and so many on that side, and the strips had to be a certain size.

One of the things I loved about Michael and the whole encounter was that I got credit for the concept, even though they would execute it without me at times. They would simply replace photos as new people came in. I wasn't involved in that, but my design credit was always there. The book was very much styled as a result of my having gone to Joe Papp on my own. I requested the art directorship of the book, saying, "The photos are going to be mixed between mine and other people's. I'd like to do as many photos as possible, but whatever are the best photos are what should be in the program. But I would like to have control over the visual concept and layout for the entire piece." And it was agreed upon that I would have that control. As the art director, they would let me select the photographic energy that went into the book, with Nancy's collaboration, and Michael would then have to sign off on it. All of my black and white pictures are from downtown; I shot color photos

from uptown. Martha Swope was doing all the hard work. I was trying to do creative stuff with color and that was how the color program cover came about, which was a few years into the run.

NANCY HELLER: Because the show was such a phenomenal hit, with successive actors playing the roles, the souvenir book was conceived as sixteen pages of standard bios, interviews with the original cast, and then this eight page center section with the Herb Migdoll photos. All you really had to do to keep it current was strip in the new photo. Herb had conceived that way of lining them up. Periodically we would redo the cen-

The second souvenir program cover, which was thereafter used throughout the run of the show

A CHORUS LINE

Above and opposite page: The souvenir program's strip photos

ter photo of the entire company as well, but it didn't always match up with the strip photos.

HERB MIGDOLL: The strip photos were 50% Martha Swope and 50% me. The center spreads of the cast on the line, except for one or two of the companies, were all mine. I took them in three groups of four on the line and one group of five. I would always do the five shot first so that I would have my distance and establish from where I would take the picture. Then I would shoot the next three groups. I stayed in the same place; each group moved into the same spot as the previous group. Then I would have prints made, put them together and go to the retoucher to work on how far apart to place each group to give a continuous look.

Those decisions would be abandoned when they let Martha do it, because they were not thinking of concept that strongly. They just knew that the pictures had to fit on each page. In the original program, the center spread was taken during the opening night performance at the Public, and it's the same picture that's used on the cover. The cover was meant to idealize these people, and I felt they should all be much taller and thinner to be absolutely extraordinary.

NANCY HELLER: Bernie Gersten persuaded Joe, saying, "This is something that usually a press agent does, and they get paid extra for it. Nancy has done it, and she should get paid something extra above her salary — a royalty or a nickel a book." Actually the royalty was for me and the designer, and that is what we implemented. But when I left the Shakespeare Festival, one of the managers proposed that if I wasn't an employee, I wasn't entitled to the royalties.

HERB MIGDOLL: I was doing it on a royalty basis which I got right through to the end. I don't know why that happened and I never fought for it. I never had to fight for my income from Michael. I was lucky, I was blessed.

ARNOLD KOHN [Lerman Graphics; Printer of Souvenir Program]: It was probably the nicest printed souvenir book that I have ever seen on Broadway. Everything was just about perfect in the production. The type style was excellent, the cover was laminated perfectly. It was just a beautiful book and it won a couple of prizes from the Printing Industries of America. It was a tough production at first but we found a way to handle it. By preparing the art in a

special way, we were able to lick the problem of the eight page inner fold-out signature, which changed every time they had a cast change. We wound up printing the outside cover and the sixteen standard pages, and holding them in stock until we changed the inside eight page gatefold.

The end of every week we delivered four or five cartons, with 800 books each, to the Shubert. In its heyday, with three companies going, our presses were tied up for weeks. The eight page inner gatefold was different for each company. There were orders of a couple hundred thousand covers at a time to laminate and print in full color. The eight page insert was so time consuming, because every time a cast member changed, we put in a new picture and name. However, I don't think it wound up being any more expensive to produce than the average Broadway souvenir book. There were over a million books printed for the Broadway edition alone and at least 1,800,000 among all the different companies over the years.

> " In its heyday, with three
> companies going, our presses
> were tied up for weeks.
> There were over a million books
> printed for the Broadway edition alone."
>
> —ARNOLD KOHN

Above: The center spread of the Original Company, photographed at the Public Theatre, was the only time the line was photographed in its entirety for the souvenir program. All subsequent companies were photographed in four groups, then put together to create the complete line.

Photos by Herb Migdoll

PHOTO/HERBERT MIGDOLL

Photo Shoots

MARTHA SWOPE [Photographer]: At the first photo call downtown we did candid shots and then we did setups. Herb Migdoll was also there taking photographs. It was unusual to have two photographers working on a show.

HERB MIGDOLL [Photographer]: I was under the impression this was my job and walked in to see Martha Swope with her assistant. Sue McNair, Michael's assistant, said to me, "I'm not sure what's going on here, but Martha is shooting the rehearsal today and if you want to take pictures,

Michael said you can." So I shot around Martha. It was very awkward — Martha doing her thing and me going off to shoot a different angle. I was there to come up with creative fresh material and Martha was there to give them the "guts" of what they needed. She had a crew and the capacity to turn out black and white photography overnight in quantity. I couldn't have done that properly and it wasn't something I wanted to do. I was invited to these sessions and although my expenses were covered, I didn't get a fee.

MARTHA SWOPE: The photo call choreo-

graphed itself. Being such a perfect show, it was really obvious what to do. You would see it in the choreography. Over the years we would often try to think of something different, but there wasn't anything else. It was obvious what made a picture and what didn't. Even fifteen years into the run, I never thought there was any other way to photograph it that captured the show's straightforwardness and honesty.

CLIFF SCOTT [NYSF Grouptix]: Martha and Herb had very different styles, but not one better than the other. Sometimes there was a bit of refereeing going on in a subtle way, because from our perspective there was very little time for the photo shoot.

HERB MIGDOLL: There was always some kind of sequence set up to make it the most expeditious for that particular cast.

LAURIE GAMACHE [Cast]: It got to be a science and was done very quickly. They always did the same things for each character. Every damn light in the theatre was turned on; it was really bright and hot. Martha Swope would take shots from the balcony and the middle of the house.

HERB MIGDOLL: I did individual studio shots at City Center. They would send down three or four people and it would be

Photo by Herb Migdoll

a ten-minute session per person. For the individual strip photos used in the center of the souvenir program, the white line was always dummied in. In studio shots, the line was not there at all; for those that were shot in the theatre, the line would not extend across the entire spread of the photos. To make it appear as if all the individuals were standing on one straight line, we would delete the line from each photograph and draw one across the whole piece containing the nineteen strip photos.

MARTHA SWOPE: I think the rules with Actor's Equity were that whenever there were "X" number of new people in the company, new photos had to be taken. We were only called in when new shots were needed. I would usually photograph the show myself rather than send an assistant because I loved A CHORUS LINE. We didn't photograph the Final Company because on a closing show, the producers are not going to bring you in. It costs money.

HERB MIGDOLL: I was lucky not to have been responsible for the press "gut'" material of the show I had the opportunity to experiment, the chance to produce work which reflected some of the brilliance of the show. You cannot get that in a press photograph which is there to serve a documentary purpose. If you want to create an image that is absolutely dazzling, you need to be able to think about it and experiment. I had that extraordinary opportunity.

A CHORUS LINE

PICTURE CALL PROCEDURE TUESDAY FEBURARY 9, 1982

1. FINALE WEDGE
    FINALE LUNGE
    FINALE 'ONE CHANGE'
2. FINALE GROUP: ZACH   LARRY
                     SHEILA   VAL
                     CASSIE   DIANA
                     PAUL

        (CHANGE INTO OPENING DRAG)

3. SOLO'S: JUDY (KERRY)
              BEBE (ROBERTA)
              SHEILA (DEBORAH)
              DIANA (GAY)

RICHIE SPLIT JUMP > 4. FULL SHOT LOGO
5. LOGO GROUPS: A) DON
                     MAGGIE
                     MIKE
                     CONNIE
                  B) GREG
                     CASSIE
                     SHEILA
                     BOBBY
                     BEBE
                  C) JUDY
                     RICHIE
                     AL
                     KRISTINE
                  D) VAL
                     MARK
                     PAUL
                     DIANA

INTERNATIONAL COMPA

A CHORUS LINE

PHOTO CALL   MARCH 30, 1989

1. OPENING - Mirror   "5-6-7-8"
2. ON LINE - hands on hats - hats in air - MIRROR
        LOSE MIRROR and HATS
3. LOGO SHOT - on line
4. RESUME SHOT - Photos
5. 4 GROUP SHOTS - on line   (2nd group - 5)
6. 3 SHOTS - everyone doing their bit
7. AT THE BALLET
8. SING - Flynn and Stephen
9. NOTHING - Arminae
10. WHAT I DID FOR LOVE - full cast
11. SINGLES: for souvenir book: Arminae, Drew, Michael G., Christine, Susan, Gordon, Stephen, Diana K., Susan Santoro
12. Paul's Soliloquy - Drew from balcony
13. Richie Number - Gordon and cast
14. Cassie number - Laurie if needed
        FINALE

Two photo call sequences

Merchandising

Photo by Michael Harvey

The original and final tee-shirts, with an original show jacket

RICK ELICE [Associate Creative Director; Serino Coyne Inc. (Advertising)]: It was the first time you saw show jackets, tee-shirts, mugs — and there were many versions of those items.

NANCY HELLER: The very first run of the tee-shirt was white with brown lettering. We gave them out as opening night gifts at the Public, and we couldn't get the beige shirts in stock until after we opened. One year we did duffle bags for the cast, and we had umbrellas, the Bloomingdale's towel and tote bags.

RICK ELICE: A CHORUS LINE was certainly at the forefront of theatre merchandising.

I'VE SEEN BROADWAY'S LONGEST RUNNING SHOW
A CHORUS LINE
AT THE SHUBERT THEATRE IN NEW YORK CITY

Complimentary bumper stickers were available in the box office lobby

Photo by Michael Harvey

A CHORUS LINE merchandise and memorabilia including the 4000th performance Finale hat distributed to the audience

THE MEDIA CAMPAIGNS

ADVERTISING & PUBLICITY

The advertisement announcing the move to the Shubert Theatre

*"I remember seeing the preview thinking, 'Shit, all of these lines
I have been writing are completely wrong — it has so much more heart.
It's not just a backstage story.'"* — NANCY COYNE

The Logo

A CHORUS LINE was represented by three advertising agencies. Blaine Thompson, the largest theatrical advertising office of its day; Case & McGrath, with no previous theatrical experience prior to the New York Shakespeare Festival; and finally Serino Coyne & Nappi, later Serino Coyne — minus the Nappi — (now the nation's leading theatrical agency), who handled the A CHORUS LINE account for over twelve years.

DON JOSEPHSON [Account Executive: Blaine Thompson]: There was no significant advertising campaign to announce A CHORUS LINE at the Public Theatre. In fact, there was no major advertising campaign two months later when they moved to Broadway. Everybody in the country already knew about it. The most popular theatre in 1975 was the Newman and A CHORUS LINE was the hottest ticket in town. We barely needed our small pro-forma campaign in *The New York Times.*

SUSAN FRANK [NYSF Freelance Graphic Designer]: Nancy Heller called me and said "We have a show here called A CHORUS LINE and it's about gypsies," and I said, "About gypsies … you mean Rumanians?" And she said "No, the dancers who go from one show to another." I saw the show and went through all my type books to see if I could use anything to create a logo. I finally found a typeface in the Letraset catalog and did a little pencil sketch with the words "A Chorus Line" stacked and centered, one on each line.

I wish I could say that I drew it and that it was mine totally — but then again, there's no point creating what's already there. The typeface was exactly what was used for the show, including the borders around it. I thought it echoed a reflective feeling of the show. I did two or three versions with other typefaces but I was sure they were going to choose this one. When it moved to Broadway I was quite surprised when they decided not to change

the look, because it almost seemed too simple.

MORRIS ROBBINS [Art Director: Blaine Thompson]: When the original logo was first accepted, we printed it on many different backgrounds, including lucite and mylar. We printed it in gold and silver as an experiment.

DON JOSEPHSON: I thought we should use colors that occur in the finale: the beige, brown, and silver, which became the color scheme for the window card and subsequently for the record album.

As much as I would like to take credit for advertising as the reason for its success, that's not the case. We used to run what we call shallow double ads — little two-column ads about two inches high, with little teaser copy, something like "You'd better get to the Public while you still can." There was very little done, really. It was a word of mouth success, more than anything else.

NANCY COYNE [Creative Director: Serino Coyne Inc.]: I was at Blaine Thompson when the account exec, Don Josephson, asked me to go to the first preview at the Public. I had something to do and didn't go. When I got in the next morning to work, Don said, "Oh, you really blew it!" I went to the second preview and was swept away. At the time the logo had already been done by someone at the Public. There were little tiny ads that ran, and I remember writing copy like "They're in it for more than just the kicks." Very show bizzy. It didn't hint at the heart at all.

I remember seeing the preview thinking, "Shit, all of these lines I have been writing are completely wrong — it has so much more heart. It's not just a backstage story." That was my first inkling that there would have to be more than this flippant approach. It was becoming clear that we wouldn't need copy lines. Press quotes were going to do the job for us, which were then followed by awards and the Pulitzer Prize.

My next assignment wasn't so much copy as broadcast and television. I was asked to come up with a television commercial for A CHORUS LINE. I knew what a hit the show was when directors who didn't get the job were furious with me. It was a very desirable assignment and we decided on Bob Giraldi to direct.

The TV Commercial

BOB GIRALDI [Director of TV commercial]: Michael Bennett and certainly Marvin Hamlisch did not as yet have respect for the commercial medium. There had only been one Broadway show commercial, for Fosse's PIPPIN, and while it was very enjoyable, the results weren't in yet. Nobody knew if it really worked. But Nancy, who always was a visionary in that field, persuaded them to do a commercial. When she brought me down to the Public to see the show, I could not believe my eyes. It was the early days of people seeing A CHORUS LINE for the first time. It was different theatre, it was emotional theatre, it was dance theatre, it was just stunning. I saw it twice. I made a professional excuse to go back and see it again only because I personally wanted to see it. And then I was ready to meet the people and shoot it. I had taken notes of what I thought were emotional scenes.

The problem with A CHORUS LINE is that almost every number has some sort of emotion to it. You couldn't do the highlights in thirty or sixty seconds, because there were too many good highlights! There was a script and a story board idea, but with Michael, God bless him, he just didn't get it in terms of commercials. He just didn't get what it could do. Michael, as an artist, was not easy to pin down any-

way. He had that style of creating by doing and by process of elimination. We clashed in that I wanted progress, I wanted something. I also knew the shooting date was coming close.

We went to Michael's apartment and met Marvin Hamlisch, who said, "We'll shoot this, then we'll shoot that, and maybe we'll try a third thing." And I said, "Excuse me, how do we get around doing three commercials when it is going to be hard enough to do one?" He said, "Relax, what do you need? A few people, a camera, you shoot this, you shoot that." I said, "No, Marvin, maybe that's the way you compose, but you don't make a film that way." It was Papp who really brought us all together. "Look," said Joe, "I want a commercial and I want a good one, so sit down, figure out a way, and come back with something that we can shoot." And we did. Starting with the pan down the line and their headshots, which I always thought was wonderful.

NICK NAPPI [Art Director: Serino Coyne & Nappi]: We were all sitting around a room, Bob Giraldi and some of his assistants, Michael Bennett, Bob Avian, Nancy, and myself. We started to throw some ideas back and forth.

BOB GIRALDI: Slowly we began to trust and like each other. I thought Bob Avian was really important at that time. He doesn't look for conflict, he looks for ways to solve the problem, so he was sort of the negotiator, the arbitrator. We tried a trick which really was not very effective, but worked in those days, of the line in rehearsal clothing and in the next frame, down and up in Finale costumes.

NANCY COYNE: Michael was not happy with my decision in the 60-second spot to show the Finale costumes. He said I was giving the ending away, which is an argument I've had with a lot of directors over the years. I've done enough commercials to know that giving a one- or two-second preview to a television audience only enhances that moment in the theatre. I remember sitting in Michael's apartment with Bob Giraldi and Bob Avian, fighting about whether that frame was going to be used or not. It was an awful night, we really slugged it out. I can't remember why I was determined, because it probably wasn't a make or break situation. The commercial needed an end, a look.

Michael thought Bob Giraldi and I were crassly commercial and were doing a real number on his show. But when it was done, he loved the commercial and was the first one to say, "Boy, do I not know anything about television!" When we made the DREAMGIRLS commercial, we used Giraldi again, and Michael said, "Don't ask

me, I don't know about commercials, I only know what to do on stage."

BOB GIRALDI: After watching over my shoulder for the first few hours during the shoot, Michael saw that the making of film is a craft in its own right. Michael really learned to respect that shot of the line with the resume photos. We laid dolly track straight across the entire line. It's a difficult dolly shot because you can't go too fast, you can't go too slow; you have to hit just when each actor is putting his photo down. It seems simple but the film shot wasn't that easy. At one point I got off the dolly and said to Michael, "Why don't you ride this?" He said, "No, it's okay, I see what you're doing." "Go on," I urged. "Get on the dolly, put your eye in the camera, and see how glorious it really looks." He tried it, although he couldn't really make it the first couple of times, because it's difficult to ride a dolly with your eye glued to an eyepiece and your two hands working a camera by the wheels. Michael got off half-way after a couple of tries and said, "It's beautiful, I love it." I think he had a certain new appreciation for the craft you had to know and do and feel in order to make film.

DON JOSEPHSON: Shortly before the Broadway opening, the New York Shakespeare Festival decided that they might change advertising agencies. Merle Debuskey, their press agent, called and

said, "Joe Papp is quite unhappy and he's thinking about going to a different agency." It was suggested that we do a presentation with some new ideas, which we did, but apparently they had already made up their minds.

NANCY COYNE: It had much more to do with Papp than it did with Michael Bennett or A CHORUS LINE itself. It was the Joseph Papp account. And Joe was very unhappy with Blaine Thompson, which he felt was formula, and he didn't want A CHORUS LINE to be treated the same as every Broadway show. This was his big splash on Broadway. He was looking at his legacy and he wanted to protect it. And he was simply not confident in the people who worked at Blaine Thompson. This was crushing to me. When they lost that account and I watched it happen, powerless to stop it, it was an unhappy day. I'd just made what I thought was a wonderful television commercial; to sit and watch some other agency air it was painful. That's a part of the business that no one in the business likes. The creative belongs to the client, not to the people who created it.

Switching Ad Agencies

JIM RUSSEK [Account Executive: Case & McGrath]: Nancy Heller was the cousin of a woman that I rented a summer house with. I had attended a few New York Shakespeare Festival productions before and said to Nancy, "If A CHORUS LINE is such a breakthrough, why is it being advertised like every other play?" A CHORUS LINE was mundane in the advertising and sensational on the stage. She said, "Don't tell me, tell Joe." "Well, set up a meeting." The show was going to move to the Shubert in July. So Gene Case, the principal and creative director of the agency, and I met with Joe extensively about everything the Festival did.

Joe was going to launch a season of new playwrights at the Booth Theatre. There were a million things that were about to go on. A CHORUS LINE, in Joe's firmament, was one little star off in the corner. He was much more interested in what we thought about the American plays on Broadway, what we thought about the season he was about to do at Lincoln Center. We really didn't talk very much about A

CHORUS LINE. It was territory that, as I learned later, he was not all that comfortable on. It was not his baby. So we had a very nice meeting, quite electric. Gene Case is an outspoken guy in his own right, sparks ignited and those two hit it off. Right after the 4th of July holiday, before A CHORUS LINE moved to Broadway, Joe called and told us we had the account, the entire New York Shakespeare Festival account.

It was the first defection of anybody ever from Blaine Thompson. There just wasn't another theatrical advertising agency out there. We had zero experience in theatre. I think the promise that we brought, to do it brilliantly and differently, is why we got the account. No presentation, just a meeting with Joe Papp.

GENE CASE [Creative Director: Case & McGrath]: Jim Russek worked for me, we had done political campaigns, and at one point he came to me and said, "I have this very good friend, Nancy Heller, who works for the New York Shakespeare

"If A CHORUS LINE is such a breakthrough, why is it being advertised like every other play?"

— *JIM RUSSEK*

A A
CHORUS
LINE

NEW YORK · LOS ANGELES · LONDON

Festival, and Joe Papp is not enamored with the advertising." So we took some work down, had a meeting with Joe and Bernie Gersten. Something just happened between Joe Papp and me, just sort of a connection, and I showed him some work that he liked. I told him he represented something very rare to the theatre and he should work with people in advertising who represent something of that quality too. And I think he was intrigued by that. So he decided to take a shot with us, and we began working almost immediately. Not on A CHORUS LINE, we worked on New York Shakespeare Festival productions, the Beaumont programs. Those were the things that we got involved in. I didn't even know what A CHORUS LINE was.

Paul Davis's rejected "glass dimensional design"

JIM RUSSEK: Once we got the account, we presented a million ideas for A CHORUS LINE. We didn't love the logo. Part of what I objected to was that you couldn't put that logo on a window card. So we broke it up into three lines of people with "A Chorus Line" centered. It ended up being printed on mylar. The original design had no visibility. It was the same tiny type a million times, as though repeating it made it more visible. It just was very bad graphically. It really was just a copy of a photograph to create, in effect, line art, and a type face that you could go buy in a drugstore. It was really ugly. As it came to symbolize the show over the years, since it didn't get changed, it developed a certain magical quality to it, but at the time it was dreadful. We adapted it. We went to Michael Bennett and said we really want Paul Davis to do an A CHORUS LINE poster.

PAUL DAVIS [Freelance Artist]: The ad campaign for A CHORUS LINE sort of existed, and we were in the process of changing the image of the Shakespeare Festival, doing the first poster for Lincoln Center. We began to work on ideas for A CHORUS LINE around that time. It was really a long-term process. This was a running show, there was no urgency about it. We wanted to do something really interesting and different. We talked a lot about putting the lettering on glass, and photographing it and doing it as a dimensional piece because we were trying to make it

identifiable with the other work of the New York Shakespeare Festival, but at the same time very unusual. And since the show had to do with mirrors and illusion, we tried to use those ideas in the poster. I was trying to figure out a way to show the whole cast, although none of the posters had ever featured Cassie. So I thought it would be a nice idea to feature her, with the red skirt.

JIM RUSSEK: Michael Bennett said, "It's not about one person, it's not Cassie's show." We had this idea of a diorama, a little box with A CHORUS LINE characters cut out that Paul painted and that was a collage idea, with a mirrored background. It would be photographed to create the poster. But it was awful. It got executed but we never did a photograph. I didn't want to show it, but we did anyway, and we got our butts kicked.

PAUL DAVIS: We showed it to Joe Papp and Bernie Gersten and they liked it, but Michael Bennett, I don't think he even wanted to look at it. His idea was this show was a huge success, if it's not broken don't fix it — just keep the art the way it is. I was just trying to add another way to do an ad, and to do it in color as well, because the previous ads were all that bleached out black and white look. I had really put a lot of work into it, and they were very quick to dismiss it. I think if it had only been up to Joe Papp we would have done it, but I don't think he wanted to argue with

Michael about it. Then we also talked about a Christmas poster. The idea was to take the concept that was used on the second poster and *Playbill®* cover of the crowd outside the Shubert Theatre and make it a snow scene. I never did it partly because I was so discouraged after the first rejection.

JIM RUSSEK: The art director, Reinhold Schwenk, did a piece which is sort of an optical illusion, that took two photographs, one with the kids in their rehearsal clothes, and the other the Finale. He cut them in little strips, about an eighth of an inch wide, and it revealed both pictures. You actually could see two pictures at once, and it was incredible, a real optical illusion. You had to stare at it to see what it was; your eye could shift to two pictures. It was amazing. Michael hated it, so it didn't get done.

REINHOLD SCHWENK [Art Director: Case & McGrath]: It was unsolicited, unasked for, no one was really much interested. I think Bennett didn't want to change anything. There was very little going on. We seemed to be so much out of the loop. I was caught in the middle. I didn't think the look actually needed to be redone.

JIM RUSSEK: We looked at the commercial again to see if we could change it for the road, and there was no way. They had shot it exactly scene by scene for the cuts in the spot. There was no long shooting of

an entire performance or any segment of the show. It was strictly shot to cut that commercial, so it was uneditable. We later did things with title crawls in a "Star Wars" kind of way, ending on the kick line turning into the glitter costumes, but we were never able to redo. Another commercial was shot later by Serino, but the first commercial was used during our entire tenure.

We did make wonderful radio commercials. We had the first "I loved it" commercials, where we interviewed people in front of the theatre and put them together along with the music from the show. I made so many versions of that commercial for so many different cities. The show had no trouble on tour anywhere. We also made the second poster and *Playbill®* cover.

NANCY HELLER [NYSF Audience Development; Marketing]: Part of what happened was *Playbill*® switched to color. I don't think everybody was thrilled with the repetition of the title as the image for the show. It was a good typeface, but all the repetition was just a practical way to fill it out. There was a photo that Bernie really liked of the marquee that was used in a tourism brochure. Part of his pride and joy was the way the exterior of that theatre looked. I think that the image of it to replace the other photo on the cover was something Bernie suggested.

BERNARD GERSTEN [Associate Producer, NYSF]: That second poster came about because of an American Airlines advertising shot taken of the exterior of the theatre. It was kind of documentary, of an audience standing under the canopy with a marquee and neon sign all starry. It was so beautiful and I said, "Let's use that as our three sheet." That also became the second *Playbill*® cover.

PAUL ELSON [Freelance Photographer]: I had taken the photo for an American Airlines brochure cover. It was a summer's evening, and I made the exposure long enough so that none of the crowd in front of the theater would appear too focused; it was just a fortuitous juxtaposi-

Paul Elson's photograph was used as a postcard, a poster, and the second Playbill® *cover*

tion of people at the right time of night, before curtain. Bernie Gersten contacted me to use the shot for the A CHORUS LINE poster and *Playbill*® cover, but wanted the words "Best Musical" to appear on the moving sign. I had to go back to the exact same spot to shoot the sign from the proper angle so it could be stripped into my original photograph. Ironically, my grandfather, Herbert J. Krapp, who was known as the "architect of Broadway," constructed the Shubert Theatre.

NANCY HELLER: The next incarnation of the *Playbill*® cover was the wedge shot. Initially Michael Bennett refused to have any shots of the Finale. There then became a point at which the Finale wasn't a surprise anymore. You constantly have to face the issue of what sells tickets.

JIM RUSSEK: We invented the half page spread for A CHORUS LINE. Because the logo was a line, we split it across two pages, so we bought a spread that was two facing half pages as opposed to a full page, and it had just as much impact.

GENE CASE: At the risk of getting myself in trouble, the show was so prepackaged, it was almost an advertisement in itself. It came with its own campaign. I think Michael Bennett resented us and didn't accept us. I wasn't trying to woo him, it wasn't important to me.

JIM RUSSEK: The honest truth is that Gene Case couldn't stand being in a room with Michael Bennett, and so he treated A CHORUS LINE like the stepchild of the account; he just wanted nothing to do with it. I ran it, did all the creative work, I wrote everything, I did it all. We went out to California, shot a commercial with Carol Burnett to run in four different cities, as sort of a testimonial that ran during the Tony® Awards. The agency wrote a commercial which was dreadful; nobody ever saw it. It was a script for Carol Burnett, and it was just embarrassing and ludicrous. Bernie Gersten came out a couple of days later, as we were doing pre-production. I showed Bernie the script over drinks and he looked at me and said, "We're not going to do this, are we?" I said, "I don't think so … I wouldn't. Let's just do what we need to do." So we sat down and wrote a commercial for Carol. Right there. And the next morning we shot it. The agency copy had been written by a woman who had never seen A CHORUS LINE. She wrote it from a couple of reviews.

This was the disdain that Gene had for that show; he wouldn't put anybody on it. I ended up garbage-canning stuff all the time and just rewriting it and getting it done. You don't have disdain for a multimillion dollar account when you're a tiny agency. I was in a very tough position, because I loved A CHORUS LINE, and I worked for a man who hated it, so I had to secretly do work for it. I kept a couple of

people in the art studio after hours to grind out ads for A CHORUS LINE.

In 1977 the entire New York Shakespeare Festival was billing about two million dollars, about $1.6 million from A CHORUS LINE, $400,000 from everything else. We didn't advertise in the papers in NY, we didn't take any display ads. ABCs — that was it. Except for events, such as "Now in its 3rd Year," but it was gratuitous.

At the opening of the Feld Ballet Studios at 890 Broadway, the ad space salesman from *The New York Post* told me that Matthew Serino was leaving Blaine Thompson with GREASE and was going to get A CHORUS LINE. I said, "Really? I haven't heard anything about that." He said, "Well, he says he has it." So I confronted Bernie Gersten that night at the opening of Feld Studios, and said, "Is it true that A CHORUS LINE is going to a guy named Matthew Serino who is starting an agency?" and he said, "That's not decided yet." I said, "You mean, you're discussing?" "Yes, we are. It's Michael's show, he created it and he has known Matt forever. He feels comfortable with Matt, he doesn't feel comfortable with Gene, and he doesn't want to make Gene money." And I said, "Yeah, but I'm there too, I'm the one who's doing all the work." And he said, "But you're not Gene Case, and Gene Case is the one who gets all the money. If you tell me you're Jim Russek and you have your own business, that's one thing, but

Gene Case is making the money, and Michael doesn't want Gene Case to make money on his show." And so we lost the A CHORUS LINE account.

GENE CASE: I know at one point Michael Bennett said, "I don't want this show to make Gene Case rich." Jim reported this to me. He needn't have worried. It was not a big account at our agency. I went over to see Joe Papp and he told me that he had to take A CHORUS LINE away. I remember crying, physically, tears coming down my face, being hurt. Not over A CHORUS LINE, but over the fact that Joe, whom I really admired very much, took something away. But not by Michael, because we never had a relationship.

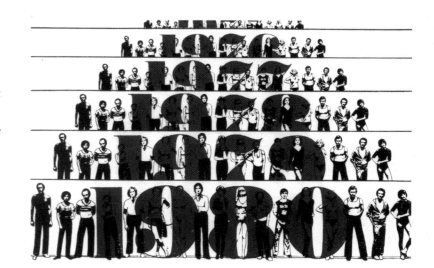

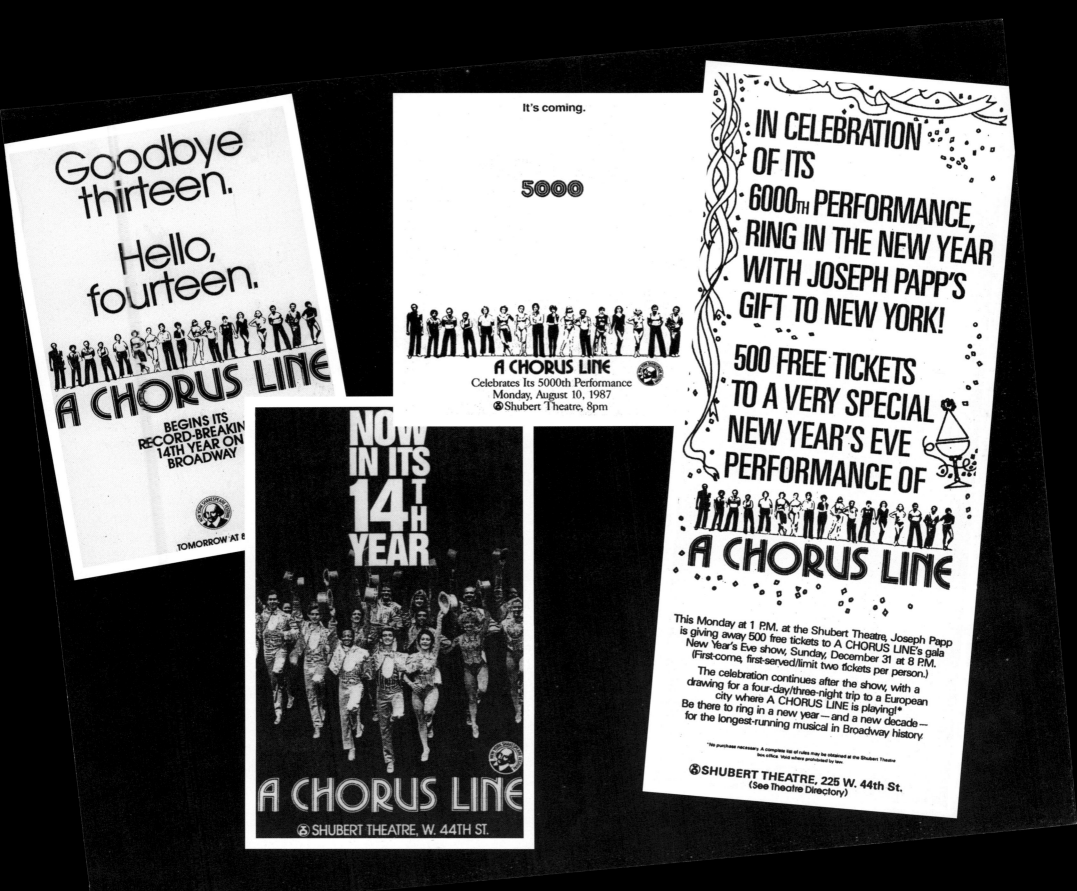

Switching Yet Again

MATTHEW SERINO [President: Serino Coyne Inc.]: I had met Michael Bennett at an opening one night at Blaine Thompson. I don't know if it was BAJOUR or A JOYFUL NOISE, but he was the choreographer. He was a young guy, I was a young guy, an assistant account executive. He came up to the office, I had never met him before, and we got talking, waiting for the reviews to come in, and became great friends. But I had never handled Michael's shows at the time. I remember going to a preview of A CHORUS LINE at the Public and walking out saying this is the greatest thing I had ever seen. It was just phenomenal. I don't know what happened, but the show moved to Case & McGrath. I remember we were all very disheartened about it, but it had nothing to do with my friendship with Michael.

I happened to mention something to Michael sometime later that I was unhappy at Blaine Thompson, and was thinking of opening an advertising agency of my own. And Michael said to me, "Well, Matty, if you ever open an advertising agency, you can have A CHORUS LINE as your first account." With that, I said, "Holy shit, what greater gift can somebody give you than say if you open an agency, I'll give you the biggest hit on Broadway."

Michael never bullshitted, he was a very upfront guy. He was like I was, a street kid. So with that, I said, "I'd have to be pretty crazy not to open an agency." At that time I was a vice president at Blaine, handling about five or six big accounts, including THE KING & I, GREASE, THE WIZ, and one or two other shows. So when he said that to me, I was very happy, obviously, and very encouraged to make that step. I was young, about thirty-two years old, and to open an agency is not an easy task by any standards.

It was the kick that I needed and I will always be grateful to Michael for that. It took about three or four months to get A CHORUS LINE because the show had a contract with Case & McGrath. We had opened Serino Coyne & Nappi in October 1977, and in January 1978 we acquired A CHORUS LINE. We took the other accounts that I was handling, but A CHORUS LINE was the premiere account.

NANCY COYNE: Blaine Thompson looked as though it were going out of business, so several of us together opened our own agency and at the time Matty called Michael Bennett and said, "Listen, you can't possibly be happy with the job that Case & McGrath is doing for you. I don't know if Joe is happy with what they are doing for the Public Theatre, but

A CHORUS LINE on Broadway and the Public Theatre are two different animals. We know how to handle Broadway shows." So Michael went to Joe and said, "I want to peel off that piece of the business. I want A CHORUS LINE to be handled by the people that I know," and Joe said, "Well, they're the people that I walked out on at Blaine Thompson." And Michael said, "No, they're not. They're not the same people at all. Just meet with them." So Joe said, "I don't have to meet with them, if you tell me that they're not the same people."

Michael gave us A CHORUS LINE and we took off. After about a year and a half we got a call from Joe Papp saying he would like to meet with us vis-à-vis THE PIRATES OF PENZANCE and his other productions. That's the first time I met Joe Papp formally. He said, "Michael is very pleased and I'm very pleased with what you've done for A CHORUS LINE; maybe you'd like to handle the rest of the business. I had you branded with Blaine Thompson; apparently you're different, so let's see if we can do business." And we handled his business until the day he died. But it was Michael who made the decision to pull it out of Case & McGrath. It was a great day when we got A CHORUS LINE.

MIKE MONES [Account Executive: Serino Coyne Inc.]: Joe Papp may have been a little unhappy with Case & McGrath because the problem with big agencies, while they do fine creative work, is everything takes a long time. They don't want to know about the front of the theatre, and all the little side things that have to be done. And I think that was beginning to bother Joe. But mostly it was Michael who believed in our new agency. You see Michael Bennett, as well as any other creative person who is very much involved with a project, can deal directly with a theatrical agency. There's contact. There was no contact between him and Case & McGrath.

NANCY COYNE: Michael wanted to shoot a new commercial and the reason that he wanted to shoot a new commercial was just because he wanted to shoot a new commercial. There was really no need for it. But as I recall the second commercial is what motivated the whole thrust of the "wedge," the famous "V" shape pose from the Finale, which became a signature look used in ads, *Playbills*®, and the commercial.

RICK ELICE [Associate Creative Director: Serino Coyne Inc.]: The wedge that was in the TV commercial became the spearhead of all the advertising. The commercial footage that featured "The reason for the line outside the theatre is the line inside the theatre" also included little testimonials for each character and interviews with them.

NANCY COYNE: It was done before the A CHORUS LINE movie. Maybe in Michael's own mind, he was playing with the concept of the film — but the concept he presented was little interviews with the characters in character. We had a two-day shoot, which was unheard of at the time, shot in various locations, in the dressing rooms, backstage, all over the Shubert Theatre, not just on stage — little bits of people talking about their roles, with the company. Then we shot some footage on stage.

When it was edited together, the only way we were going to get all the information that Michael wanted in a commercial was to make a 4½-minute spot. When we cut it down and had a little bit of Cassie offstage and a little bit of Cassie onstage, Cassie onstage was a hundred times better than Cassie offstage. And so somebody had to bite the bullet and say, "Michael, the better commercial is the one with the footage onstage. The backstage stuff just doesn't work."

> *" Radio was always effective in very narrow targeting.*
> *We spoke very specific messages*
> *to very specific audiences."* — NANCY COYNE

RADIO SPOT

Kiss Today Good-bye
(Written by and reproduced with the permission of Serino Coyne Inc.)

Background Music: "What I Did For Love"

A CHORUS LINE, because theatre should thrill you. A CHORUS LINE…the One musical you've got to see. The One that won nine Tony® Awards and the Pulitzer Prize. The musical *The New York Times* calls "A brilliant accomplishment…rare and irresistible." You will find yourself very much moved by A CHORUS LINE. The show described by *The New York Post* as "Dazzling, driving, compassionate, and yes, thrilling." The hit Metromedia is calling "A miracle." The show *The Daily News* calls "Uninterrupted magic." A CHORUS LINE…the best musical ever. And the best part is…it's here.

IKE MONES: Radio was more effective in the summertime. We put together quite a few spots once the music was recognized. In the first eight or ten years, radio spots were used mostly in the summertime and television was used more in the fall.

NANCY COYNE: The television commercial remained pretty much the same for quite a while and the radio changed.

MIKE MONES: For the first few years of the show we advertised in the Sunday *New York Times* for events and occasions more than anything else. We didn't advertise "just to be in the paper." For the first seven years it was strictly anniversaries and holidays. I remember one ad with the kids forming a Christmas tree — all different kinds of Santa things. I would say if we ran seven, eight ads over the course of a year, it was a lot.

NANCY COYNE: There were two groups of people coming to see A CHORUS LINE. The out-of-towners, which was a huge group. We really didn't have to sell to those

RADIO SPOT

One
(Written by and reproduced with the permission of Serino Coyne Inc.)

Background Music: "One"

A CHORUS LINE…the One musical you've got to see. A CHORUS LINE …the One musical that won nine Tony® Awards and the Pulitzer Prize. The One musical *The New York Times* calls "Tremendous, terrific, devastating, the show that dances, jogs and whirls its way into the history of the musical theatre. One of the greatest musicals to ever hit Broadway." A CHORUS LINE…the One *Newsweek* calls "An explosive hit…dazzling theatre…the most exciting thing ever seen on the stage." The One *The Daily News* guarantees "Will lift you right out of your seat," provided you can get one. And the best way to guarantee that is to call right now.

---

people, because this was the first show they wanted to see when they got to New York. And then there were the New Yorkers. After we exhausted every New Yorker, we were

RADIO SPOT

White Line
(Written by and reproduced with the permission of Serino Coyne Inc.)

Background Music: "One"

The reason for the line outside the theatre is the line inside the theatre. That long white line that stretches from one end of the stage to the other. Every night. Seventeen people put their lives on that line. A CHORUS LINE. Winner of every award Broadway could come up with. Every Tony®. Even the Pulitzer Prize. A CHORUS LINE. The only show on Broadway every single critic acknowledged as the best, the one singular sensation. A CHORUS LINE. The only thing better than seeing it for the first time is seeing it for the second time. Or the third. A CHORUS LINE. Second best to none. Give it your attention. Do I really have to mention? A CHORUS LINE. It's the one.

left with people who were going to see it for the second, third, fourth, fifth time. I can clearly remember the moment in which we came up with the campaign, "Remember the first time you saw A CHORUS LINE," and that was very effective. "It wasn't all the awards that got you there, it was knowing that we were all on that line."

RICK ELICE: In 1984 or 1985 we made the decision to go back to the very first commercial, the Giraldi spot. The original life of that commercial was relatively short, it was on over a summer, and that was it. Because the show was so hot then, there was no point in advertising it. I remember the last time we had lunch with Michael, we brought him up to the office to see the original Bob Giraldi commercial with the new voice-over. In summer of 1987, when the show was about to celebrate performance 5000, we went back and found all of that interview footage from the second commercial and thought about turning it into a spot. At that point the show could no longer afford to shoot a new commercial. We were looking through everything to see what we might be able to recirculate as potential new advertising material. No one had ever seen this footage before. But it never transpired.

NANCY COYNE: The obstacles were the longevity. The Broadway audience and the New York audience had already been totally saturated. Once the film came out, we had that challenge of saying "forget the movie, it never happened, just let it go away."

RICK ELICE: The wedge continued to live on to the pre-movie advertising, which was "Live on stage … Where it Belongs." The copy was specifically designed to counter the film-going experience.

NANCY COYNE: Once it was out on the road and exposed to every market, the challenge became getting those people to see the original Broadway version. With any show that runs this long, you have the challenge of having eaten up your audience. Unlike a show like GREASE, for instance, A CHORUS LINE isn't necessarily a youth market. A show that markets itself to a youth audience has much less of a problem because it keeps growing its audience. People keep getting old enough to see it. As a matter of fact, that was one campaign we did for A CHORUS LINE: You're now old enough to see it. We targeted that group. We needed everyone we could get. Fourteen-year-olds certainly weren't a primary audience for A CHORUS LINE, but we got to the point where it was one audience we hadn't talked to, so we talked to them. Radio was always effective in very narrow targeting. We spoke very specific messages to very specific audiences through radio.

Taxis, Trains, Buses ... and More

MIKE MONES: A CHORUS LINE was the first show to use bus ads. They were plastic illuminated panels that went the full length of the bus. All it said was A CHORUS LINE. THE BEST MUSICAL. EVER. I remember the colors we used were white on brown.

RICK ELICE: That was part of a three pronged campaign ... train, bus, and taxi. The taxi read "Just say 'take me to A CHORUS LINE'," the bus read "Take the bus to the best," and the train read "Leave from this station for the Singular

Sensation." It was all done in tandem with the transit authority.

NANCY COYNE: We got the transit authority to pay half of the cost of the promotion. That's how we stayed in business, by working with these small budgets and trying to maximize by using Broadway shows as landmarks. And A CHORUS LINE was, without question, the first really legitimate Broadway landmark that was promoted as such.

MIKE MONES: I had the idea, and Nancy came up with the copy, to do post-

cards in the theatre. Treat A CHORUS LINE like the Statue of Liberty. So we printed maybe 100,000 cards and people sent it off as a "having a wonderful time, wish you were here." We had three different postcards over the years.

RICK ELICE: Except for the ad for Donna McKechnie's return in 1986, the only thing we did with an original cast member — and it was not about them coming back into the show — was the end-of-the-line ad, with Priscilla Lopez and a little bit of Sammy Williams, but that was simply because their characters were positioned

142

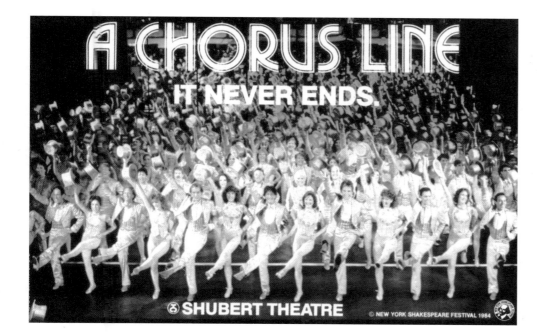

A CHORUS LINE
IT NEVER ENDS.

⑤ SHUBERT THEATRE
© NEW YORK SHAKESPEARE FESTIVAL 1984

at the end of the line. That was the only "end-of-the-line" ad. We also did a TV commercial for the closing that was a pan down the logo of the line with a voice-over copy that read "See it one last time before it closes."

NANCY COYNE: I would say the advertising was 50% broadcast and 50% print, outdoor, and ancillary publications. This was a show where the creative was never difficult. Basically what the advertising always did for A CHORUS LINE was tell the truth.

The last of the three postcards created for A CHORUS LINE

Just say– "Take me to
A CHORUS LINE"
⑤ SHUBERT THEATRE, 225 WEST 44TH ST.

T!

A CHORUS LINE

⑤ **SHUBERT THEATRE**

The end of the
LINE
MARCH 31, 1990
The final performance of
The Best Musical. Ever.

Buy tickets now
for the last six weeks of
A CHORUS LINE
Ⓢ Shubert Theatre Call (212) 239-6200

*The final two ads for
A CHORUS LINE*

Saturday, April 28th

The grandest finale
in Broadway history.

A CHORUS LINE
The Last One.

8PM • Tickets: $80–$500
Proceeds benefit the
New York Shakespeare Festival.
Seats now on sale.

TELECHARGE (212) 239-6200 Ⓢ SHUBERT THEATRE W. 44th St.

 RADIO SPOT

Come Say Goodbye
(Written by and reproduced with the permission of Serino Coyne Inc.)

Background Music: "Kiss Today Goodbye, the sweetness and the sorrow…"

Due to the overwhelming demand for tickets, A CHORUS LINE, Broadway's longest running musical ever, has extended its run through April 28 at the Shubert Theatre. Between now and then, get yourself a ticket and come say goodbye, to the sweetness and the sorrow, to the songs and the glorious dancing, to the people whose lives have been on that line for the past 15 years. A CHORUS LINE. See it one last time. Call 239-6200 for tickets.

Music Fade: "What I Did for Love."

THE NEW YORK TIMES, TUESDAY, AUGUST 7, 1984   C11

How 'Chorus Line' Keeps Its Kicks After 9 Years

By ELEANOR BLAU

orus Line': Still high-stepping

BARLEY

Theater Review

A Chorus Line

CAST

'Chorus Line' still its own biggest star

By CLIVE BARNES

BROADWAY REVISITED

Curtains for 'Chorus'

ong line s ending

Mitzi Hamilton, center, who has appeared periodically in "A Chorus Line," with other cast members Christine Barker, left, and Chris Marshall.

NEW YORK POST ON THE TOWN

'A CHORUS LINE' MARCHES ON

Highest Kicker Is 'A Chorus Line'

By PATRICIA O'HAIRE

DAILY NEWS, WEDNESDAY, MARCH 24, 1976

Lynn, Yes; Vanessa, No

Cassie's Bittersweet Encore

After 10 years and a bout with arthritis, Donna McKechnie is dancing again in 'A Chorus Line' on Broadway.

Stars turn out for big celebration

POST SALUTE TO 'A CHORUS

Darla Hill (left) and Jennifer Ann Lee look over their souvenir copy of The Post's special midnight edition after "A Chorus Line" became the longest running show in the history of Broadway.

way history is made — and The Post is there!

st of 'Chorus Line' Wonders About Taking Its Next Steps

Angelique Ilo   Gordon Owens   Michael Gruber   Laurie Gamache   William Mead

The New York Times

ARTS AND LEISURE

On the Town

END OF THE 'LINE'

British Equity Nixes McKechnie; London 'Chorus' Takes Rece

By JACK PITMAN

London, Jan. 25.

Broadway's one singular sensation

IT WAS incredible! It really was.

Slipping ticket sales force closing of 'A Chorus Line'

By MATTHEW FLAMM

THE BOTTOM LINE

OPENING	JULY 25, 1975
PERFORMANCES	6,000
BROADWAY ATTENDANCE	6,600,000
GROSS TO DATE	$146,463,780
GROSS TO DATE	$277,000,000
AVG. WEEKLY GROSS (wk. Market)	$122,826
AVG. WEEKLY GROSS (wk. Market)	$40,000
N.Y. FESTIVAL SHARE (wk. Market)	$37,000,000
CHORUS LINE	810
SHOES WORN OUT (Per)	20,000

A SINGULAR, SENSATIONAL SEND-OFF

By CLIVE BARNES

nett's last curtain

The tribute opened with "What I Did For Love," the pop hit from "A Chorus Line."

MICHAEL BENNETT
Loved by many.

JOSEPH PAPP
Gave final tribute.

MARVIN HAMLISH
Played "Chorus" hit.

Form New Group To Raise Backing For Goodman, C

Chicago, Jan. 22.

The spectacular chorus line in "A Chorus Line" steps out on glittering gold top hat and tails in the hit musical's rousing closing number, "One."

'Lonely Lady,' but not in bed

By ARCHER WINSTEN

Director Michael Bennett's genius made this ticket — for the record-breaking performance Thursday night — one of Broadway's most-prized items.

Publicity

MERLE DEBUSKEY [Press Agent]: I was the Festival's publicist from its prenatal days at Tompkins Square in the Croation Church. I represented A CHORUS LINE because I represented the NYSF and everything it did. I was there when the prospect of a workshop came up. I was interested in it because although I was known as a press agent for serious works, my heart was in the musical part of show biz.

BOB ULLMAN [Press Agent]: I had been with Joe Papp since 1970 and worked on A CHORUS LINE for the first six years of the run. Michael wanted me to continue when the show moved to Broadway, but Merle said, "You can only work on it on Broadway if you work out of my office uptown." I loathed to leave Joe Papp and the Public Theatre and said, "The only way I will continue is if I can stay downtown at the Festival and handle the shows at the

Photo courtesy Merle Debuskey

Merle Debuskey

Public plus A CHORUS LINE," which is what I did.

The buzz didn't really start until previews began and the buzz was strictly from show biz, not the media. Before A CHORUS LINE opened at the Public, I couldn't get any media interested. The only person the press was interested in was — not Marvin Hamlisch, who had already written music for Streisand — but Jimmy Kirkwood. Everybody adored Jimmy Kirkwood. Once it opened, of course, first and foremost it was Michael. And then the people in the show who made the biggest hits, like Donna McKechnie, Kelly Bishop, and Priscilla Lopez. I couldn't get the rest of the cast very much, because their parts weren't showy enough. The showy parts got the publicity.

MERLE DEBUSKEY: Downtown, the word spread like wildfire. For press purposes, we used Michael and the elements of the show that were so superior — the concept of no scenery, the bare stage. At some point after that, the thrust became "This is a musical that is rooted in show biz, but it's about life." Those kids standing on line were everyone, whether you were standing on line for morality, law, or civil rights, whatever it was. We kept pushing on that principle and got out of just being a show biz story.

BOB ULLMAN: When A CHORUS LINE opened, it was absolutely overwhelming. I mean it was the biggest hit I had ever worked on in my life. The number of requests for interviews was staggering. The first two years on Broadway, everyone I called was fascinated by what I had to sell. They would usually go along with story ideas — they were always interested. I initiated a lot of articles that were based on what the show was all about — the gypsies, the original cast, and what happened to each one of them. When you work on a show of the magnitude of A CHORUS LINE, you are never at a loss for ideas to publicize.

MERLE DEBUSKEY: We tried to spread the press around through the cast as much as we could. The three ladies all got attention — Priscilla, Kelly, and Donna. The others were pretty satisfied to be in a show. These kids were all gypsies. I don't remember anybody being upset about the others getting more publicity, because the Original Company all got something. When subsequent companies came in, it was inevitable that Cassie would get the major attention. But we promoted the show, not the individuals in it. We would sit up in the office every day trying to get the kids something. Can we get them to represent the city of New York in some-

thing like the "I LOVE NY" spots?

When we opened in Baltimore, we had the idea of opening the box office at 10:00 a.m. and remaining open for twenty-four hours a day until every ticket was sold. This was in winter at the Mechanic Theatre. And it was cold. The line at the box office was still there at 2:00 a.m. We stayed open until we were sold out, which was covered on the local news. In San Francisco we sold out the show before it opened. Our big display ad was "Thank you" and we had the cast sign it, "Sold out — we will be back," which was a theme we kept repeating. And that used to feed back to New York. We just kept plugging and repeating. We didn't do much: they didn't want to spend a lot of money. We held back deliberately.

BOB ULLMAN: People were constantly calling me for house seats. It was the hottest ticket on Broadway. A couple arrived at the Shubert one night, got out of the car, and the wife just started beating up the husband, physically abusing the man. He'd left their precious A CHORUS LINE tickets at home.

Whenever there was a celebrity in the house, I made it a point to get them on stage and photograph them with the company. I brought people like Laurence Olivier and Gene Kelly; it always made the front page of *The New York Post.* Laurence Olivier couldn't have been more charming about it. We put one of the hats on him and he posed with the kids on the line. The celebrities were all like that, very gracious, willing to go on the line with the people from the show.

Celebrities came back to see it constantly. It was a show that perpetually enriched itself. I was never afraid to invite critics to come back and see it. I never had any qualms about inviting them for one basic reason: Michael and his production staff kept the show at such a peak level. The thing that amazed me quite honestly is the creative and brilliant job done by Bill Schelble after I left the show.

BILL SCHELBLE [Press Agent]: I was just trying to keep the show out there. But not column items. It's a hard show to do column items about, as everybody wants dirt and there wasn't that kind of dirt on us.

I tried to do things with THE FANTASTICKS, such as a pie-eating contest in some East Side restaurant between the two longest running shows. We weren't technically the longest running show at the time, OH! CALCUTTA! had more performances, but everybody knew we were going to make it. OH! CALCUTTA! was being such a bastard about things even then.

Harvey Sabinson of the League of American Theatres and Producers would call and say, "Can you get me anybody from the show?" The kids were always so wonderful about it. It was a hard show to do because it's difficult to pull individual numbers out. *Tits and Ass* and Paul's speech are not the things people would want to see in the nursing homes! I got the various Dianas to do *What I Did For Love*. I took Roxanne Caballero to Radio City Music Hall where she sang *What I Did For Love* standing all by herself on that big stage with Nick Archer playing

Photo courtesy Bill Schelble

Press agent Bill Schelble dressed up as Santa Claus for the Company every Christmas (pictured here with "Cassie" Laurie Gamache)

Above: "Laurence Olivier couldn't have been more charming about posing with the cast." — Bob Ullman
From left: Michel Stuart, Kelly Bishop, Ron Kuhlman, Nancy Lane, Thommie Walsh, Trish Garland, Robert LuPone, Olivier, Donna McKechnie, Cameron Mason, Renee Baughman, Wayne Cilento

Upper right: "We had twenty to fifty people a night waiting for autographs." — cast member Deborah Geffner

Right: A celebration
From left: set designer Robin Wagner, cast member Cynthia Onrubia, Joseph Papp, author James Kirkwood, Michael Bennett, cast members Wanda Richert and Mitzi Hamilton, lyricist Ed Kleban, and cast member Eivind Harum

*Above: Academy Award winner Greer Garson
paid a backstage visit to the line
From left: George Pesaturo, Mitzi Hamilton, Justin
Ross, Kurt Johnson, Garson, David Thome, Tim
Cassidy, Paul Charles, Rene Ceballos*

*Right: A photo opportunity with the line
Back row, from left: Kevin Chinn, J. Richard Hart, Tim
Millett, Pam Klinger, Michael Danek, Danny Herman,
Rene Clemente; front row: Susan Danielle, Lily-Lee
Wong, Pam Sousa, Poster Child, Marvin Hamlisch,
Christine Barker, Mitzi Hamilton*

*A promotional event
for the 5000th performance*

150

---

the piano for her.

I would call up the media and say, "You need some new photos. I want you to throw the old pictures out, get rid of them. I've got new photos for you. Keep the original cast photos, but please …" There were so many turnovers.

I always felt terrible that it was so much easier to get stuff on the women than the men. Get a woman in a pretty dress in or out of costume, they all looked pretty good. Newspapers like the *Post* and the *News* want pretty ladies and leggy ladies; you could always get press on them. It was almost impossible to get Zach anything; Paul was a little easier because of all the gay publications that would be interested in a new Paul. But the women were definitely easier.

When Donna came back in 1986, Bob Ullman said I made her a bigger star than he did. He said I got more stuff on her return than when she won the Tony®. The night she was going in, I got Channel 5. I said, "Why don't you come and do the interview and then stay, shoot her number and show it on the late news" — which they did and it was lovely. It helped our box office — the next day there were people there. She got the Sunday *New York Times* piece. Donna was difficult on that. I don't know why. She just hated that photo. A lot of the press she got was because of her coming back. Also it was the timing — September, when there is not a hell of a lot happening here. I'm not taking anything away from Donna, because people in the industry love her. She did have a little bit of a following, but it wasn't like Shirley MacLaine coming to Broadway.

BOB ULLMAN: One of the things I hated about publicity then and still hate to this day is that you are everybody's patsy. The first person called when a show is a hit is the press agent, whether from a television station or the mailroom. You are everybody's dumping ground. That's why an experienced press agent on a hit show is so important because he knows whom to kowtow to and whom to kiss off.

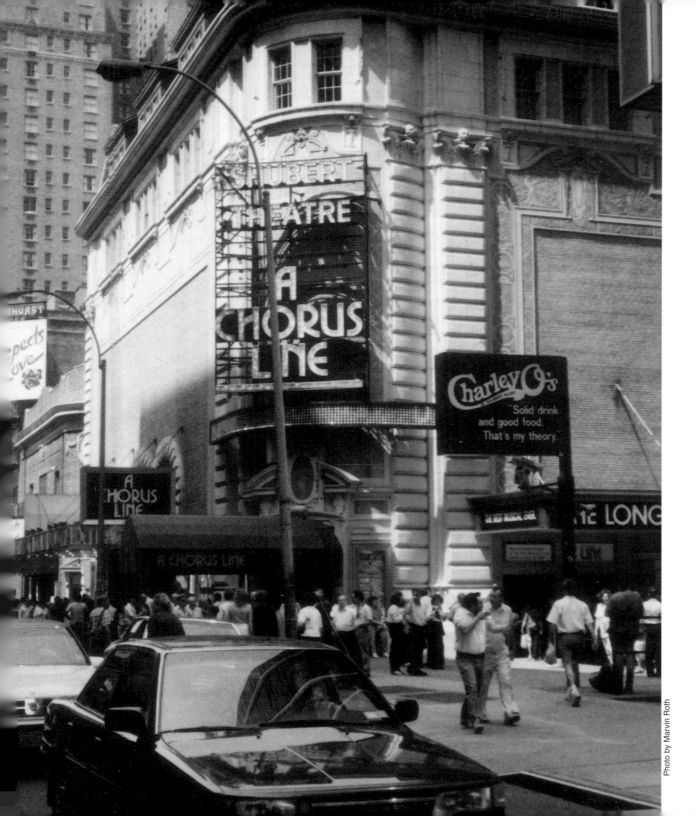

CHAPTER 7

THE SHUBERT

INSIDE AND OUT

Planning the Move to the Shubert

GERALD SCHOENFELD [Chairman, Shubert Organization]: The primary mover in our involvement was Bernie Jacobs. Before the production commenced downtown, there was a question as to whether or not it should close at the Public due to a lack of funds. But Bernie offered to advance the funds, which became unnecessary to do.

*Shubert heads:
Bernard Jacobs and
Gerald Schoenfeld*

Photo by Steve Friedman

BERNARD JACOBS [President, Shubert Organization]: It was the first performance downtown; Michael told me I should not have come — it was too early. He called me the next day to get my "laundry list," as if he needed it, and I gave him a long list of things that should be done. Alex Cohen, Phil Smith, my wife, and I went to Pearl's Restaurant after the performance where Alex lectured us about how he could fix the show. He knew exactly what was wrong with it. It was really kind of ludicrous for him to be so presumptuous as to think he could fix the show and do things Michael would not see. When I gave my laundry list, I was equally presumptuous, because whatever was wrong with the show, I'm sure Michael saw way before we did. We went back to see it again and had a conversation about possibly moving the show to the Winter Garden. Michael thought Hal Prince, coming in with PACIFIC OVERTURES, would throw him out of the Winter Garden. I told him that I didn't think dynamite or hell could blow this show out because it was such an over-whelming hit. Clive Barnes, critic for *The New York Times*, called and asked, "Have you seen A CHORUS LINE?" "Yes." "Is it true it's the second coming?" I told him that A CHORUS LINE was as close to it as he was ever going to get.

GERRY SCHOENFELD: We wanted to see A CHORUS LINE come to Broadway. It was always going to be a Shubert house — Michael was very loyal. The only question was which theatre. David Merrick had Tennessee Williams' THE RED DEVIL BATTERY SIGN booked into the Shubert, and Michael, in a marvelous gesture, said he would take the Broadhurst, even though he thought the Shubert was the right theatre for the show.

PHIL SMITH [Vice President, Shubert Organization]: Michael originally didn't want the Shubert, he wanted the Barrymore. We spent a weekend with him talking about theatres and showing him different houses. We were thinking in terms of putting it into the Winter Garden.

But Michael said, "The theatre is too wide, it has to have more of a tunnel effect, and I don't want any obstructed views because the auditorium isn't properly raked. I want to rake the last five rows and create a stadium kind of effect that you have in the Majestic or the 46th Street." If we did that, there would be no head room. So the Winter Garden was ruled out.

Then Michael said he wanted the Broadhurst, which was booked with a David Merrick show. Merrick was in his craziest state, and at first told Bernie Jacobs, "I'll give you the Broadhurst, no problem, I'll move to the Shubert." But as soon as he read about it in the newspaper, he said it was libelous. "You can't move me out, I have a signed contract. You have to give me the Broadhurst." We had heard that Merrick's show wasn't even coming in. It was in serious trouble in Boston. The chief critic for the *Boston Globe* had given it bad notices, and suggested they close the show.

The Broadhurst is really the Shubert without a second balcony. If you have a show that is strong enough, the Shubert has that added benefit. Then we were tossing around the Barrymore because it

had the tunnel effect that Michael was looking for. But it made all the sense in the world to go with the Shubert. The Shubert has the straight-on look that he wanted to keep from the Newman. The Shubert isn't a wide house; it doesn't fan out, it is rather tight in, and the mezzanine is the same. And the distance from the last row to the stage is just fine.

But Michael needed that process, and eventually after a lot of battles had been fought, Merrick refusing to move and many negotiations going on, Michael said, "I'll take the Shubert." He told Bernie Jacobs confidentially, "Don't worry about it — keep pressing for the Broadhurst, but I'll take the Shubert." It was Memorial Day weekend. I made some thirty-odd calls that weekend between Bernie, myself, and Merrick.

GERRY SCHOENFELD: As it turned out, THE RED DEVIL BATTERY SIGN closed in Boston, freed up the Shubert, LuEsther Mertz put up the money for the move and the rest is history.

BERNIE JACOBS: Joe Papp didn't dirty

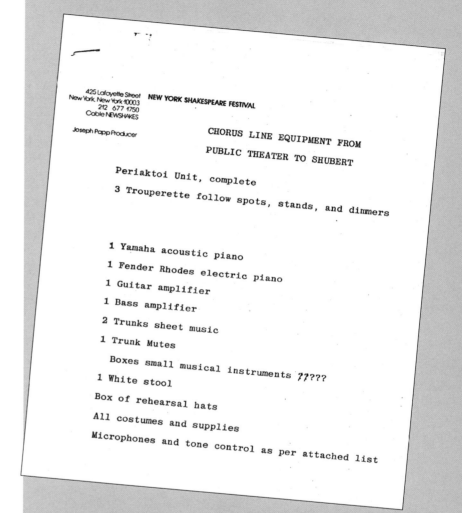

425 Lafayette Street
New York, New York 10003
212 677 4750
Cable NEWSHAKES

NEW YORK SHAKESPEARE FESTIVAL

Joseph Papp Producer

CHORUS LINE EQUIPMENT FROM
PUBLIC THEATER TO SHUBERT

Periaktoi Unit, complete
3 Trouperette follow spots, stands, and dimmers

1 Yamaha acoustic piano
1 Fender Rhodes electric piano
1 Guitar amplifier
1 Bass amplifier
2 Trunks sheet music
1 Trunk Mutes
  Boxes small musical instruments ?????
1 White stool
Box of rehearsal hats
All costumes and supplies
Microphones and tone control as per attached list

"Merrick was in his craziest state, and at first told Bernie Jacobs, 'I'll give you the Broadhurst, no problem, I'll move to the Shubert.' But as soon as he read about it in the newspaper, he said it was libelous. 'You can't move me out, I have a signed contract.'" — PHIL SMITH

Photo by Marvin Roth

his hands too much with business. Our initial meetings were more with Bernie Gersten. Joe would come into the high level meetings, but in all of the negotiations that took place for the presentation of A CHORUS LINE, I doubt if Joe was at 10% of the meetings. Mostly it was Bernie and Michael. Even though Michael did not really fully understand the business as a business, Michael loved to participate and loved to think he was manipulating all of the pawns in the business deal. He got a great kick out of doing that. I don't know how much ever really stayed with Michael, because he was essentially an artist, not a businessman. In business, he just wanted

to be sure that Michael Bennett got a better deal than anybody else. That was the one assurance he was always looking for. Nobody else got a deal like him.

We revolutionized booking terms because of our agreement with Papp. Producers and theatre owners had historically shared receipts and expenses. A CHORUS LINE was the first show in which we established the principle of theatre owners making a percent of the gross, while the producer paid for all the expenses, which the theatre owner had previously contributed to. It was something that I had always wanted to do and this show became the perfect opportunity

to do it. We made a 90/10 deal, in which we got 10% of the gross, instead of 70/30 or 75/25, which is the way the deals had been constructed up to that point. It seemed to Michael particularly attractive that he was only paying 10%, but of course, he was absorbing a lot of costs that we absorbed when he paid 25% or 30%. That was the deal at the Shubert that changed our booking terms forever.

We agreed at the time to compare the percentage of the gross deal with the 75/25 deal. For the first ten weeks, we tracked the two deals. If the old-fashioned terms were to work out better for the producer, we would go back to those terms. At the end of the ten weeks, the show's general manager, Bob Kamlot, told me my formula worked so well it resulted in essentially the same kind of deal for the producers that they would have had in the old terms. We thought when we did this, we invented the wheel. When we started producing in Great Britain, we discovered the Brits had been doing this for a long time, so we didn't actually invent anything.

BOB KAMLOT [Original General Manager]: It became the benchmark for the arrangements theatre owners made with producers. It was a change of philosophy. All of that shared bookkeeping disappeared. The show paid its costs and the theatre paid its cost and were subsequently reimbursed for whatever those costs would be.

The Shubert Exterior

BERNARD GERSTEN [Associate Producer]: The mylar outside the theatre was my idea. I had always admired the way that the British used the exteriors of the theatres as points of display in such a flamboyant fashion — far more than Broadway ever did. Crowds walking by get strong impressions from what they see.

When the NYSF did TWO GENTLE-MEN OF VERONA, our first Broadway show, we did the first exterior theatre treatment at the St. James with huge color photographs. We also did full color *Playbill®* covers. With A CHORUS LINE, we wanted to cover the theatre with our fantastic quotes. I said "Let's do it on mirror," because mirror is the medium.

One of the wonderful things, especially at the Newman, was that great portions of the audience could see themselves in the mirror. The idea of seeing yourself seeing the show and finding yourself in the show is very metaphoric. And the universality of A CHORUS LINE, in no small measure, was the extent to which people identify with the people on stage. You didn't have to be a dancer competing for a job in the chorus. It was the idea of using the outside of the theatre to lure people inside the theatre by giving them a scent of the experience: There you were, standing in front of a theatre, reading these fantastic

quotes — and there you were in the quotes and behind the quotes and in front of the quotes. You were always there. We took great pains to do it. Even the mirrors that were above head height were tilted so that when you looked up to read them, you saw yourself as well. It was all very carefully calibrated for that purpose. It was an idea that held up remarkably well. During the entire occupancy of the show at the Shubert, those mirrors remained; they never redid them.

GERRY SCHOENFELD: Bernie Gersten couldn't find enough space for mirrors. He had mirror mania! That was Bernie's great ambition: to put as many reflective surfaces on the exterior of the theatre as he could find. But it dressed it up very nicely and, of course, it was compatible with the mirrors in the show. That was Bernie Gersten's major contribution, I think — dressing up the front of house.

BERNIE JACOBS: Our initial reaction was that it was not going to sell a single ticket. We have never believed that there is much to be gained in decorating the outside of the theatre. By the time we get somebody in front of the theatre, they're already there to buy the tickets. Fancy displays in front of the theatre is usually an expenditure which only satisfies the ego of the

Photo courtesy Artkraft Strauss

producer or the artists, but really doesn't generate business for the show. However, other people disagree with us. Cameron Mackintosh and most of the Brits believe that decorating the outside of the theatre is very important.

WAYNE SAPPER [King Displays]: My father, Jerry Sapper, was the one who really worked on the show. The whole front of the theatre was one big mirror. The only things that weren't mirror were the color photographs.

The type of material for the mirrors was undecided. First they were talking about a bronze mirror. Regular mirror was too bright, which would make the quotes

"Before I left the Festival in 1978, I revised my concept of what should be done on the plastic marquee: it should have nothing but the A CHORUS LINE title."
— *Bernard Gersten*

The mirrored cast board featuring the names of the Final Company. The authors bought this display at the auction and it now hangs in their home.

unreadable. Originally it was going to be black letters on the mirror. But we decided to go with white lettering because white stood out more.

Everything was done by hand. The lettering had to be sketched, laid out, painted, and then double coated. Then the entire piece was built up on frames. It took about two or three weeks. Pieces went up a little bit at a time — the top panels, then the side panels, then the doors.

The original marquee was a light beige background with the line logo itself. The mirrored letters of A CHORUS LINE were cut out in silver mylar and glued on to the plastic marquee. They were heat-cemented on and couldn't be pulled off. After a couple of years, the mylar started to get worn and the Festival didn't want to go through the expense of re-creating it again, so we made the marquee a dark brown background with white letters, without the line logo. The marquee was five feet high by nine feet wide.

BERNIE GERSTEN: Before I left the Festival in 1978, I revised my concept of what should be done on the plastic marquee: it should have nothing but the A CHORUS LINE title. No line logo. We moved to a very dark background with the light shining through on the letters. We stacked the words on three lines to get the largest possible type to make it more powerful.

WAYNE SAPPER: Through time and the elements, it naturally got dirty. The Shuberts were very strict about keeping everything clean so we used to have to wash the mirrors with plain soap and water and then polish them up. We also had to retouch the mylar. The back of the sign is a blue film over plexiglass. When the blue started coming through, we had to take small strips of mylar and attach it. 99% of the repairs were done at our warehouse early in the morning and put back up for the evening show.

Every time someone new came into the company, we made a name plate for them, which in those early days cost five dollars. We had boxes and boxes of mirrored strips, just waiting. The names were all hand painted. Even the lettering on the mirrored price scale that hung in the box office was hand painted.

FRASER ELLIS [Assistant Stage Manager]: When a new person would come in, we'd add the mirrored name plate. We needed one for the cast list, and one for the understudy board. We had extra mirrored strips at the theatre, so if we needed one in a hurry, I "hand painted" the names in with white-out.

BERNIE GERSTEN: I also had the idea of doing the big neon sign with lights. Neon was never used on Broadway. In London, again, neon is commonplace. So I said, "Let's do a neon sign. Let's take the logo and rearrange it to be on three lines." It may have been my idea to put a zipper [running message lights] on the sign, to give information and to show quotes. Robin Wagner's contribution was to make it a much larger zipper than I had imagined. That was part of the exterior display, so we had this combination movie-type sign, and the zipper to boot. I never thought the zipper would leave the Shubert, but they took it down for some reason after the show closed. It wasn't at the Shubert before A CHORUS LINE. The Sunburst in Shubert Alley was again the idea of the largest possible place for a big photo display.

FRED OLSSON [Shubert Organization Facilities Director]: The zipper traveling sign was put up by Artkraft Strauss. It was a very expensive sign and maintenance was high. Only Artkraft could maintain it because it was on an automatic lighting control console that only they understood. It was housed up in the manager's office; all the wires came through the wall with traveling tape that would control the flashing of the signs.

KEITH MARSTON [Shubert Organization Projects Coordinator]: The zipper used hundreds and hundreds of bulbs. Later in the run, we had to determine whether or not we were going to refurbish and maintain the traveling sign or let it go after A CHORUS LINE closed.

FRED OLSSON: We couldn't burden other incoming shows with a built-in cost of an electrical sign. And the Shubert Organization is not keen on having what you might call "movie type" signs. They were so happy with the show, we lived with the sign. But it's just not the kind of sign that legitimate theatres use. We like the idea of staying a little old-fashioned with less neon. You wouldn't get my boss to put neon anywhere, it's just not legitimate.

JIM MANFREDI [Artkraft Strauss Signs]: The words A CHORUS LINE had neon light all around it. The message sign ran on 25,400 watts. We used to update the message sign weekly, with cast changes, whatever they wanted to advertise on the sign. This was an old type of machine, a Motorgraph, that used to have a tape; it looked like a band with a lot of perforated holes. You would type in the message, tape the band, put it together, bring it out to the job site and actually install it in the machine, something like a typewriter ribbon. After a while, the machinery became obsolete. The message unit was one of a kind; it was one of the industry's first

back then. I don't think there is a house now that has one, especially that size. It wrapped around the Shubert Alley corner, so it gave a good view from Broadway.

The running light was on all day until the theatre closed at night. A house electrician monitored it for failure, or broken tape, which was only like a heavy paper. We housed two or three spares inside the room right behind the sign at the theatre. We upgraded the system in 1984 or 1985 and changed the components to send messages out by phone modem. Then it all became computerized, state of the art. We put in different controllers, and got rid of that old tape machine — we couldn't get parts for it.

For the words A CHORUS LINE, there were about 175 bulbs in the total sign. For maintenance back in 1976, we would make a nightly inspection of the sign, replace all burned out incandescent lamps, replace all malfunctioning neon tubing, replace any transformers, faulty wiring, and the flasher effects of the sign. We'd get $175 a month — that was a lot of money in those days.

GENE KORNBERG [Artkraft Strauss Signs]: The message sign for the Shubert had to be made special because it was a round face sign on the corner of the building. Alex Cohen was the first one to use a message sign for SHERLOCK HOLMES at the Broadhurst. A CHORUS LINE had an old style traveling message sign. It used a

The message on the traveling zipper sign was changed frequently

The neon lights of A CHORUS LINE

tape, similar to Western Union's. We used Western Union equipment, and every once in a while the tape would get stuck, or wear, or get torn. Somebody had to physically type the message onto the tape using a Western Union code, then it was proofread and installed in the machine.

BERNIE JACOBS: Bernie Gersten spent all that money on the electric sign, which we loaned them because the Festival didn't have any money. I think that sign was about $150,000, $175,000.

BERNIE GERSTEN: Whatever Michael wanted, Michael got. And whatever I wanted that Michael wanted, we got. How could they say no to us? I mean it wasn't their show, it was ours. They thought it was their show, but it was ours.

GERRY SCHOENFELD: When somebody with a major show wants to do work to

the outside of the theatre that is compatible with the exterior and can be rectified after it's removed, we would be agreeable. If there was going to be some permanent damage, we would not have done it.

MITCHELL WEISS [Company Manager]: Years into the run, we put up a new mirror in the lobby — the only curved one. Since there had been critics coming back to see the show many years later, we looked for a place to put a few more up-to-date quotes. Inside the lobby, there was a curved piece of wall between the main two doorways and, of course, everyone asked, "How do you get a mirror that's curved?" But we found someone to build it; the Shuberts gave us the okay and we put it up.

Joseph Papp cordially invites you to attend the Broadway Opening Night of

A CHORUS LINE

Sunday evening, September 28, 1975 at seven o'clock Shubert Theatre

R.S.V.P.   Formal Dress S.V.P.

The scheduled Broadway opening on September 28th was postponed to October 19th due to the musicians' strike. However, the original invitation (above) was never revised.

Building the Set at the Shubert

PHIL SMITH: When the Cassie mirrors were brought on at the Newman, it was done by actors. You could never get away with that on Broadway. Stagehands would claim that as their work, and you'd have to hire extra stagehands. Something really had to be done about it. I called Robert McDonald, who was with Local 1, and asked him to see the show downtown, which he did, and asked him how he would treat the mirrors so as not to become involved with five extra stage-hands on Broadway. He said, "Fly them in, and you won't have to get involved with the stagehands pushing them on."

When Michael was told "fly them in," he said, "No, I don't want to fly them in, I want to pop them up from underneath." Do you know what that involves? You have to rip apart the stage, change all your plumbing — the Shubert has sprinkler systems that run under the stage which would all have to be rerouted. Michael insisted, "I want to pop them up." I guess Bernie Jacobs was the one who made him reconsider. Flying the mirrors in was an enormous savings to the show, because otherwise it would have amounted to five stagehands for the fifteen years. Stagehands cost roughly $1500 a week, $75,000 a year, so for 15 years, that's $1.25 million — a lot of money.

ARTHUR SICCARDI [Production Carpenter]: When I got involved with Robin Wagner moving the show to Broadway, certain things needed changing to fit the Shubert. We tried to keep the same basic black box look of the show. It was a simplistic look, but a very delicate hang. We put a whole new stage on top of the existing one at the Shubert, because it was not in good condition.

BERNIE JACOBS: Michael complained that the stage floor was not in the best shape, and we put in a new one for him, which cost about $40,000 at the time. He was as proud as punch that he got a special stage floor just for his show.

ARTIE SICCARDI: Even though the Shubert has no traveling deck, the way the masonite was put down unwittingly became the way the decks for the road companies would be built. The actors used the tiny cracks in between the masonite as guidelines for their positions on stage. So we replicated those "guide-lines" in the road company decks. The white line was painted at least once a month.

The actors couldn't warm up on stage because we had no house curtain. So we built a little dance floor in the basement for them. And then Michael naturally wanted mirrors! He always thought about the dancers — he cared about everybody. There were no problems, only solutions.

RON STAFFORD [Assistant Stage Manager]: A CHORUS LINE has some of the greatest masking. It was masked within an inch of its life. As the mirrors were turning, if it hadn't been masked so neatly, you could very easily have seen the backstage area. The back of the flats were masked, which gave it such a clean line.

ARTIE SICCARDI: Michael always wanted to have a periaktoid. He wanted mirrors and he wanted black to hide the mirrors. He said, "I don't want to see mirrors flying out, I don't want to see black flying in." Because the mirrors went right to black, it was faster with the periaktoid than flying them in and out. The periaktoid was cranked by one person, which in the beginning was me. It was a matter of just timing it to the music. Everything was manual; it was more economical. I had a cue card made — a big color-coded chart. We had green, yellow, and orange, one color for each side of the periaktoid. I put arrows on the colors, and arrows on the handle of the crank, and when you looked at the

Seven mirrors were lowered from the fly space for the slow section of the Cassie Dance (Deborah Henry pictured)

chart you knew which way to turn the crank. We used a clothespin to mark positions, so when you finished a cue, you moved the clothespin to the next cue. Since there's a long time between cues, when you'd hear a cue coming up, you'd look at the clothespin and know which direction to turn the crank. It was operated from the upstage right corner in back of the periaktoid.

Finding out exactly what material to cover the orchestra pit was trial and error. We needed to keep the light from coming out but at the same time not kill all the sound. It basically ended up being a double layer screen of black scrim material.

There was this famous Artie Siccardi line: "Wear your white gloves and watch the mirror." Sometimes when the dancers walked back to the mirrors, they would kick one. Then we would have to put tape on the mirror and use this heavy duty hair dryer to smooth it out. They would just bump it and it would wrinkle. It was very delicate. I spent hours up on the ladder smoothing out the repairs. And then we had to clean it all the time because sweat would pour off the actors and get all over the mirrors. Even cleaning was trial and error. You had to wipe straight down, using almost like a cheesecloth or a baby's diaper. If you went up or in circles, you would make a scratch. It was very delicate. Marty Fontana, the person who replaced me in the show, was a fanatic at keeping the mirrors clean.

The actors kicked them so hard that we had to keep spares at the theatre against the back wall in a cardboard box. We always had two spare panels and two spare mirrors. They were universal and could fit into any of the slots. We were never caught with a broken mirror. The Cassie fly mirrors weren't, however, interchangeable with the periaktoid; they were much higher. We had to keep the Cassie mirrors clean and trim. They all had to come in and touch the floor at the same time. They were on cables with little weights at the bottom to keep the tension. A CHORUS LINE made Mirrex, the company that made the panels, famous.

Michael was adamant about keeping it consistent on the road. The show was playing the big cities and this was the "A" version. It had to be. We did surveys across the country for houses for the show. There were some houses the show could not play in as is, unless Michael would make changes. And he would say, "I'm not going to change the 'A' version." There were theatres that we could not play because of our tiny little black box. Our little black box needed enough room upstage and offstage and enough fly space for the mirrors.

People who saw A CHORUS LINE on tour saw the whole works.

GERRY SCHOENFELD: A CHORUS LINE not only had a major effect in New York, but it also established the Shubert Theatre in Los Angeles. Up until that time, we were struggling in L.A.; this was the first major hit we had there. A CHORUS LINE established a precedent that a show could run open-ended in L.A. The Shubert then became known as the long-running theatre for shows. The show always played Shubert houses in other cities as well. That was the nature of the relationship with Michael and with Joe. We were very loyal to them, and they were loyal to us.

It's like anything else — you get involved in a show, it becomes very intense — and then you move on and you give that intensity to the next show. With us, it lasted a lot longer because of the success of A CHORUS LINE. For the first year or so, every night was New Year's Eve. A CHORUS LINE was the most wined and dined and toasted show in the history of the theatre!

"Flying the mirrors in was an enormous savings to the show; otherwise it would have amounted to the cost of five stage hands for fifteen years." — PHIL SMITH

Hats off to the 4000th performance

Photo by Cliff Lipson

Giving notes to the Company
From left: longtime stage manager Tom
Porter, Michael Bennett, and Bob Avian

CHAPTER 8

MANAGING THE LINE

HIRINGS, FIRINGS, & ONGOING BUSINESS

"A lot of the people from the New York Company who went to California started getting delusions of grandeur. They thought they were going to become big stars and negotiations were very difficult." — BOB KAMLOT

Money

BOB KAMLOT [Original General Manager]: Joe Papp never worked with budgets. We spent what we needed to spend. If you gave Joe a budget and said it's going to cost $500,000, Joe would say, "It's going to cost whatever is necessary." He was unique in that fashion. Whenever something needed to be done, he would raise the money. As it happens, LuEsther Mertz put up $250,000 as an outright gift.

There were no investors in A CHORUS LINE. Nobody was ever a participant in the profits, except Michael Bennett as the conceiver; he had a share of royalties and a 25% interest in the production. The rest all went to the NYSF. Profits never went into anyone's personal pocket. In the decade from 1975 to 1985, the Festival was the most prestigious performing arts organization in the world, all made possible by the money that was generated by A CHORUS LINE.

We were supposed to open right after Labor Day but a three-week musician's strike intervened when we had to suspend operation. We kept the company intact, but we didn't pay them. We gave them a stipend instead, a kind of weekly subsistence, rather than a salary.

The nineteen people who were basically the principals were each to get $650 a week and the people who were dismissed in the opening would each get $425. It was a favored-nations contract with everybody and an easy negotiation.

The original weekly break-even for the show was about $80,000 or $90,000. Break-even figures for us were a little difficult to deal with because the NYSF had an administrative force that functioned not only for A CHORUS LINE but for its other shows as well. As general manager, I received an annual salary that pertained to everything I was doing. We actually separated our operation into the regular program and the extended program of all the Broadway spin-offs, obviously including A CHORUS LINE.

BERNARD JACOBS [President, Shubert Organization]: Manny Azenberg had always managed the NYSF when they moved anything to Broadway, and I had wanted them to use Manny again for A CHORUS LINE. But Michael did not want Manny because of some big argument Michael had with him during GOD'S FAVORITE. Eventually, Manny, Michael, and I had lunch at Sardi's and Michael agreed to Bob Kamlot handling the show on Broadway and Manny handling the tours.

BOB KAMLOT: There was no way I could ever have managed those two road companies; I was swamped at this point. Michael decided to rehearse the International, National, and "New" New York Companies all at the same time. Five of the Original Cast decided to stay in New York, along with the understudies; the others went to California. There must have been seventy-five people rehearsing at the same time at City Center: three sets of company managers, nine stage managers, and three

sets of dance captains.

Michael wanted to make a determination at the end of the rehearsal period which actor would go with which company — he wanted that freedom — but Actor's Equity wouldn't let him do that. For obvious reasons. You cannot tell the actors after they've started working whether they're going to Toronto, or whether they're going to California. Initially we were signing the contracts reading "Zach in A CHORUS LINE" without saying which company, but we eventually had to make the actual designation.

Manny negotiated the tour salaries, I did all of Broadway. By this point, it was strictly by negotiation as everybody had agents. The favored-nations arrangements went down the tubes. A lot of the people from the New York Company who went to California started getting delusions of grandeur. They thought they were going to become big stars and negotiations were very difficult.

PETER VON MAYRHAUSER [Stage Manager]: In the early years the "swings" had what we called the "Golden" contract. If one of the understudies in the opening went on for one of the line roles, somebody had to replace the understudy in the opening. If anybody was out in the show, one of them was sure to be on. They were never *not on*. Going on for even those little opening roles, they got an additional one-eighth of their salary — which is what you

get if you go on for a principal role. They were getting double salary constantly because they were always on for somebody, at least in the opening. But Equity stepped in about a year and half into the run and said contracts had to be divided up into chorus and principal roles. Those people in the opening that were eliminated became chorus roles.

BOB MacDONALD [Company & General Manager]: The dancers who are eliminated at the beginning were originally on principal contracts, but Equity wanted them to be on chorus contracts. There was a big fight with Equity about that. There were a number of fights with Equity.

BOB KAMLOT: When the Original Cast decided to go to California, we signed the new people to so-called conversion contracts, which permits you to sign an actor for a two week period with an option to either change it into a run-of-the-play contract or leave them on a two-week contract.

RICHARD BERG [Assistant General Manager]: It was more like four or eight weeks, as I recall. There were conversion contracts in the first year I was on the show, and then they disappeared. The period I was there [1978-1983] was mostly three- and six-month contracts.

BOB KAMLOT: The conversion right was the producer's to be exercised by the fifth

performance along with a mandatory 10% increment in salary. When Barbara Luna took over for Priscilla Lopez, Michael didn't like what she was doing, so we did not convert her contract. Michael said, "Don't convert her, just leave her on the standard minimum." Barbara got upset and quit. Once you're on two-week contract, the actor can quit on two weeks notice, which she did.

One of the general manager's functions is to give the bad news. The producers give the good news. The general manager announces when the show is closing, the producer announces when the show is being extended, or when they're having a party. That comes with the territory. Michael decided to let Carole Schweid [the original understudy] play Diana, and she played the part for five months. One day Michael came to the theatre, saw her and said, "She's not a Morales, she just can't play Morales, get rid of her. If she wants to go back to being an understudy, that's okay with me." My office at that time was up at Lincoln Center and I called Carole and said, "I've got to talk to you." She came to the office and it was the toughest thing I ever did. "Carole, I have to let you go." I explained to her that it had nothing to do with her ability, it was strictly miscasting. "Why did Michael let me play it for five months?" "That's Michael," I said. "Carole, because we don't want you to be unemployed, Michael said if you want to, you can stay on as the understudy; there

Longtime A CHORUS LINE company manager, later general manager, Bob MacDonald

will be no diminution in your salary." She turned it down and said no — screw you, basically. And I have got to give her a lot of credit for that.

Unfortunately, there were many firings, because the show had a way of slipping and sliding depending on people's energies. When Michael came to see what was going on, if he saw some sloppiness, he would fire people. And Michael kept firing people on A CHORUS LINE. Now that has changed. The "just cause" provision was directly attributable to something that happened at ANNIE, with Martin Charnin. He went in one day and fired about twenty people in one block move, for the same reason, the deterioration of the production.

PETER VON MAYRHAUSER: Michael became unhappy with many people for one reason or another after they had been playing for a while. There was no "just cause" clause and there was a lot of firing going on, a lot of tension, a lot of nerves. The stage was packed with it. I was very young, probably the youngest stage manager on Broadway. It was exciting, but terrifying, because it was such a huge hit.

There was so much tension when that "New" New York Company was formed.

RICHARD BERG: Shortly after BALL-ROOM opened, Michael came to see A CHORUS LINE over the weekend. He was really upset. The show had gotten a little undisciplined and we terminated several people on what was to be termed "Black" or "Bloody Monday." It wasn't just the A CHORUS LINE event that brought about the "just cause" provision. Martin Charnin had done it and I think somebody else did it. But Michael wasn't given to firing people. He was just not happy with what he saw and Michael Bennett was very strict about how his show was performed.

BOB KAMLOT: At that point Equity negotiated an agreement whereby people could only be fired for "just cause," not because of whimsy. A procedure was set up to first advise someone that they were not performing properly, and then be given a chance to fix it, before they could be fired. The firings diminished considerably.

BOB REILLY [Company Manager]: Tom Porter, our stage manager, was responsible for firing somebody. But I gave the news. It was awful. Terrible. But ultimately it was better for me to do it because I was not involved in the process. I was not the one who made the decision. I just had to tell them, basically, "We're not renewing your contract." It was always done after the final performance of the week. We would give them two week's notice, and it would be a Saturday night after the show. I would have a last minute talk with Tom about the situation, and he'd say definitely do it tonight. Then I'd go off to Charlie's or Sam's, have a drink, and go back to the theatre to watch the Finale. Afterward, I'd go backstage and once they finished dressing, I'd go into the stage manager's office and either page or pull them aside. They knew when their contracts were up, but it still came as a surprise. Some nights I would watch the Finale from offstage, and people would see me in the wings, and all of a sudden it became, "Uh-oh, he's waiting. Who's going to get it?" So I stopped going into the wings.

"There was a lot of firing going on, a lot of tension, a lot of nerves. The stage was packed with it. It was exciting, but terrifying, because it was such a huge hit." — PETER VON MAYRHAUSER

BOB KAMLOT: The most difficult thing during the run of the show was the revolving door, the constant replacement performers. Casting basically became Joe Nelson's job. Auditions were almost constant. Movement from the International Company to the National to the New York Company, and back and forth, was frequent. That was ongoing, coupled with many people being out of the show because of illness and injuries.

JEFF HAMLIN [Original Production Stage Manager]: We didn't have a casting department for A CHORUS LINE. I spent a lot of my time calling agents, setting up auditions. When we made this big tour around the country, auditioning people for the National Company, I helped set up the audition space, deal with the theatres, coordinate and organize all the hundreds of people who would appear at the theatre. By that time I had left the Broadway production as stage manager.

PETER VON MAYRHAUSER: The stage manager is always there for casting, but has only the most minimal kinds of input. Pat Carney, our original company manager, found some money in the weekly operating cost to give me a little extra for casting, because, literally, I would be there at 10:00 in the morning on the phone, setting up appointments, for hours and hours, which stage managers never do. That only happened for about six months or so. They

Photo by Cliff Lipson

hired George Martin, who was an old stage manager friend of Michael's. He was the first casting person on A CHORUS LINE. He only did it for a few months as a favor to Michael. Then they hired Joe Nelson.

TROY GARZA [Dance Captain]: Michael Bennett made a big mistake in choosing Joe Nelson and Sue McNair, in my opinion. Sue started out as a secretary who became "Ms. go out and maintain the companies with Joe Nelson." I don't think

either one was qualified. Joe would have been fine except he was abusive. But Michael was the kind of man who loved to delegate, so consequently a lot of the management were less than qualified to maintain this show. It's not like a regular musical. It was rare the stage manager or company manager was really great. When the National Company closed, I was on the plane coming home with Joe Nelson and Michael Bennett, and Michael, who loved to do this to people, said, "Joe, by the way,

Prepping for the Gala From left: Bob Avian, Baayork Lee, Michael Bennett, Troy Garza, T. Michael Reed, Fran Liebergall, and Don Pippin.

167

you're fired. The company is closed and I don't need you anymore." And I am sitting in the seat next to him thinking "Good grief," but secretly enjoying it.

RICHARD BERG: Michael controlled the show very, very tightly. Nobody got a five-dollar raise without Michael's approval. This was Michael's show, there were no two ways about it. You did nothing on the show without calling Michael; he was an active producer. Joe would stop by and see the show once a year and would see all the financial reports but Michael really stayed on top of the show.

BOB KAMLOT: The late seventies and early eighties was also a time when there was quite a bit of drug abuse in the company, and that created a lot of outs. We finally had to go to Equity, which stepped in, and a lot of people were fired because of it.

ANONYMOUS: We had major, major problems with drugs in all three companies. Equity sent a representative who not only spoke to the Broadway Cast, but flew out at Equity's expense to talk to the other two casts. People who were high on stage during the choreography in that show could harm other dancers. Equity tried to be helpful with the drug scene, but, as they explained, they can't be a policing organization. They unfortunately had very little impact.

RON STAFFORD [Assistant Stage Manager]: It was an innocent time when people didn't really know all the consequences of drugs; it was the seventies. I don't think it was worse with one company or the other. It affected a lot of people's performances. We certainly didn't know then what we know now. There were people who did drugs because it made their show easier, or so they thought. And it did — for a moment. But after doing it for a period of time it was wearing them down even more.

TROY GARZA: It was just popular. And some people became addicted; that's what happens. The cocaine problem was terrible in the Bus & Truck Company. It was never too bad in the New York Company; we went through a cocaine phase but eventually it just fizzled out. As time went on, people lost interest in drugs. 1983 was the last drug year.

MITCHELL WEISS [Company Manager]: I remember two serious drug interventions, both of which were resolved to the benefit of the show and to the benefit of the performers. They took some time away from the show, and when they came back everything was fine. They were guaranteed their job back. It was done quietly and always with the individual in mind — as long as they were willing to do it right.

BOB REILLY: Bob Avian basically left it to Tom Porter to hire replacements. Tom would run them by Bob and I would negotiate the contract. But in the late eighties, when I was involved in the show, there were no negotiations. They took it at minimum, "Here's what we're offering, do you want the job or not?" We kept a drawer which held everybody's contract from the very first performance. If you were rehired, the contract came out of the "dead contracts," and the new contract was attached to that one. You could look through the history of the person's employment career — when they got a raise, if we let them go for drug rehab — it was all there in one drawer.

RICHARD BERG: We had the current cast files, the past files, and the touring files. Some of these people had very thick contracts, like books, because we would staple each new one to the previous any time they had a renewal or new rider.

BOB REILLY: People who came in brand-new sometimes were only given three-month contracts to see if they worked out. Those who had a run-of-the-play contract, we couldn't get rid of. Once a week I would give Tom a list of whose contracts were coming up for renewal, based on five, six, or eight weeks in advance. Tom kept that list on his desk; he made those casting decisions.

It was difficult if you had to audition outside of the company. All of a sudden the actor who is playing the role hears

about it; it's hard to hold auditions in Shubert Alley without anybody knowing. Tom Porter and Jeff Lee, who was the production stage manager on CATS, were always calling one another asking, "Do you have anybody who can play Maggie?" and "Do you have anybody who can play Rum Tum Tugger?" And Tom would say, "What does he have to do?" Tom hated CATS and refused to remember any of the character names. Tom Porter's famous take on CATS, when he finally saw it, was "You mean to tell me the Shuberts spent $5 million to put a bag woman through the roof of the Winter Garden?" Saturday nights when Tom would try to get the cast up for the performance he would go to the speaker and say in his dry, monotone voice, "Energy, energy, energy." Just like that, and we'd all howl. He didn't understand why we were all laughing.

MITCHELL WEISS: It sometimes felt as if whoever Tom Porter had in his memory banks at that moment, whom he was willing to deal with, he would call. We were out of the loop. We were just told who was available and Michael or Bob Avian decided. The years I was company manager, Bob was pretty much doing the casting.

RON STAFFORD: There was a file drawer of people who throughout the years had sent in their resumes. Half of the people

had left the business, some of them had put on weight, and certainly everyone had gotten older. At one point I said, "This filing cabinet is outdated. Can't we at least update this system? We'll ask for resumes to be sent." That's how we finally got started getting a new influx of pictures and resumes. They started hiring people from these photos that were coming in from new people in town.

FRAN LIEBERGALL [Original Pianist; Vocal Supervisor]: There was a time when we really didn't want to teach the show again. We would bring in people who had paid their dues, whom we felt would be beneficial to the New York Company. There was a loyalty to certain people, like a home they kept coming back to.

TROY GARZA: Michael and Bob were not around enough. They were rarely ever present at an audition, so we didn't always make the greatest choices. But we would try to follow our instincts as best we could and Tom Porter, Fran, and I usually gave them our recommendations. If we ever had a chance to hire somebody who had not done the show before, I welcomed it. But we had an influx of people from the road who had earned places in the Broadway Company. When someone in New York would finally give their notice, the word spread like wildfire.

MITCHELL WEISS: After the Gala was long gone, we had to think of how to keep the show going. Is it time to bring in stars? Is it time to reconsider how to reduce costs? Which direction do we want to go in? It's now ten years down the line and we were concerned the show not lose either its quality or its audience.

The show's star is Donna McKechnie, and her return in September 1986 came out of that kind of strategic thinking. From day one, when I called she was willing to consider it. We were actually trying to bring back Donna and Robert LuPone at the same time. Although they weren't available concurrently, we started the negotiations. Once we got confirmation that they both would do it — even though at separate times — and the price range they'd consider was something we were willing to pay, Joe Papp had to get involved.

BOB REILLY: When I first came into the show, I saw that nobody had ever tallied how much money we would owe in sick pay when the show ultimately closed. That became one of my first jobs. At one point Tom Porter was owed $10,000 because he had never taken a sick day. It ended up about $60,000 or $70,000 we had to start accruing, so that when the show closed we could pay it out. Everyone got their money by the time the show closed.

Assistant general manager Richard Berg

MITCHELL WEISS: When I first got into the management office, just trying to familiarize myself with certain contracts, I pulled out the original cast album contract. As I looked through it there were a number of questions that did not make sense to me, especially in the accounting of money that was due us. I called the accounting office at CBS and said, "The contract says we are supposed to have a piece of paper for each of these special deals you do in Europe or Australia. We only have three of them and according to your accounting there are approximately fifty-four. Where are the others and what kind of deals are happening?" CBS called me back a week later and said they had found some discrepancies and the following week we received a check for $98,000. And the week after that a second check for $98,000. All for back royalties for the cast album and foreign rights. Very often they take *What I Did For Love* and put it on a Broadway show compilation. Those are special deals that have been all around the world and no one had bothered to check. Joe Papp said I paid my salary for my entire life.

Ticket Prices

BOB KAMLOT: I tried to keep prices lower than other shows. Bernie Jacobs accused me of losing a lot of money for Michael because I didn't raise prices as quickly as the other shows. But because we were a nonprofit organization, we didn't want to be the leaders in terms of price hikes. We were always a shade or two behind everybody. Ultimately as costs go up, since there are a finite number of seats, you have to raise your prices. The largest expense was labor. Stagehands' costs and actors' salaries went up, as did advertising rates in the *Times;* they don't give you any great bargains.

PHIL SMITH [Vice President, Shubert Organization]: Bernie Gersten wanted the balcony in two prices. People don't want to sit in the rear of anything, so once you divide the balcony, they buy the front, they won't buy what's considered the rear. We put the seats on sale, we weren't automated at that time, and the box office had a couple of hundred tickets at this lower price, which I think was $6.00, almost virtually untouched. Bernie Jacobs and I kept trying to persuade Bernie Gersten to change the price, but he was reluctant to do it. He wanted to keep that $6.00 price, to have something that was inexpensive — but nobody was buying it. One day, Bernie Gersten looked at the racks in the box

office, and saw all of these tickets lying around. The orchestra is sold out, the mezzanine is sold out, the front balcony is sold, the boxes are sold — and these rear balcony tickets are just lying there. People were jumping over the dates rather than purchasing rear balcony. Bernie said, "OK, you might as well order all the new balcony tickets at $8.00 and put them on sale." That became the standard.

BERNARD GERSTEN [Associate Producer, NYSF]: The Shuberts always wanted to raise prices, and it was very tempting because the money came to the NYSF. The Shuberts had a secret weapon, which was to follow the market trend. Why should A CHORUS LINE, which is the best show in town, be cheaper than other shows?

BOB MacDONALD: The Shuberts had a lot of influence on ticket prices. They would always be on me or Joe or Bob Kamlot, "Raise your prices, raise your prices. The higher the ticket prices, the more you're going to get at Duffy Square."

BERNIE JACOBS: As costs kept going up, we kept pushing Bernie and Joe to raise prices, and they always resisted us because they thought it was their function to provide theatre at as cheap a price as possible. But it was also their function to make money out

of A CHORUS LINE so they could keep all of their activities going. I think at the time we were pushing them to go to $40 or $45, and Joe, in a fit of hysteria, said, "Oh, raise all eight performances," not keeping lower prices for Wednesday and Saturday matinees. It was not the right thing to do, but since they were discounting tickets at the TKTS booth, they increased their income to that extent. You didn't get rational decisions down there.

GERALD SCHOENFELD [Chairman, Shubert Organization]: It was a new experience for Joe to be on Broadway. It was sort of an ironic chapter in his career that the NYSF would ultimately find its financial rewards and success on Broadway. And it changed the whole relationship between nonprofit and profit theatre in their attitudes toward Broadway as being another place for the presentation of shows. Joe's attitude towards ticket prices and their sale and distribution changed as he became more accommodating to the idea of the NYSF on Broadway. His relationship with us preceded A CHORUS LINE because we have always been a sponsor of the NYSF.

Joe became much more entrepreneurial. But there was nothing that could be done about ticket prices without Joe's consent. As the show starts to run down, you get involved in twofers and the discount ticket booth and other discount arrange-

ments. The idea is to try to keep the show alive as long as you can. Of course, we started to make major concessions in rent and other terms, or the show would have closed much earlier than it did.

RICHARD BERG: I got a telephone call from the box office saying they wanted to send tickets to the TKTS booth for the first time. Our general manager was out of town, and I couldn't reach Joe Papp. So I got hold of Michael Bennett, because I didn't want to send tickets to the booth. I don't remember how many they wanted to send over, maybe 50 to 100. This was in late 1978. Michael said, "Go ahead and do it," so we did. A few months later it became a routine, because the decision was made to keep the audience there.

PHIL SMITH: A CHORUS LINE established very strongly the value of the half price TKTS booth. And the booth is one of the reasons the show was able to survive fifteen years. I was very instrumental in organizing the TKTS booth. The League of New York Theatres had appointed a three-person committee to create a TKTS booth in Duffy Square. Well, the other two people didn't show up, so I organized it alone and gave them a budget of what it would cost for a ninety-day trial ending Labor Day. John Lindsay was mayor at the time, and he was very pro-theatre, saying, "You can have Duffy Square." I met with a man

from the Parks Department who had a trailer he would let us have, all we had to do was cut windows in it, paint it, and make a box office out of it. The Parks Department brought it to Duffy Square and we were nearly off and running.

The League asked what the three-months projection could turn out to be and I suggested a possible $20,000 loss. I couldn't say it would be an instant success, that it would hit the ground running. They took a vote and said they were not willing to take the loss. A few days later, Anna Crouse, an original board member of TDF, called to meet with me. She had met someone the night before from the Ford Foundation who said the foundation would give a grant to go ahead with the project. With waivers and some concession from the treasurers' union, we set up. Dick Barr, then President of the League, asked if he could negotiate a salary for me to be the operator of the booth. I said, "I'll do it for nothing."

The whole idea of the booth was audience development, not dollars. People who never otherwise went to the theatre would suddenly see a show. We were making theatre accessible. You could go on impulse, you didn't have to plan months in advance, and you could buy it reasonably. It was important to get a new audience that had never been to the theatre, get them into the habit, and those that had been going to the theatre would

go more often than before, because you were making it so affordable.

TROY GARZA: Management decided to take Tuesday nights off because that was our worst night at the end of the run, so our week started with a Wednesday matinee. Equity approved that without realizing you can't start a week with a matinee; it caused a huge uproar.

BOB MacDONALD: We did Sunday matinees, then we dropped them. Dropped Thursday nights, did Tuesday matinees, and at one point got in trouble with Equity in that you can't have a matinee after the day off. We were grasping at straws, searching.

BERNIE JACOBS: Bernie Gersten had billing as the Associate Producer of A CHORUS LINE. When Joe and Bernie split, Joe took it away from him for about a year, until finally Michael convinced him to restore the billing. Joe, in a strange kind of way, resented the success of A CHORUS LINE because it really was not his so much as it was Bernie's. As time went on, he became more and more the parent of the show, because once he caused Bernie to exit from the NYSF, it was all Joseph Papp. There was no Bernie Gersten.

BERNIE GERSTEN: The trouble with A CHORUS LINE is the same trouble with

anything that lasts too long. There's a point where it becomes mechanical, redundant, repetitious, and you don't want to spend your life there. I feel lucky I was finished with A CHORUS LINE after three years, but I didn't feel lucky at the time. It wasn't my choice. Nonetheless, I have no regrets that I didn't have to spend years four through fifteen there. I went on and did other things.

I was fired, Joe took my name off the billing board and took my name out of the program. I protested, others protested, and eventually billing was restored. The pain and trauma of being fired from the NYSF and the termination of a friendship with Joe that had begun in 1948 far transcended separation from A CHORUS LINE. The show was part of a spectrum of loss. I lost the theatre I had worked in and helped invent and discover, in which A CHORUS LINE was only one manifestation.

BOB REILLY: A CHORUS LINE was always thought of as that step-sister we don't talk about. It existed, but everybody at the NYSF was focused on the Public Theatre and the Delacorte during the summer. So when Bob MacDonald became the Festival's general manager after being A CHORUS LINE's company manager, he remembered that he loved the step-sister. He kept close watch and paid very personal attention to the show.

"You take the basic blueprint of the dance, you use the right steps, and you let their bodies make the variations." — TROY GARZA

The Dance Captains

RICHARD BERG: When we were switching between the three companies, we had people on planes frequently going from one company to the other to cover vacations and short-term absences. Some people would just hop on a plane and go out and do it. T. Michael Reed, one of the dance captains, had a lot to do with coordinating all of that; he was very good. He really kept the dance tight in all three companies.

TROY GARZA: I had been assisting Tom [T. Michael] Reed on the road starting in London. Michael hired me on his recommendation to take over in New York. On December 12 1977, I became the dance captain of the show on Broadway while understudying the roles of Mark, Mike, Larry, and Paul. I continued for the show's fifteen year run.

As dance captain, I was primarily concerned with musical staging. Tom Porter and I collaborated well together. We only clashed when I would direct the actors. It was impossible for me to teach the show without giving them some of the acting along the way. But I would always preface everything with, "When Tom gives you

directions, do what he says because he is responsible for this, not me. I am just trying to give you a guideline." I rarely saw a stage manager who took charge of the acting in the show. The cast came to the dance captains with their problems because it's such a dance oriented show. That's really where their trust was.

CLIVE WILSON [Dance Captain]: I knew every aspect and step in the show for each character. Aside from the steps, it was working somebody through a song. It wasn't just the physical stuff. I would interface in the best way with Peter Von Mayrhauser and Jeff Hamlin. They would get more involved in the real "scene" stuff — the Cassie / Zach confrontation; the Paul monologue; all the dialogue. But when there was an overlap on dialogue leading into a song, I would get involved too. In A CHORUS LINE, dance captaining was about a lot more than just steps.

TROY GARZA: If everyone in the opening danced perfectly then you don't have the play. People then look like they are dancing choreography they've known for years. It's supposed to be an audition and

if there's not some variation in the way they do it, then your reality goes out the window. And even though the show is about enhanced reality, the audience shouldn't know that. They should only perceive it as reality. Especially in the jazz combination, I did allow a lot of variation. It had to look natural. Some people kicked a little higher, a flexed foot here and there, a hand turned the wrong way, little things. The jazz combination is so athletic and modern in its content that everyone's body looks different doing it no matter what. So often I let their own bodies make the variations until something was so blatantly wrong that it pulled my eye.

With the solos and monologues, I tried to give them as much leeway as possible. You start with basic staging and a few given gestures. There are variations in the choreography plus there are different versions of the choreography. The way Wayne Cilento did *I Can Do That* is not the same as Michael taught me, so it depends on the dancer. You take the basic blueprint of the dance, you use the right steps, and you let their bodies make the variations. Of course, there are the numbers where the movements are plain. Diana does

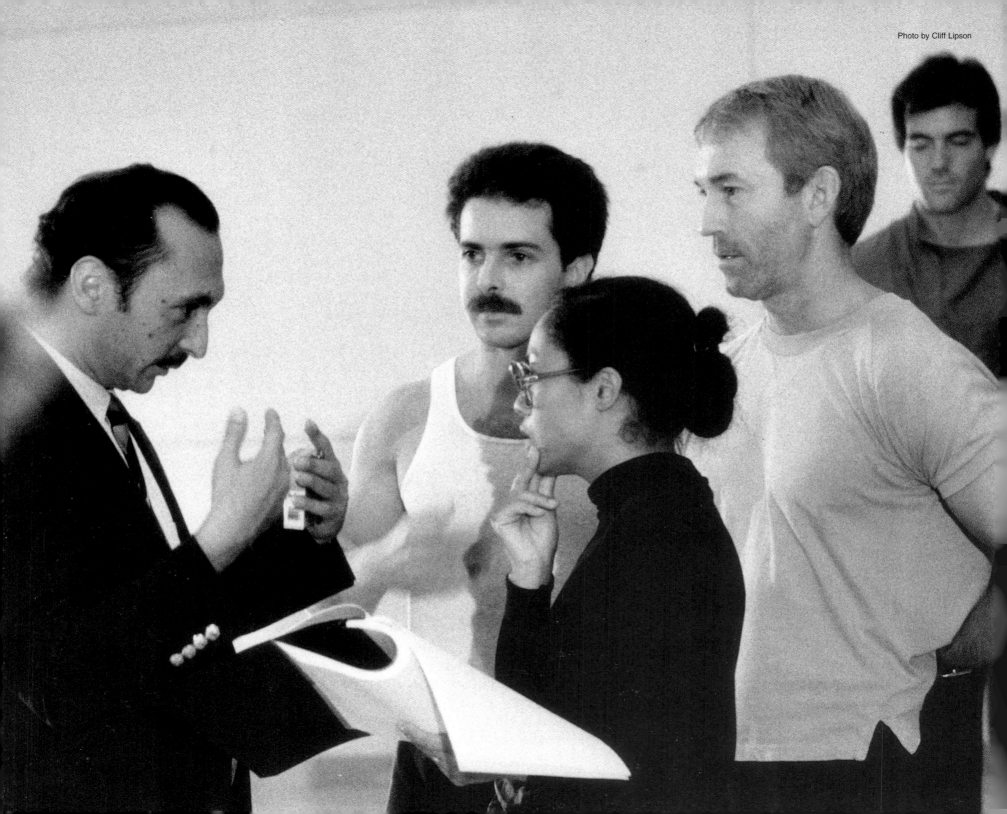

"whoosh, whoosh" in *Nothing,* but one Diana might do it with her fingers together and one might do it with her hands open It doesn't make any difference to me as long as it is an organic gesture from her. With Cassies, it's the basic dance, they all have to find their variations and what works best on their bodies. The main problems we had in New York were when people on the road had been directed by Joe Nelson and he had been cloning them, telling them, "You must do this gesture here." There was a great deal more space for expression in the Broadway Company than in the road companies. The road stage managers were afraid to let anything change because they were afraid they would get in trouble. We were in closer contact with Bob and Michael, so nobody argued much with us.

FRAN LIEBERGALL: You didn't mess with the formula There was certain leeway in the solo numbers, but if it overstepped the boundary, it wasn't A CHORUS LINE anymore — it was musical comedy, and that was the bane of our existence. We wanted it to be a reality piece, about a real audition. We did everything we could to keep it that way.

TROY GARZA: Sometimes people would come into the New York Company and Tom Porter and I would have to deal with attitude such as, "Michael Bennett directed me six years ago in Chicago, so this is my performance." I would say, "I know, but this is here and now and you have to trust me."

PATTI D'BECK [Dance Captain]: We had a convention where Michael flew in all the dance captains. We broke things down, trying to get the one-and-only version of everything so when it is taught, it's all the same. He wanted us all to be teaching exactly the same version.

RON STAFFORD: Michael got together stage managers from all of the companies — casually referred to as the "Cassie Camp." He taught the entire show from beginning to end. What he did was to make each company uniform — exactly the same.

PATTI D'BECK: I relied a lot on Baayork Lee and the original people, who let us know where stories came from. We tried to be true to what they really meant. It was easier then, because we were closer to when it happened. The information was still close to the surface.

CYNTHIA ONRUBIA [Cast]: When they brought Troy in from the International Company, I started assisting him in auditions. Troy really got me started on dance captaining; I think he saw I had the mind for it. Cliff Lipson and Dean Badaloto were coming into the show and I put them in when Troy was away. I was sixteen, scared to death, but I knew I had to do it.

PETER VON MAYRHAUSER: Cynthia was amazing. At some point we were actually considering hiring her as dance captain, but she was only about seventeen. You can't have a dance captain who's seventeen.

"You didn't mess with the formula. There was a certain leeway in the solo numbers, but if it overstepped the boundary, it wasn't A CHORUS LINE anymore — it was musical comedy, and that was the bane of our existence." — *FRAN LIEBERGALL*

A Chorus Line of motorcyclists. Eight production staff members commuted to work on motorcycles. From left: Bob Kamlot (general manager), Harris Goldman (company manager), John Mineo (original cast member), Gary Shevett (production electrician), Martin Tudor (lighting), Steve Cohen (NYSF production supervisor), Steve Terry (sound operator), Tommy King (Public Theatre guard). Adorning the motorcycles are cast members Rene Ceballos, Loida Santos, Kate Wright, Donna Drake, and Cynthia Onrubia.

Photo by Martha Swope

CHAPTER 9

THE GALA

A CHORUS LINE BREAKS THE RECORD

> *"Michael said, 'I want to do something absolutely fabulous.*
> *Bring everybody back!'"* — BOB KAMLOT

Becoming the Longest Line

BOB KAMLOT [Original General Manager]: As we got closer to breaking the record, Michael said, "I want to do something absolutely fabulous. Bring everybody back!" I said, "Michael, that's not possible, how are you going to do that? Who knows where everyone is? Some people are no longer in the business." "I don't care, I want everybody here." So we made an arrangement with Actor's Equity wherein we would bring performers back with no pay, except for a $50 honorarium. Naturally, we would pay their transportation and hotel expenses. We had an enormous amount of help from Bob MacDonald, Richard Berg, Wendy Mansfield, Tom Porter, and Joe Nelson in contacting all the people who were in the show.

BOB MacDONALD [Company & General Manager]: We had meetings every two weeks, then every week, then every day. It probably took a good four to five months to put it all in place.

MITCHELL WEISS [Company Manager]: I was involved from day one. Bob Kamlot,

Richard Berg, and I were in charge. We did the seating charts, hired all the security, arranged for the catering, the carpeting, and the tents for Shubert Alley. We called the actors all around the world and coordinated their travel arrangements. They were showing up at different times over a period of three days. We housed everyone at the Milford Plaza.

TROY GARZA [Dance Captain]: Michael didn't formally plan which dance captain was going to handle which section. It all just fell into place. I was responsible for the opening and we all ended up working on the Finale. Wendy Mansfield, Tom Porter, Fran Liebergall, and I did most of the casting. We tried to assemble as many people from each particular company; when we couldn't, we had to shuffle people around.

PHIL SMITH [Vice President, Shubert Organization]: The responsibility for the whole event really belonged to the Festival. The only aspect the Shubert Organization was involved with was the party afterwards in the Alley — getting the permits, security, electricity.

BILL SCHELBLE [Press Agent]: We had photos of the Original and Current Companies, which were sent to the press with a production-facts sheet that included statistics of cities played, costume data, how many people were going to be on stage that night, etc. Michael wanted to list which actor was doing what section in the *Playbill*® but there was no way because he kept switching people around during rehearsals. It worked out much better with the Supertitles.

MERLE DEBUSKEY [Press Agent]: We had to rent a trailer just for press. We knew what we were in for and we had to prepare for it properly — because the world wanted in. I've never seen anything like it for the theatre. It was set up like a military camp; we had charts, theatre positions. The back row of the orchestra had the seats removed so we could put in platforms and plant cameras.

BILL SCHELBLE: We really didn't have to do anything for press follow-up because the Gala hit every newspaper in the country.

BOB KAMLOT: Right before the Gala, A CHORUS LINE had slipped a bit in terms of the grosses, and the show looked like it was going to ease out. That event created such an incredible amount of international publicity that the very next week, the show grossed over $300,000. It started grossing $340, $350, $360 and renewed its life beyond belief. It was eventually what was responsible for the fifteen-year run.

TROY GARZA: We didn't get a bonus or extra money for putting the Gala together. We all just did it because it was for the New York Company. We didn't even think about it.

THARON MUSSER [Lighting Designer]: We had to bring in lights for the aisles of the theater, but other than that, we didn't change anything for the show. We added a little bit of light from the front of house to satisfy the camera. They were supposed to give us a monitor inside the theatre so we could see how it looked on the screen, but the monitor never worked. We had to watch from a truck in Shubert Alley to see where we needed a little lighting help.

TONY D'AIUTO [Spotlight Operator]: There were so many Cassies dancing, at rehearsal it was like "Where's my Cassie coming from?" We had seven front-light men. We didn't know which Cassie we were spotting, they were coming out of the walls! There were five of us on the bridge,

Photo by Cliff Lipson

and two men in back of the balcony. They put the balcony guys up on a platform, which worked fine until the audience in the balcony stood up and they were right in front of the spotlights! It was such a crazy night.

BERNARD JACOBS [President, Shubert Organization]: There were going to be over three hundred people on that stage. We built supports underneath to make sure the stage would not fall in.

FRAN LIEBERGALL: The first day of rehearsal, everyone sat in the house, and

Michael said, "Let's start with the Finale." This Mormon Tabernacle Choir of people started singing with perfect cut-offs, perfect crescendos, decrescendos, phrasing. Perfect everything — as if they had just done it yesterday. Don Pippin was conducting, and it was the most amazing thing. The kids were trained so precisely — it all came back to them.

WANDA RICHERT [Cassie]: I put it in my contract for NINE that I would be off for that night and any rehearsal time that was needed. I would have not taken the

The National Company rehearsing the Third Montage

Photo by Cliff Lipson

In rehearsal

RICHARD BERG [Assistant General Manager]: Rehearsals were run like clockwork; nothing was done behind closed doors.

JUSTIN ROSS [Greg]: We're all dancers, very insecure and egotistical. It was a little scary. I did Greg's monologue, which was the highest compliment Michael could have paid me, but I was a wreck. First, I was scared to death I wouldn't be asked to do the bit, then once Michael chose me, it became "Oh my God, now I've got to do it."

SCOTT PEARSON [Zach]: We had several Zachs that night. I was pissed off because Michael gave me a section where I was the voice at the back of the house, and naturally I wanted to do one of the scenes on stage. There were three of us who did the offstage Zachs, dressed in full Zach costume as if we were going to be

on stage, but, of course, we weren't. My vanity was slapped down.

KERRY CASSERLY [Kristine]: When I saw my name posted in Kristine's spot during *Sing*, I was so excited. I knew Michael liked me but that was really special.

KATE WRIGHT [Sheila]: The rehearsals were the best part — the schmoozing and the crying and doing all those steps again that we had put away in our memory banks somewhere. It was the best party and it lasted a whole week.

LAURIE GAMACHE [Final Broadway Cassie]: I was in the Current Company playing Lois in the opening number. When they were dividing things up, it was announced that the original Bus & Truck Company would do the *Fourth Montage*, and I assumed I would be in that

job if I was going to miss the Gala. Rehearsals were incredible. The first day at the Shubert, when everybody came together after all those years, we sat in the house and sang the Finale. I sat there crying, couldn't even sing. It was so intense and wonderful and loving.

RON STAFFORD [Assistant Stage Manager]: At the first rehearsal, we made an announcement to bring valuables to the basement. A security guard stood behind me as people tossed their wallets into a huge trash can. When they broke for lunch a couple of hours later, it was announced that "Ron will be in the basement with your valuables." It was a mess! I took all the wallets out and laid them on the floor. Lunch hour was practically over by the time everybody got their valuables back.

Photo by Cliff Lipson

"We didn't know which Cassie we were spotting, they were coming out of the walls!" — Tony D'Aiuto

Above: The Pauls

Opposite: Karen Jablons, Mitzi Hamilton, and DeLee Lively asVal

group because I was in the original Bus & Truck. But I had also joined the Las Vegas Company for about a month, and for some reason, that's the company I was put into, doing the *Rehearsal Ones*. I wanted to dance with my Bus & Truck Company, but as it turned out I got to do more with the Vegas Company. I danced

center stage next to Ann Reinking, who was doing Cassie in the confrontation scene, which was a lot of fun.

WAYNE MELEDANDRI [Paul]: Michael created the Paul monologue as sort of a Greek Chorus. It was difficult because most of us weren't doing the bulk of the monologue. Sammy Williams was the focal

point. The rest of us echoed Sammy and had individual lines throughout the speech. It was disconcerting, being used to doing the whole monologue with all the emotion going on, and suddenly the concentration was on "Where is my word, when do I move?"

DEBORAH GEFFNER [Kristine]: I wasn't allowed to be with any of my pals. I was with the "young" crowd doing *Shit Richie* with all the dancing. I didn't get to say a word, and didn't get to do Kristine's bit, although I was dying to. Everyone wanted to be in their part.

The feeling of being on stage with all those people doing the final kickline and having the stage shaking under our feet while we were kicking — the aisles came alive and then the balconies came alive, this golden mass of everybody kicking! There was nothing like that experience. I loved every minute of being on stage.

DeLEE LIVELY [Val]: Michael made me the "Ass." Originally, the Val monologue and *Dance:10, Looks: 3* were supposed to be the two Vals that it's about, Mitzi Hamilton and Pam Blair, and me. Karen

> *"All those people doing the final kickline and having the stage shaking under our feet — the aisles came alive and then the balconies came alive, this golden mass of everybody kicking!"* — *DEBORAH GEFFNER*

Above and opposite:
The Cassies

Jablons, we were told, was brought in to teach it to Pam, and the next thing we knew, Pam wasn't going to do it. So it was me, Karen, and Mitzi who ended up doing the number. It was a thrill!

JANET WONG [Connie]: I ended up doing the *Rehearsal Ones*, and had to do the Finale on the opposite side, which I was not happy about. At that point, I couldn't remember the Finale anyway, so Laurie Gamache taught it to me on the other side.

TROY GARZA: As captain of the Broadway Company I was mainly responsible for the opening. Roy Smith was doing most of the *Montage* with his group, Baayork did the Foreign Companies. T. Michael Reed and I staged the Finale in collaboration with Michael and Bob Avian. They wanted to bring everyone on, and Tom and I coordinated that effort. We brought four people on at a time, two lines from both sides of the stage. Everybody coming on from stage left had to reverse their steps, because the entrance is normally from stage right. That was a wonderful, wonderful time.

PATTI D'BECK [Understudy]: I remember watching Michael in one of the big rooms at 890 as he watched Donna do the Cassie speech. She was speaking to Michael as if he were Zach. Seeing the love in Michael's face for Donna was overwhelming.

CYNTHIA ONRUBIA [Connie; Understudy]: Donna was running a scene and everybody was sitting on the floor, in tears, watching that happen.

ANN REINKING [Cassie]: Michael directed us for the Gala with the same measure of care and respect as if we were all doing the show for the first time. I was thrilled when he asked me to do the confrontation scene. Somebody else rehearsed me to refresh my memory and then Michael came in and we rehearsed again. It was so well done, a real theatrical moment.

CHERYL CLARK [Cassie]: For the Cassies, it was great. We're all girlfriends. We all knew the choreography, and Michael broke it up into sections. There were only three of us out of all the Cassies who had lines. Annie did the confrontation scene, Donna did the names section and the dialogue surrounding *The Music and The Mirror*, and I did the "call a doctor" lines in Paul's accident scene. It was all very smooth.

VICKI FREDERICK [Cassie]: Some of us

hadn't been in the show in years. Michael got all the Cassies together and took each section one at a time. He honed the number down for each one of us to do certain things. He had us all go through the number to see what stage of stamina we were in and to determine who should do which section.

ANGELIQUE ILO [Cassie]: Michael thought of the Cassie dance as sort of a relay race. Two girls came on to join Donna, then they went off and were replaced by two other girls. This "on and off" continued through the entire dance until we all came on after the "heat wave" section at the end and everyone finished the number together. I don't remember any feelings of competitiveness.

LOIS ENGLUND [Val]: I felt very much removed at the Gala. It was a painful and difficult experience. An enormous amount of unhappiness and competition.

SCOTT ALLEN [Original Understudy]: I was going to be a part of the Gala, but I took an opportunity to go away instead. So I didn't do the show, but I saw it. Talking to some of the understudies, they said, "You didn't miss a thing, same old shit. Stand in the back of the room, we'll get to you later."

KAY COLE [Original Maggie]: At the Gala, Michael said to me very candidly

and honestly, the reason he wanted the Originals to do *At the Ballet* was because he felt that's when the show started. It was really a great gift to hear that from him.

RON DENNIS [Original Richie]: It was horrible for me. I had taken my vacation from MY ONE AND ONLY to do the Gala. Michael

Photo by Cliff Lipson

was the thorn up my ass. He was on my case and not very pleasant at all. The only reason I can figure was that a year earlier, before MY ONE AND ONLY opened, Michael came in to do some doctoring. We were doing a lot of intricate cane work that was supposed to go in that night. At one point I asked him, "Michael, is it possible that we can get gloves soon so we can practice with them?" He said, "Ron, don't worry about the gloves, just do the steps." "I'm just asking so there won't be an accident later on." Obviously, he didn't like that.

Everyone from MY ONE AND ONLY was pissed because of all the changes and

having to deal with Michael's attitude. I guess he just didn't like me speaking up. But please, I was thirty-two and had a right to say anything I wanted if I thought it was affecting my performance in my show. The number went in that night and was gone the following night. It was terrible.

When this Gala happened a year later, I come to find out during the rehearsals that the song I had created Michael gave to a kid who had done it on the road. I didn't get a chance to do my own number! Well, I was just miserable. Afterwards, I split quickly and went home to

Alyce Gilbert and her wardrobe staff prepping costumes for the event

Cast. Everyone else found their costumes hanging alphabetically from these bars. There was also a bag containing their Finale hat and shoes, together with the line costume they would be wearing that night. Before it was over, we had also appropriated the area behind the balcony seats and the standing room area behind the orchestra section as dressing areas. The Cassies all had new costumes for the Gala because we couldn't find eight sets in storage that matched perfectly.

RON STAFFORD: I made sure the various companies got from the Booth Theatre to the Shubert. It was actually very easy because everyone wanted to see as much of the show as possible. We set up back-stage monitors at the Booth, so everyone was very involved with what was going on. It was such a fever-pitched atmosphere backstage.

bed. It took me years to figure out the connection between that incident with MY ONE AND ONLY and him seeking revenge on me. I don't think he did it to make the show any better. Michael was just being bitchy Michael and decided to piss in my face and call it rainwater.

BILL JONES [Dresser]: The stage of the Booth Theatre became our wardrobe room. The bars that normally hang scenery were lowered to hang all the Finale costumes. The current Broadway cast stayed in their dressing rooms at the Shubert. The dressing rooms in the Booth were given to the Original Broadway

DON PIPPIN [Original Musical Director]: I said to Michael, "I haven't done the show in so long, are you sure you want me to do the Gala?" "Yeah, I like your tempos." He wanted to go back to the way the show had originally been played. I needed to get it back in my head. Michael gave me a printout of what

"At 5:00 on the day of the performance, Michael said he wanted to wear tails for the event. I reached Barbara Matera and said, 'Send the tailor, we have an emergency.'" — THEONI ALDREDGE

would be happening that night. I thought I would have to mark in cues, but I tried it once without marking anything, just using my instincts, and it came out exactly the way it was supposed to.

Michael didn't happen to mention that *Nothing* was going to be sung in Japanese. I hadn't rehearsed with Chikae Ishikawa, who was doing Diana at that point in the show. I only rehearsed parts that had changes. Suddenly she came down stage and started singing in Japanese. I thought she would definitely switch back to English — but she didn't. I could still tell exactly where every key change was; it was all in the inflection.

With the switching of the companies, the evening was absolutely spine tingling.

BOB ROGERS [Conductor]: I was conducting the New York Company at that time, but I sat the Gala out. I felt sidelined in one sense, and relieved in another. I understood that it was an impossible situation. What do you do after everyone has been invited back, including the original conductor, yet only one conductor can be in the pit? Somebody's got to give. But I really wound up enjoying it immensely. In fact, I got the best seat in the house for the show. I got to drink champagne in the alley and Don Pippin had to do all the work.

FRAN LIEBERGALL [Original Pianist; Vocal Supervisor]: Don Pippin asked me to play the opening with him. After the opening, I switched with the regular pianist and he finished the performance.

THEONI ALDREDGE [Costume Designer]: At 5:00 on the day of the performance, Michael said he wanted to wear tails for the event. I found myself in Michael's car with his driver, calling Barney's and pleading with them to put aside any small tails and to please stay open until I got there. Once I arrived, I grabbed everything in sight, flew out of there, called the costume shop, which was closed, then I reached Barbara Matera and said, "Send the tailor, we have an emergency." Michael had tails on that night.

MITCHELL WEISS: We were in tuxedos for about seventeen straight hours before the Gala. I was playing "security guard." The only way someone could get into the theatre was if they had a ticket or if I okayed them.

I had a book with three different ways to find people in their seats; we were covering all bases. I got a call from security that someone was trying to break in at the front entrance. I walked up and standing in front of me was Helen Hayes. The security guard turned to me and said, "She tried to get in with this." I looked at the ticket, which was from the Helen Hayes Theater, and she said, "I'm so embarrassed but I left my tickets at home and thought maybe if I tried this, I'd still get in." I told Helen Hayes it was no problem.

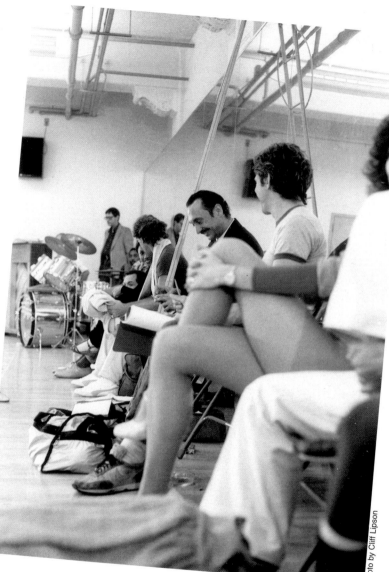

Photo by Cliff Lipson

Michael Bennett at 890 Studios

BOB MacDONALD:
One of the biggest problems we had during the performance itself was to keep people out of the back of the theatre, because the place would fill up like you wouldn't believe with stagehands,

ORCHESTRA SEPT. 29, 1983
A CHORUS LINE   2:00 p.m. and 10:00 p.m.

1. "OPENING"
   Bar #367 (Timp) is played 3 TIMES

2. #9 - "AT THE BALLET"
   Original key: G minor (2 flats, concert)

3. #13 - "NOTHING"
   Eb - and in Japanese !!

4. #16 - "TITS (6) + ASSes (3)"
   High key (5 flats throughout)

5. #18 - "MUSIC + MIRROR"
   Original key (F♮ concert)
   Watch for different licks, fills, voicings —
   particularly bars #122-123, and key
   relation at #124
   SAME NOTES: VERY DIFFERENT PACING

6. #22A - "ALTERNATIVES"
7. #23 - "WHAT I DID FOR LOVE"
   Ab - Priscilla Lopez returns

8. #25 - "BOWS" - in 3 stages
   Ⓐ Play as usual till cut-off
   Ⓑ Immediate D.S. to bar #111, play to end.
   Ⓒ On cue, play final 4 bar vamp till cut-off.

(8A. Take a bow!)

An outline of the only musical changes made for the Gala performance

> *"I got a call from security that someone was trying to break in at the front entrance. I walked up and standing in front of me was Helen Hayes."*
>
> — *MITCHELL WEISS*

wardrobe people, ushers, box office. We had to keep that area clear. The fire department was all over our butt, because we were violating so many rules.

FRASER ELLIS: I got to do the opening, which was really incredible. The lights go out, your back is to the audience, there is adrenaline like you've never felt, and you start the show. You turn around, the audience is on its feet, there in the front row is Ruth Gordon, Garson Kanin, Liza on the aisle jumping up and down, Helen Hayes, Patti LuPone, Baryshnikov. These stars are on their feet crying and applauding. What a thrill! It just doesn't get better than that.

DONN SIMIONE: There were monitors set up at the Booth Theatre so we could all see the show. We were like a football team, everybody was so excited and rooting for each other. For the Finale, I danced in one of the aisles of the orchestra. The audience didn't know what hit them! They kept

looking around at all the dancers in the mezzanine, the balcony, all over the place, beaming, going crazy.

RICHARD BERG: We broke our backs making sure that nothing would go wrong. The only really upsetting thing was something we couldn't control: the torrential rain later that night. It was just a mess. $15,000 worth of flowers, ruined. The rain was so heavy, the tents offered no protection and Shubert Alley is such a wind tunnel that it came right through. $24,000 worth of Antron floor carpeting, donated by Antron, was totally destroyed. We were going to use the carpet this one night and then give it to the Actors' Home.

The clean-up was pretty light, but the destruction was a great sadness to everybody. We were all wiped out afterwards; everyone had worked so hard. Michael called us all personally to thank us.

BOB KAMLOT: On stage, following the show, Michael publicly thanked a zillion people, except two he left out — me and Bob MacDonald. Both of us were very hurt. But the following day he called *The*

New York Times and they ran an item where Michael said, "Forgetting them was the only mar on a perfect night. It was the one thing I did wrong."

RICHARD BERG: It was not just a celebration, it was also a promotional event. They spent half a million dollars which we recouped at the box office within two or three days. The national publicity was just phenomenal.

MITCHELL WEISS: Michael set the tone. This was going to be the most wonderful, positive event — or else. There was such a feeling of everyone working together; no union problems, nobody saying, "Oh, they are trying to cheat me" or "Who cares about this?" Everyone was happy with their work and egos were left at home. That was Michael's doing. He was powerful enough that nobody would dare challenge him.

BOB MacDONALD: It was a half-million dollar evening, but in the long run, it netted $3 or $4 million. It will remain a highlight of my life and of my career in the theatre. All that genius, the Paul monologue, the Cassies, the duplication and number of actors, *Nothing* sung in Japanese, the integration of the foreign companies. It was mind-boggling.

Hanging out
at the Booth Theatre

189

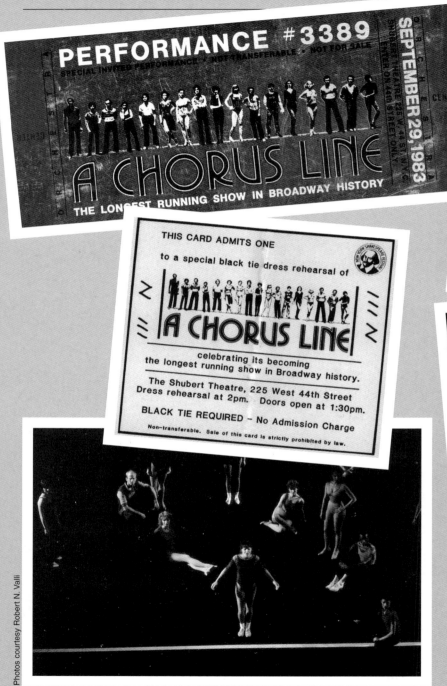

Bottom two pictures: Priscilla Lopez sang What I Did for Love *with the Foreign Companies and was joined by the Original Cast and several "ghosts" of each character*

Top: The post-performance acknowledgments onstage

Michael's Speech to the Company

Excerpts from Michael Bennett's speech to the entire Company following the Invited Dress Rehearsal for the Gala (courtesy of Otts Munderloh):

My heart can't take it! I mean really, you can do no wrong! They [the audience] know what it's about, they're thrilled, they got tickets and they're going to be in the theatre tonight. We could do anything, they'd love it.

I did this for *us*. And I went to all the money people and I said, "It's so big, it will get all the press in the world, and it will justify spending a half million dollars." I just wanted us to have a great party, but I didn't want you all to die and think, "Omigod, my career is going to be over if I'm not brilliant."

I also want to tell you that I never intend to do another show that doesn't have a cast of at least three hundred. I mean it's just more fun than thirty.

I went and I edited the film for LIVE AND IN PERSON, the Finale. It's unbelievable. It's good we did it twice this afternoon because they didn't believe it the first time they saw it. I'm serious. I still don't believe it when I look at it. It's fabulous.

Now let me tell you what happened. First of all I would like to tell the Current New York Company that I have not seen the opening of this show danced or played as well as it was done today since the show opened in London — and T. Michael Reed had beaten everybody to death for months! New York Company, you were fabulous! The tempo was fabulous. Then the Original Company got to stand there suffocating behind their pictures for thirty-two bops. Now, we never got thirty-two bops. The longest was thirteen. Thirty-two bops!

Let me tell you about tonight's audience. Liza's here, Misha's here, Gregory Peck's here … you know, a lot of stars, and then there's all the press. But the point is, tonight I don't want you to do it for them, I want you to do it for you. That's what I want.

This is what happened to the show. Every Company came out and played their chunk of the show like it was the first scene. We're going to play the play. Remember, it's an audition. Just because you didn't play the three scenes before doesn't mean you have to go out and establish yourself as some new character. Theoni Aldredge did a great job, you walk out in the same clothes as the person before you, and they go, "that's the same character," and they're in the play.

We have nothing to worry about, we cannot do any wrong … you are fabulous.

I want to tell you that there is a great deal of paraphrasing of the play going on. Lines are not exactly the way they were. Who cares?!?! You're making the statement, so don't worry about whether you're saying the line exactly right, say it loud enough to be heard.

I'm not stoned, I'm not drunk, this is happiness. Really.

New girls coming on after *Ballet*, when you come back on, don't come back on and sing the end of the number like you didn't sing the whole number. Emotionally, be at the end of the number. That's the trick you have to do as actors tonight. Pick up where the other company left off, not start over.

Chikae, they love you. So wait 'til they finish applauding to say the line that goes into Don's entrance. As long as they applaud, take it.

Tits & Ass girls. So we rehearsed it. So the idea was great. All you've got to do is stop worrying about it now. Girls, stop worrying. As long as the three of you are the three hottest, sexiest, funniest girls that ever lived.

The audience thought, "Oh, this is all the people coming back to sing *What I Did For Love*," and all of a sudden you were gone, and then zillions of people hit the stage for the Finale! They were shocked … it was one of my favorite reactions in the theatre.

I love you.

Directed by Michael Bennett

Michael Bennett and Bob Avian

The Show

Performance #3389

SEPTEMBER 29, 1983, 10:00 PM

SHUBERT THEATRE, NEW YORK CITY

As Company replaced Company, a screen was lowered from the flies and
projections identified which Company was performing.

SONG / SECTION OF SHOW	COMPANY / SOLOIST
The Opening	
I Hope I Get It	The Current New York Company
The Photo and Names Section	The Original Broadway Company
	(Terri Klausner replaced Rene Baughman as Bebe;
	Karen Jablons replaced Pam Blair as Val;
	Eivind Harum replaced Robert LuPone as Zach)
I Can Do That	Wayne Cilento (Mike)
Bobby Monologue / *And*	Thommie Walsh (Bobby)
	(with the Original Company)
At the Ballet	Kelly Bishop (Sheila), Terri Klausner (Bebe),
	Kay Cole (Maggie) (with the Original Company)

Ballet Blaze (last verse of *At the Ballet*) . . . . .The International Company

Sing! . . . . .Kerry Casserly (Kristine), Scott Plank (Al)

Mark Monologue . . . . .Timothy Scott (Mark)

Four Foot Two . . . . .Jennifer Ann Lee (Connie)

Nothing (sung in Japanese) . . . . .Chikae Ishikawa (Diana)

Don Kerr Solo . . . . .David Thomé (Don)

Judy Solo . . . . .Sandahl Bergman (Judy)

Mother Montage . . . . .The National Company

Greg Solo . . . . .Justin Ross (Greg)

Monster Montage . . . . .The Bus & Truck Company

Gimme the Ball .Gordon Owens (Richie) (with the Bus & Truck Company)

Dance: 10, Looks: 3 . . . . .DeLee Lively (Val)
                                                                                      Mitzi Hamilton (Val)
                                                                                      Karen Jablons (Val)

JOSEPH PAPP, MICHAEL BENNETT, THE
BOARD OF DIRECTORS OF THE NEW YORK
SHAKESPEARE FESTIVAL AND THE
SHUBERT ORGANIZATION INVITE YOU TO
THE 3,389TH PERFORMANCE OF A CHORUS LINE
ON THURSDAY, SEPTEMBER 29, 1983
WHEN IT BECOMES THE LONGEST RUNNING SHOW
IN BROADWAY HISTORY.

8:00PM
HORS D'OEUVRES AND CHAMPAGNE IN SHUBERT ALLEY.
9:15PM
SPECIAL CEREMONY CELEBRATING "A CHORUS LINE DAY."
10:00PM
RECORD-BREAKING 3,389TH PERFORMANCE: SHUBERT THEATRE.
12:30AM
THE CELEBRATION CONTINUES IN SHUBERT ALLEY.

BLACK TIE

Short Paul Monologue . . . . .Wayne Meledandri (Paul)

The Music and the Mirror . . . . .Donna McKechnie (Cassie)
(scene, song, and first dance break; the Cassie fly mirrors were
lowered for the slow section, but raised almost immediately
to reveal seven Cassies: Cheryl Clark, Vicki Frederick,
Deborah Henry, Angelique Ilo, Wanda Richert, Ann Louise Schaut ,
and Pam Sousa, who completed the dance with Donna)

Paul Monologue . . . . .Sammy Williams (Paul)
(joined by nine Pauls in a "Greek Chorus":
Tommy Aguilar, Rene Clemente, Steve Crenshaw, Drew Geraci,
Wayne Meledandri, Evan Pappas, George Pesaturo,
SamViverito, and Timothy Wahrer)

One Rehearsal Scene including Cassie/Zach Confrontation Scene . . . . .The Las Vegas Company
Ann Reinking (Cassie)
Joe Bennett (Zach)

The Tap Combination / Paul Accident Scene . . . . .The Chicago Company

The Alternatives Scene . . . . .The Foreign Companies
Each character spoke in a different language,
with Zach's responses in English.

What I Did For Love . . . . .Priscilla Lopez (Diana)
(Original Company joined the Foreign Companies,
along with numerous "ghosts" of each character)

The Elimination Walk . . . . .The Original Company

One (The Finale) . . . . .338 Cast Members
filling the stage of the Shubert and the aisles of the orchestra,
mezzanine and balcony. After the final chorus, the entire cast
for the evening assembled on stage to form 15 rows of
CHORUS LINERS, each row bowing individually, one after
the other, culminating in all 338 dancers coming up from
their bow on one singular sensational count.

Acknowledgments and Thanks . . . . .Michael Bennett

Schedule of Activities for September 29th Celebration

FRIDAY, SEPTEMBER 23RD:

	Costume alterations and fittings continue	Alyce Gilbert
8:00 a.m.-5:00 p.m.	TV lights arrive from Vanco; to be hung and focused by Shubert Electrics Dept.	Bob Valli / John Caggiano
10:00 a.m.	Carpentry Dept. call for shoring up stage, installing extra platform, rehanging black velour, installing projection screen, and building platforms for TV cameras at Messmore	Doc Rennman / Andy Benzinger
	Pick up dressing room lights from Times Square Lighting	Bob Valli
	Set up of dressing room tables, chairs, dividers, mirrors, intercom sound system, and lighting at Booth Theatre	Booth House Crew
	Empty Vanco electric boxes stored in the rear orchestra right at the Booth Theatre	Booth House Crew

Photo by Mitchell Weiss

Setting up Shubert Alley for the party

Chorus Liners on the Shubert stage with the Originals in foreground

Photo by Cliff Lipson

SATURDAY, SEPTEMBER 24TH:

10:00 a.m.	Costume alterations and fittings continue	Alyce Gilbert
12:00	Security badges for cast and Shubert crew prepared at Public Theatre	Mitchell Weiss

SUNDAY, SEPTEMBER 25TH:

All Day	75 actors checking in at the Milford Plaza Hotel	Mitchell Weiss
	No costume work	

A Finale rehearsal

MONDAY, SEPTEMBER 26TH:

9:30 a.m.	Delivery of cast and crew ID badges to Shubert Theatre	Mitchell Weiss
	First rehearsal at Shubert Theatre (full company except Current NY Cast) — 296 actors	Tom Porter
	Juice, coffee, danish, and croissants for above	Alan Bell
	Explanation of dressing room setup, use of Booth Theatre, distribution of badges to cast and crew, posting of sign-up sheet for Tuesday and Wednesday evening performances for all company members not currently on contract (no guests)	Bob MacDonald
	Explanation of financial arrangements for taping of Finale by LIVE AND IN PERSON	Robert Kamlot

11:00 a.m.	Current NY Company joins rehearsal	Tom Porter
	Full rehearsal begins under work lights with explanation of staging and logistics / rehearsal of Finale	Michael Bennett / Bob Avian
	New awning installed outside Shubert	Peter Entin / Bob MacDonald
	Finale hats fitted	Woody Shelp
	Costume fittings continue	Alyce Gilbert
3:00 p.m.	Rehearsal ends at Shubert Theatre:	
	All actors are given some or all of the following:	
	a. Tickets for Thursday matinee and evening performances	Mitchell Weiss / Richard Berg
	b. Posters and tee-shirts	Tim Fischer and assistant
	c. Subway tokens	Chris Gregory and assistant
5:00 p.m.	Rehearsals recommence in smaller groups at 890 Broadway	Michael Bennett / Bob Avian
8:00 p.m.	Regular A CHORUS LINE performance #3385	NY Company

A hug from "Sheila"
Susan Danielle; "Bobby"
Matt West, far left

Warm embraces at the Gala reunion party

TUESDAY, SEPTEMBER 27TH

8:00 a.m.	Projection equipment arrives and is installed at the Shubert	Bob Valli
10:00 a.m.	Rehearsals continue at Shubert and 890 Broadway	Michael Bennett / Bob Avian
	Costume fittings continue	Alyce Gilbert
11:00 a.m.	Still photographers at 890 Broadway	Diane Judge
Afternoon	Orchestra rehearsal	Don Pippin
8:00 p.m.	Regular performance #3386	NY Company
	Rehearsal at 890 Broadway without NY Company	Michael Bennett / Bob Avian
11:00 p.m.	Painting of stage deck at Shubert	Lou Edson

WEDNESDAY, SEPTEMBER 28TH

7:00 a.m.	Apple Security begins with four men	George Maggio
	Police barriers arrive	Sarg. Walters of Manhattan South
	Carpet installation begins	Fred Williamson
All Day	Deliveries of party supplies, food, beverages, etc. to be stored in Booth Theatre lower lounge	Alan Bell / Tom Pritchard
	Management person on premises all day	Robert Kamlot / Bob MacDonald / Richard Berg / Mitchell Weiss
10:00 a.m.	8' x 30' operations van to be delivered by Cerco Products to be stationed in the west bay of Minskoff Bldg. loading dock to serve as command post for security, management, and press	Bob MacDonald
	Banner rigging on 44th and 45th Streets (no traffic interference)	Capelli Erectors
	Installation of 16 A CHORUS LINE three sheets (without snipe) on west side of Shubert Alley	Shubert Bill Postet
10:00 a.m.- 12:00	Tech rehearsal at Shubert Theatre	Michael Bennett / Bob Avian
2:00 p.m.	Regular performance #3387	NY Company
4:30 p.m.- 6:00 p.m.	Tech rehearsal at Shubert Theatre (without NY Company)	Michael Bennett / Bob Avian
8:00 p.m.	Regular performance #3388	NY Company
	Possible rehearsal at 890 Broadway (without NY Company)	Michael Bennett / Bob Avian

11:00 p.m.	Shubert Alley closed	George Maggio
	Tent erection begins	Tom Pritchard

THURSDAY, SEPTEMBER 29TH

6:00 a.m.	Unitel Star mobile truck arrives / to be parked on 45th Street in front of Booth	David Nash
7:00 a.m.	LIVE AND IN PERSON crew begins camera load-in / lighting call	David Nash
8:00 a.m.	Lincoln Center mobile truck arrives / to be parked on 45th Street in front of Plymouth	Betty Corwin
	Decoration inside tent continues (has been going on throughout the night): installation of mylar panels, bars, tables, chairs, flowers, etc.	Tom Pritchard

Photo by Cliff Lipson

An expectant Carol Marik

	Sound and electrics installed in tent	Tom Pritchard / Bob MacDonald / Bill Dreisbach
	Signs redirecting public to Ma Bell's set-up	Bob MacDonald
	Lincoln Center load-in begins	Betty Corwin
9:30 a.m.	Full tech rehearsal call: all actors except NY Company	Michael Bennett / Bob Avian
	Breakfast for cast	Alan Bell
	Checks issued to cast for TV payment	Robert Kamlot / Bob MacDonald
	Management person on premises all day	Kamlot / MacDonald / Berg / Weiss
10:15 a.m.	NY Company joins rehearsal	
10:30 a.m.- 12:30 p.m.	Blocking of Finale for TV cameras	Michael Bennett / Dick Stucker
12:30 p.m.	House clean up at Shubert	Alex Witchel
1:00 p.m.	2 additional security men (now 6-man total)	George Maggio
1:30 p.m.	44th Street exit doors open to admit audience for special black tie dress rehearsal	Alex Witchel
2:00 p.m.	Black tie dress rehearsal begins / Michael Bennett will ask audience to remain for second taping of Finale (rows J and K emptied) — LIVE AND IN PERSON shoots two takes of Finale / TV news crews shoot news footage	Michael Bennett
3:00 p.m.	TV monitors and 9' x 12' projection screen installed in Booth	Richard Ryan
	Half of catering crew arrives for set up in Booth and in tent	Alan Bell

Kerry Casserly in a moment with Cher

5:00 p.m.	Skytrackers and generators arrive to be set up on 44th Street	Joe Macada
	LIVE AND IN PERSON cameras removed from Shubert	David Nash
	Second house clean up in Shubert	Alex Witchel
6:00 p.m.	LuEsther Mertz dinner party at Algonquin Hotel	
6:00 p.m.	Security to full 12-man crew in black tie	George Maggio
8:00 p.m.	Shubert Alley party begins — champagne and hors d'oeuvres	Alan Bell / Tom Pritchard and all management
	2 men to open limousine doors	Richard Berg
9:15 p.m.	Ceremony on platform begins with various speakers	Joseph Papp, M.C.
10:00 p.m.	Scheduled time for SPECIAL INVITED BLACK TIE PERFORMANCE #3389 to begin. Actual performance time to be between 10:15 and 10:30. Performance to be taped by Lincoln Center for the Performing Arts for archival use	Michael Bennett et al. / Betty Corwin / Dick Stucker

1:00 a.m.	Approximate time performance ends / Party resumes in Shubert Alley with full buffet dinner and open bar	
2:30 a.m.	Skytrackers depart	Joe Macada
4:00 a.m. - 5:00 a.m.	Party ends and load-out begins	

FRIDAY, SEPTEMBER 30TH

Party cleanup continues / load-out of supplies, removal of tent and carpeting, removal of operations van	Bob MacDonald / Tom Pritchard / Alan Bell / Fred Williamson
2 security men remain until completion	George Maggio
At a time to be determined, but in no event earlier than eight hours after the end of the Thursday night performance, the company and house crews will be called for takeouts	Robert Kamlot

Joel Grey, Terri Klausner, and Thommie Walsh

Performance 3389 — One Singular Sensation!

*D*uring a rehearsal of the **Montage**, something was going wrong musically on stage; it just wasn't working. So I stopped the orchestra and said, "We'll start from here and continue." That's what an opera conductor does, and what I was used to. We got through the end of the number and Michael called a ten-minute break. I was standing in the pit, looking over the score, when Michael leaned over my shoulder and said, "Uh, Maestro, at the Metropolitan <u>you</u> stop the rehearsal. On Broadway, <u>I</u> stop the rehearsal. You got it?"

ALPHONSE STEPHENSON
Conductor

STATIC ON THE LINE

SURPRISES & THE UNEXPECTED

People

When Betty Ford came, the Secret Service asked if there was anything unusual that happened in the show. Thinking they were referring to gunshots, I said, "No." Then I remembered that Zach comes running down the aisle, right past where the First Lady was sitting. They said, "It's a good thing you told us; he would have never made it to the stage. We would have tackled him."

PHIL SMITH
Vice President, Shubert Organization

Somebody who looked like me was sitting in the front row of the orchestra, script in hand, mouthing the words. I was furious, thinking this was someone up for my role, watching me. I got paranoid. While offstage for the *Nothing* break, I told the stage manager how upset I was. Later, I saw him talking to this person. The stage manager reported back as follows: "The guy is hearing impaired and when he bought his tickets, he requested a script so he could follow along." Talk about feeling three inches tall!

JUSTIN ROSS
Greg

"There was a whole diagram on paper of who does what lines, who does the vocals, who does the accident scene. But of course, there was always this scramble of "What the hell am I supposed to do now?" — PATTI D'BECK

The State Department called and asked for forty free tickets to the show on Friday night for the Iran Hostages, who had just returned to the United States. Joe Papp, as only Joe could be, said, "These poor people — I want them to see the show, but I do not want them to be harassed. No media publicity stunt. I want it to be for them." But of course, Thursday night the hostages saw SUGAR BABIES and got media coverage like you wouldn't believe. Friday morning, Joe called Bob Kamlot: "We have to make a statement, we have to do something." Kamlot called me and said, "Joe wants an American flag to fly in at the end of the show, instead of the sunburst. It has to be the whole size of the stage." I remarked, "I thought we weren't going to do anything!" Here it is Friday morning, they are seeing the show that night and Joe wants an American flag that's forty feet wide! Fortunately, we obtained a flag from a recently closed show and it was a great statement.

BOB MacDONALD
Company & General Manager

Lights, Leaks, & Mirrors

The night the President and his wife came to see the show, the lighting board went crazy. I got a call about 6:30 that it just blew up. The backup system gave about 75% of the show, so we lost a lot running the show that night. Since we were using preset boards, I had to cut many cues through the show. When the lighting board failed, the lights would all come up full; they would fail on, not off.

THARON MUSSER
Lighting Designer

I remember our electrician on the phone to Oregon patching this computerized lighting system with chewing gum, scotch tape, and paper clips to keep it going.

JEFF HAMLIN
Original Production Stage Manager

In London, during the Cassie dance, as we brought down the fly mirrors, the supports in the grid gave way and all the mirrors fell all over the place.

JEFF HAMLIN
Original Production Stage Manager

I was there the night of the Con Ed blackout. Everyone was ready to go on after Paul's monologue and the lights in the basement started to fade in and out. All of a sudden, everything went black. George Pesaturo, playing Paul, stood on stage for the longest time because he just thought the lighting computer went out. They got flashlights and the next thing was, "Done, go home."

CYNTHIA ONRUBIA
Connie; Understudy

July 13, 1977. George was out on stage doing the Paul monologue when all of a sudden the spotlight went out and the emergency lights came on. We thought it was us, of course — that the power went out in the building for some reason. I made an announcement to the audience, "We're experiencing some power problems and have to momentarily delay the continuation of the show." Then someone looked out the door and saw there were no lights at all on the streets. I had a quick talk with our company manager, and we decided to explain the situation to the audience. When we first said it was just the building, the audience was fine. But when we said that the blackout affected the whole city, people started panicking and everybody headed out of the theatre into the darkened streets.

PETER VON MAYRHAUSER
Stage Manager

It rained inside the Shubert Theatre. There was a leak either in the skylight or the roof. Rainstorm after rainstorm, it would literally rain on our set. The actor playing Larry would have to come offstage, get towels, and mop the floor during the show. The cast had to avoid this big puddle upstage left. The audience could hear water dripping during quiet moments when there was no musical underscoring.

BOB REILLY
Company Manager

It tended to leak on top of Al's head. It would actually be raining on Al and Kristine during the show.

LAURIE GAMACHE
Cassie

Once on the road, I was looking up to sing "Listen to you mother," and a pocket of water from the rafters gushed down on me. I was totally soaked. Another time, in a theatre in Wisconsin, three bats came at me during my entire Cassie dance. It was really frightening. I never did so many head pops in my life.

DEBORAH HENRY
Cassie

On opening night at the Pantages Theatre in Los Angeles, I did the Cassie dance with no mirrors. They didn't turn around, nor did they come down from the flies. That's a terrifying feeling because there is nothing to spot and nothing to look at, just pitch black. It throws your equilibrium off.

WANDA RICHERT
Cassie

Threats

We had done the opening, and I was downstairs in the shower when we heard an announcement, "Everyone get dressed and leave the theatre immediately." I didn't know what was going on, so I towelled off and waited with the Company across the alley. We were eventually told it was a bomb threat. They moved everyone out of the theatre. Zach made some announcement, "Everyone on stage please leave immediately. Audience, please, in a calm fashion, collect your belongings and go out into the alley until further notice." We waited forty-five minutes while they looked through the theatre. We were then able to come back, and resumed the show from where we left off.

FRASER ELLIS
Understudy

During one performance on Broadway, all of a sudden Zach called to Paul out of context. "I would like you to turn to your left and lead the line offstage immediately. Do not ask me any questions. Would the line please follow Paul and walk directly out the stage door." We were out in Shubert Alley and told there had been a bomb threat. They cleared out the audience and it was a good half hour before we were brought back in.

LOIS ENGLUND
Val

About the time Lauren Bacall's movie, THE FAN, came out, I had problems with someone calling the theatre. One morning, Wendy Mansfield, a stage manager, phoned and asked if I was all right. She said they had just gotten a call at the theatre that I was hurt in the subway. I hadn't even left the house that day. Wendy told me they were getting other strange calls about me, but I never listened to them. That night, right before I stepped forward to do my name, I saw someone walking down the aisle towards the stage. Where I stood on the line as Connie was right in front of the aisle, and I remember thinking, "I can't just run off." The guy was just going to his seat.

JANET WONG
Connie

There was a lunatic who threatened to come in with a machine gun and kill us all. For several months, the wires were tapped and we had undercover agents at the Shubert. Michael Bennett said, "Finally, we have tension on the line," because something would move and we would jump.

DEBORAH HENRY
Cassie

Injuries

Mark Fotopolous, an understudy who was on for Paul, hurt his knee in the opening jazz combination. The music kept going ahead but Mark had to be carried off and the opening got totally messed up. The orchestra was out of synch with what was on stage. Cheryl Clark, playing Cassie, handled it.

CYNTHIA ONRUBIA
Connie; Understudy

Eivind Harum was on for Zach but didn't control the situation. Something needed to be done quickly, the orchestra continued playing, but nothing was happening. So I took charge. I didn't scream into the orchestra pit but rather told Eivind to, "Take it from the *funky chicken*," so he, as Zach, could relay the message to the conductor and we could wrap up the opening. It was a perfect spot to pick it up from.

CHERYL CLARK
Cassie

I was the first one to have a knee injury. I was the one in the Original Company who lived out the Paul story and that's when I left the show.

TRISH GARLAND
Original Judy

The strap on my shoe broke and I had to finish the Cassie dance with one shoe on and one shoe off. In stocking feet, you're just slipping all over the place. I re-choreographed instantly, but thank God it was toward the end.

I got my heel caught in my skirt, and went straight down into a "dying swan" position and did a backward slide almost into the wings.

ANN REINKING
Cassie

I wasn't really in shape, I hadn't tumbled a lot, and standing on the line was rough. I actually had to ice my knees every night. My number, *I Can Do That*, was like being shot out of a cannon because it's running back and forth, singing and acrobatics. My body wasn't used to it and I ripped a stomach muscle about two weeks into the run. I couldn't get up from a chair for a week; it was probably the worst injury I've ever had. Of course, I was mortified — my first Broadway show and injured two weeks into it. But then I went six and a half months without missing a show, which was great for that particular role. So I felt like I redeemed myself.

MICHAEL GRUBER
Mike

I went through two knee operations because of the show — or because of my lack of warming up. My knees got seriously screwed up.

SCOTT PEARSON
Zach

The Show Must Go On

I was on the night Kelly Bishop walked off the stage. It was my first time performing on the line as Bebe and I was horrified, thinking my performance was so terrible that Kelly left the stage! Zach tried to keep her on, but Kelly left. You could hear pages flipping in the orchestra, because we were obviously cutting *At the Ballet* and skipping to *Sing*. Michael felt the audience got so in touch with the characters that if we were up to or through *At the Ballet* and an actor couldn't finish the show, the understudy would not continue for them. There was a whole diagram on paper of who does what lines, who does the vocals, who does the accident scene. These were scenarios that we were supposed to be prepared for. But of course, there was always this scramble of "What the hell am I supposed to do now?"

PATTI D'BECK
Understudy

Tracy Shayne and I, the understudies, were in our dressing room, the Bungalow, after the opening number. I had just showered and was looking pretty shabby — no bra, just an A CHORUS LINE sweat shirt, dance pants, and these ridiculous silver slippers. Somebody ran up to the dressing room saying, "One of you has got to get dressed, Bebe's just left the stage." By this time, Sheila was already into her verse of *At The Ballet*, with Bebe's solo coming up next. I ran down the stairs in my silver slippers, flipped my sweatshirt inside out and made it to the stage just in time.

DIANE FRATANTONI
Understudy

One day at the beach I didn't realize I was getting too much sun. That night on stage, just before we turn around and walk upstage for *At the Ballet*, I felt this flush. I thought, "Oh no, I have sunstroke." We had learned that if something dramatic or traumatic was happening on stage, pass the information down the line towards Baayork, our dance captain. Then somehow it passed offstage to stage management. So it was passed down the line that I was feeling really sick, and they rushed to get my understudy ready. Upstage, in the dark, I walked off, the stage manager caught me as I fainted, and Donna Drake replaced me.

KAY COLE
Original Maggie

After I got pregnant with my daughter, they thought it would be best if I left the show because I was getting heavy, I was tired, and my voice was very low. At times, I was pushing to produce sound in the songs. I knew I couldn't continue performing that way. When I lost my voice, the Maggie would sing the rest of *What I Did For Love*. We planned it out: I'd signal when I would feel my voice going, she would look at me, walk in front and sing the rest of the song.

LOIDA SANTOS
Diana

Photo by Troy Garza

CHAPTER 11

REFLECTIONS ON MICHAEL

> *"He was the perfect person, a national treasure.*
> *He put names on the map that never were there before*
> *and never have been since."* — STEVE BOOCKVOR

Michael Bennett: The Boss Is in the Wings!

THARON MUSSER: Michael's shows were sheer heaven for a designer because on his first teching a show he wouldn't leave a scene until he was satisfied. He could take quite a while to tech a show that way, but when it was done, it was done. Working with him was the most fun I've ever had in the the-

Photo by Cliff Lipson

atre, or ever will. Bob Avian once asked me, "How do you always know what Michael is going to want?" "I pray a lot."

JONATHAN TUNICK: Michael had that quality of leadership you associate with dictators and great generals. I know a lot of people assigned him the role of more than a leader, almost a parent figure. Some got involved emotionally with him on one level or another. They would expect more of him than he was prepared to give and he let a lot of people down that way. I always understood where Michael was coming from. He would throw his arms around you and say, "Darling, I'll never do a show without you." I didn't take him literally — I just thought, "He likes what I did *today*." I always had a great time with Michael and was happy when he asked me to work with him.

JEFF HAMLIN: Michael would call me at 2:00 in the morning: "How was it? What do you think?" I felt he valued my opinion and thought of me as special — until I

realized, as we went along, that this was just a habit of Michael's.

BOBBY THOMAS: At 1:30 every morning we would discuss what we were going to do the next day.

ANGELIQUE ILO: Michael was the best ego-stroker in the world. He would call you at 2:00 in the morning and talk to you about what he was doing and how wonderful and fabulous you are. It would make you work harder for him. He knew exactly how to operate and get what he wanted.

STEVE BOOCKVOR: Always waking you up with the three o'clock call. I guess he felt he had an edge on you. Michael, to me, was the perfect person, a national treasure. He felt he knew better — whether or not you should still be in the show. He put names on the map that never were there before and never have been since.

BERNIE JACOBS: During the take-in at the Shubert, Michael told Bob Avian to see

if Otts Munderloh would handle the sound for the show. Bobby came back and reported that Otts would love to do the show, but he's working for Bob Fryer on CHICAGO and doesn't know how to tell Bob he wants to leave. Michael said to Bob Avian, "Tell Otts to tell Bobby Fryer that he's sleeping with me and I insist he come over to work my show." I said to Michael, "When will you pull that kind of shit on me?" and he said, "You're too smart, I would never try that with you." But he was full of shit — he was playing me. It was a matter of manipulating all of us. He loved to manipulate.

MATTHEW SERINO: Michael was a very generous person, just a fun-loving guy. And if you were his friend, you were his friend.

OTTS MUNDERLOH: In 1978, when my building went co-op, I didn't have the down payment. Michael gave me a loan. I paid him back, but he was really there for me.

SCOTT ALLEN: There was a huge blow-up at the theatre, right out of the blue. All of a sudden Michael stood up screaming, "I want everybody out of the theatre. Except my line — I just want my line on stage." All the understudies went down to the dressing rooms. The creative staff was by the elevator, asking each other, "Did you do something?" People were crying and carrying on. It was at that point I saw what Bob Avian's real role was, aside from being a good choreographer. He was soothing and stroking, saying, "It's just Michael, don't get upset."

ALPHONSE STEPHENSON: Michael used to wear Acqua di Selva cologne. It's nothing exclusive, you could buy it over the counter. I would keep a bottle of it in my locker downstairs. Any time the show would get sloppy, I would go backstage at around 6:30 and spray Acqua di Selva in the wings. Everyone would think Michael Bennett was around somewhere. It would change the complexion of the show. We had a stage hand that looked very much like Michael. One of the stage managers put a baseball cap on this guy and had him peek out from the wings like Michael would do — and all of a sudden, the whole show changed.

WANDA RICHERT: Everybody had such heightened energy when Michael was watching and, I think, a certain fear. I always felt, "Thank God he's here. I feel so calm." I always loved being around Michael's energy. Even though he had some really mean things to say to me and everybody else, in directing, he knew how to get something out of a person like I've never seen before. If you needed to be put down to get the result out of you, he would do it. He'd get the emotion and say, "Now, hold on to that." Then he'd be loving again.

SCOTT PEARSON: Michael would monitor the show in New York but only let Tom Porter know he was coming. Michael's technique was to come in stage left, which was next to the stage manager's office, and slowly move closer and closer to the actual stage in the wings. Playing Zach from the back of the house, I could see as the awareness of his presence swept through the Company. All of a sudden people got taller and straighter. They were scared to death.

Photo by Troy Garza

Michael vacationed with Betty and Bernard Jacobs through China by train

JUSTIN ROSS: It was creepy. Michael was so intimidating. Everybody's spine grew six inches longer. The boss is in the wings!

STEVE BOOCKVOR: Everybody was on key. The musicians were playing better and the dancers jumped higher, everything was tighter when Michael was in the wings. I wasn't afraid of Michael, he was my friend, a father image. I'd be in my Zach chair in the back of the theatre and Michael would talk to me and give me directorial notes as the show went on. I would get crazy because I had to concentrate on lines.

DONN SIMIONE: I was sitting in the Zach chair during a matinee and felt something punch me in the arm. I thought it was an audience member. Then I was hit a little harder and finally looked over and it was Michael, smiling at me. He stood next to me the entire show and directed me as it was going on. I remember him telling me during the Cassie scene, "Give it to her, really give it to her." Whatever Michael said was always correct. He had an uncanny ability to know what would work and all you had to do was just listen to him.

ANTHONY INNEO: The show *should* have been the juice. Unfortunately, the fear of Michael became the juice, the fear of being fired. Someone being fired meant a shot of terror that would get the show going and Michael always knew it. It would always goose the company up, get that extra spark, that energy.

RICHARD BERG: The most incredible moment was on the first day of rehearsal for the Gala when Michael did the Cassie dance. It was magic. Seeing him dance the number, you realized that although it was designed for Donna McKechnie's body, there was a lot of Michael Bennett in it. He did it the best.

GERRY SCHOENFELD: Michael wasn't very receptive to input. He knew what he was doing, and he knew when it was not right. But Michael was not one who solicited opinions. I never really "hung out" with Michael, although he was a very

good friend. As he proceeded from A CHORUS LINE on to other things, the number of friends — court attendants, sycophants, the entourage — grew and grew, so our relationship became less intimate than it was earlier on.

BERNIE JACOBS: One day Michael told me, "We really shouldn't be such good friends because I want to be a producer, and I want people to think I'm independent. I don't want everyone to think I only work for the Shuberts."

BERNIE GERSTEN: What Michael got from me was support, up and down the line. But Michael didn't need second guesses. He demanded and got what he needed and wanted from anybody.

BERNIE JACOBS: Michael always said he was neither homosexual nor heterosexual, he was just sexual. Back in the seventies, we were naive about the whole subject of homosexuality and I stupidly made the comment to Michael, "Why don't you straighten out and marry Donna?" About ten days later, Michael invited my wife and me to dinner. He picked us up in the white Rolls Royce he just had given to Donna as an engagement present, and announced they were going to get married. I asked my wife, "Do you think I'm responsible for this marriage? Because God knows what will happen." I look upon that "straighten

out" comment as the most absurd thing I could have said.

KATE WRIGHT: Michael would come into rehearsals and at times be a maniac, screaming at people. It was terrifying. When he was nice, he was adorable, but he was very unpredictable back then and, hence, the terror.

MURPHY CROSS: You learned the fear factor because Michael could be intense, so biting and sarcastic. He was never that way to me because I assume he knew how vulnerable I was.

ANTHONY INNEO: If you kissed his ass, you were in trouble. If you showed him who you were, he gravitated to you. Michael liked individuals. He liked people who knew who they were. He did not like the people who bowed, he would destroy them.

ANN REINKING: Michael was so quiet, sometimes he was perceived as being cold — but he wasn't, he was very sweet. I had dinner with him once; he was taking his "next" Cassie to dinner, saying welcome. And he was quite chatty. The dinner wasn't anything other than what he was supposed to do.

DEBORAH HENRY: He was shy, but I couldn't get enough of him. If he were living today, I would devote twenty years of

my life to him, because I know working with Michael Bennett, I would be the best.

VICKI FREDERICK: At one point during the rehearsal period, all the Cassies — this little sorority in red skirts — were doing the number over and over. Michael would have two or three of us do it together in certain segments. One day as we were going to lunch he said, "Vicki, can you stay for a minute," just like in the show. He asked me to do the scene, the song, and the number all alone. I don't think Michael was really serious about me taking over anybody's role. I was part of his manipulation. He announced it while all the girls were milling around, so that the people who would be mostly affected by it could hear. I knew I was an understudy somewhere, so I didn't feel the pressure that Ann Reinking and Sandra Roveta [International Company Cassie] were feeling. I didn't know why he was doing this, other than to say "shape up" to the other two girls. Their double turns got real good after lunch. That's why he did it. I'm not saying anything negative about Michael. Bob Fosse did the same thing. You do what you do to get what you need out of your dancer.

"The most incredible moment was on the first day of rehearsal for the Gala when Michael did the Cassie dance. … He did it the best."
— Richard Berg

Photo by Troy Garza

BOB ULLMAN: Michael took a lot of minor talent and pulled them up to his level of creativity. From a press standpoint, Michael constantly said, "I want you to take care of all of those people. To me, they are all important." He was talking about the "line" and he couldn't have been more supportive of them.

BOB MacDONALD: Michael hadn't been to the theatre in a long time, and the stage doors at the Shubert had changed. He tried to open the old stage door, which was still there but locked. He didn't even notice the new door, and finally someone said, "Mr. Bennett, the stage door is on this side." He came in screaming at Tom Porter and me, "Don't ever change the stage door without telling the director you've changed the stage door. How dare you do that!"

FRASER ELLIS: The night he died, July 2, 1987, I remember a lot of people came to see the show, and backstage, we decided on our own to change the words from "She" to "He" in the finale of *One*. It was our way of doing a tribute, independent of anybody and without anyone's permission.

BOBBY THOMAS: I hadn't heard from Michael, and couldn't make contact with

Michael's photo was lowered at the final Actors' Fund benefit which was held on his birthday, April 8

him for a year. He passed away, and there was no closure. There was no saying, "It was good knowing you, thanks for being a part of my life."

FRAN LIEBERGALL: Michael was magical. He could say two words to a performer that would change their entire performance. The cast felt a loss when he didn't come around during DREAMGIRLS. After Michael died, Bobby [Avian] couldn't handle being around. So it really became Tom Porter, Troy Garza, and myself. It was our responsibility to make the show what we hoped Michael would like.

LAURIE GAMACHE : Tom Porter called me an hour before I was leaving for the airport for my brother's wedding. He said, "Could you please not go, we really need you to be here tonight because Michael died this morning. I'd like to have the whole company here so everyone can just hang on the best they can without any added pressures." All the creative staff and people who had any connection with the show came back. I was angry because I waited all those years to prove myself to Michael. I hoped he would see me as Cassie someday and give me the recognition I'd been waiting for. He was gone and I never got that. I was the Cassie he never knew.

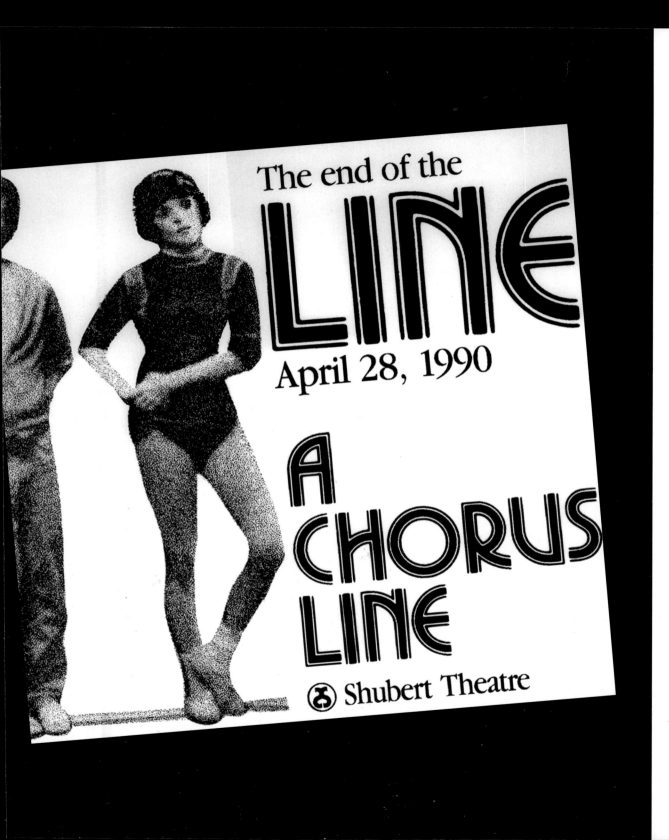

CHAPTER 12

THE
END
OF THE
LINE

> *"When we talked to Joe about closing, it was like sticking a dagger into him. He just loved the idea of having the longest running show on Broadway."* — BERNARD JACOBS

Deciding to Close

SCOTT ALLEN [Original Understudy]: A CHORUS LINE should have been Broadway's answer to THE FANTASTICKS.

BOB MacDONALD [Company & General Manager]: Everyone thought it was going to go on forever. But with Joe's illness, a lot of the will of the Festival towards A CHORUS LINE subsided. As long as Joe was there to fight the battles, we would have gone on. But the Festival was facing financial problems in general; we weren't having great seasons at the Public either. And we had lost a lot of money. The Festival put up all its own bucks on SECRET RAPTURE, PLENTY, and SERIOUS MONEY. Our $30 million endowment was dwindling quickly. We got to the point where A CHORUS LINE was a couple of hundred thousand dollars down that year, and we finally thought about closing the show.

It was actually a very quick decision. We briefly considered moving the show to Off-Broadway, but Joe just didn't want to do it. He wanted it to be over and equally wanted to capitalize on its closing. Of course, there were other practical factors involved. We would soon need to replace costumes, mirrors, sunbursts, piano, deck, flats. We had always kept the show in peak condition. We were looking at a big investment of money, and with the prospect of Joe not being there, it was time for it to go.

We still retained first class touring rights within the U.S. The negotiations for the Visa-sponsored national tour which followed were very strong. It was really a question of whether the Festival should produce the tour, as it had in the past, or farm it out. We knew about touring people; they were notorious for pocketing the dollars. But it was a matter of us putting up another million dollars, and Joe just didn't want to do that.

BOB REILLY [Final Company Manager]: We all saw it coming and were working on ways of keeping it alive. One of the ideas was to negotiate a long-term lease at the Music Box Theatre, get a corporate sponsor like AT&T or American Express, put their name over the title, on the signs, in the programs. I forget the numbers involved, but it wasn't much to subsidize the show. The idea was to negotiate a special Equity contract to get costs to a certain point where the show would literally run forever. But it all fell through because Irving Berlin, who owned the theatre and was still alive at the time, wouldn't give us the lease on the Music Box. We all knew it was going to close unless we did something, so it was no surprise when the inevitable happened — but I didn't think it would happen so quickly. I was involved with the closing night party, and all of the press, which was crazy. We were a media phenomenon, and it was an absolute feeding frenzy as the date got closer. Every night we would post a sign announcing what news crew would be filming backstage.

At one point we had four camera crews in every nook and cranny. Closing night we took a row of seats out from the back

to get an extra row of cameras in. We had something like twelve cameras back there, and CNN out on the sidewalk.

BERNARD JACOBS [President, Shubert Organization]: What should have happened with A CHORUS LINE was about four or five months before it closed, going into that summer, they should have announced last 10, 12, or 15 weeks. They would have done banner business. They did good business when they did announce it, but they would have done better if it had been much earlier on.

When we talked to Joe about closing, it was like sticking a dagger into him. He just loved the idea of having the longest running show on Broadway. But it could not have stayed open. It was consistently losing money at the end, even with all kinds of royalty breaks and rent reductions. It had reached the end of the line. Unless you had Michael around to do something spectacular again, like the record breaking performance to give it a new shot in the arm, A CHORUS LINE was over. It had really worn its audience out; fifteen years is a long time. We thought at one point moving it would have been a good thing to do. But it was Joe's show, he had to call the shots, not us. I would have closed it earlier, but when I suggested it to Joe on a couple of occasions, he suspected we wanted the theatre for something else! Toward the end of the run, the producers of 3 PENNY OPERA

with Sting desperately wanted the Shubert Theatre. We duly passed that information on to Joe. He said he wasn't going to close A CHORUS LINE, and that was the end of the discussion. 3 PENNY went to the Lunt-Fontanne, and it was a big flop.

We then made up our minds that we were never going to close A CHORUS LINE. If the show closed, it would be Joe's decision. Of course, he closed it a couple of months after that anyway, but he made the decision all by himself. The last week it did capacity, we suggested to him perhaps he could do another five weeks, and he said, "No, it's closing."

PHIL SMITH [Vice President, Shubert Organization]: We told Joe he had to announce the closing, to give people the chance to see it. He committed to four weeks, and we started to do very well, and said, "Joe, you have to do it again." He said, "How could I? I've already said it's closing. How do you know they'll come?" He was reluctant, worried he was deceiving the public, that people bought tickets thinking it was closing and it wasn't. I told him, "You haven't deceived them, you've done them a big favor — you've gotten them to see it." The show probably should have announced "Last Six Months." We got him to extend once, but it could have been longer. Joe was definitive: "That's it, I'm closing the show."

Top: "A CHORUS LINE may run forever," said Joe Papp in a New York Daily News *article January 4, 1990*

Bottom: Ironically, Mr. Papp held a press conference announcing its closing just seven weeks later

Papp: 'Chorus Line' will keep kicking

Fifteen years. Over 6,000 performances. An institution as revered as, well, the chorus line. "A Chorus Line" may run forever, said producer Joseph Papp yesterday. So don't believe what you may've heard that 1990 will mean curtains for the longest-running show in Broadway history.

When he *does* decide to call it quits, Papp will give the public ample notice — "six months."

"The fact is that we are making money," said Papp. "And as long as we're making money, we're going to run. It's true we're not making as much as we once did, but we *were* in the black in 1989. We made over $300,000 profit."

During Christmas week, the show pulled in more than $330,000 on a weekly operating budget of $160,000 — minuscule compared with other shows. And to stimulate business, Papp yesterday announced a January weekday reduction of mezzanine seats to $15.

But Papp admitted that the show may eventually have to move to a smaller theater so that the Shubert may be refurbished.

"In a smaller house, with union help, we could lower our costs substantially," said Papp. "If that happens, we could run forever."

A CHORUS LINE

TO: NEWS, PHOTO & TV ASSIGNMENT EDITORS
FROM: Merle Debuskey/ Bruce Campbell (212)

JOSEPH PAPP INVITES YOU
TO A PRESS CONFERENCE
ON WEDNESDAY, FEBRUARY 21, 1990
AT 12:15 P.M.
AT THE SHUBERT THEATRE
ON W. 44TH STREET (CORNER OF SHUBERT ALLEY)

THE NEWS ANNOUNCED WILL COMMAND INK AND AIR TIME, IMPELLED AS IT IS BY A SIGNIFICANT MOMENT IN THE MOST CHRONICLED, LUSTROUS, SCINTILLATING AND BELOVED SAGA IN THE HISTORY OF THE BROADWAY THEATRE.

MERLE DEBUSKEY & ASSOCIATES
Publicity/300 West 55th Street/New York, New York 10019

NEW YORK SHAKESPEARE FESTIVAL

Joseph Papp Producer

April 16, 1990

A CHORUS LINE Company
Shubert Theatre
225 West 44th Street
New York, New York 10036

Dear Company:

In compliance with Actors' Equity Association and the other unions, this letter will serve as your official one week's notice of the closing of the production. A CHORUS LINE will have its final performance on Saturday evening, April 28, 1990.

Sincerely,

Joe Papp

BERNARD GERSTEN [Associate Producer, NYSF]: I had been in to see it some time before the closing announcement, and it was very depressing for me. The orchestra section was only half full, there were no laughs, there was no reaction, and I thought, "Why are they doing this?" It was too painful. I was relieved when it closed.

THARON MUSSER [Lighting Designer]: It was time and I think Michael would have thought it was time. It certainly didn't owe us anything.

NANCY COYNE [Creative Director: Serino Coyne Inc.]: Closing was not the wrong thing to do. Because of the number of touring companies and the length of time it had run in New York, it really had exhausted both its primary audience and its secondary audience. I'm not saying the show was dated, but the show was fixed in a time, and that time was gone. I don't think it was the wrong decision; it was just a real sad feeling.

DON PIPPIN [Original Musical Director; Vocal Arranger]: It was a show everyone thought would run forever and ever and ever. Not CATS, but A CHORUS LINE. Somebody, it may have been Joe Papp, wanted me to conduct closing night, and I refused to do it only because I thought it would throw the cast. But I said to Fran, "Let's do the opening number. Let's start it." We played the opening number, and we both came back in the pit for the bows. I was so aware at that point of the people who are no longer with us, dancers whom we had lost to AIDS. That was very much on everybody's mind that night.

"It was very depressing for me. The orchestra section was only half full, there were no laughs, there was no reaction, and I thought, 'Why are they doing this?' It was too painful." — *BERNARD GERSTEN*

Last Weeks

BOB REILLY: The Actors' Fund Benefit for Equity Fights Aids (EFA) on April 8 was such a proud night. Kevin McCready, Larry in the show, was the one who brought it up to us. We tried doing one before the first announcement of the closing, but there was no date that we could clear, so when we got the extension, Kevin pushed for it. Joe gave us the go-ahead and it coincided with Michael Bennett's birthday, a special reason to do it that night. Kevin worked his butt off trying to sell every ticket in the house. Going backstage to all the theatres, handing out flyers at TKTS. The rest of us jumped on the bandwagon and did what we could, but it was Kevin's benefit as far as I was concerned.

KEVIN McCREADY [Final Larry]: I basically just got the ball rolling and Tom Viola of EFA did everything else.

KEITH BERNARDO [Final Don]: That performance was the most incredible evening I've ever spent in the theatre. Everyone in the audience was throwing so much love to the people on the stage, who in turn were throwing the love to the audience. It felt like the reason I went into theatre. Nothing has ever come close to that.

JACK NOSEWORTHY [Final Mark; Last cast member hired]: To perform a show

about gypsies for all the gypsies on Broadway was absolutely the most thrilling performance in the entire ten weeks I ended up doing the show.

RON STAFFORD [Assistant Stage Manager]: It was the beginning of rethinking no job, no security — all of the things you hate in the business. On top of all that, knowing there would probably never be anything like this again.

By the time the final event rolled around, Tom Porter, who had been out front, reported that you couldn't see the stage from the back of the house because of the television cameras completely lined up where standing room was. I remember Tom backstage saying, "I just want you to know it's a madhouse out there. I feel like this show doesn't belong to us anymore; the afternoon performance was our last show."

KEITH BERNARDO: We were all called downstairs and told there's a big meeting tomorrow. They didn't say anything about the closing, but the next day Joe Papp came to the theatre and made the announcement to the press. The first thing was tears, then shock set in, then you felt incredibly special because you knew you were in the Final Company of A CHORUS LINE. Suddenly the whole Company bonded. As

A CHORUS LINE

FROM: Merle Debuskey

FOR IMMEDIATE RELEASE, PLEASE.

FOUR MORE WEEKS FOR "A CHORUS LINE"!!
RESPONDING TO OVERWHELMING DEMAND, PRODUCER
JOSEPH PAPP AVERS "POSITIVELY" FINAL PERFORMANCE ON APRIL 28
****

Due to the overwhelming response to the announcement that A CHORUS LINE will close on March 31st, Joseph Papp announced today that A CHORUS LINE, Michael Bennett's landmark musical will be extended an extra 4 weeks, and will now positively close on Saturday evening, April 28th. Mr. Papp noted that performances until March 31st are virtually sold out.

The New York Shakespeare Festival producer Joseph Papp went on to explain, "In my original announcement I made it clear that if box office pressure warranted I would extend the closing a few weeks, which is what I am doing. Naturally I am pleased that the public has rallied so splendidly. The extension will permit some 50,000 more people the opportunity to see the show before it closes and provide much needed revenue for the programs of the not-for-profit New York Shakespeare Festival."

The 33 additional performances will include 2 benefits. The final performance on April 28 will be a fundraiser for the New York Shakespeare Festival. On Sunday evening, April 8, in memory of A CHORUS LINE creator Michael Bennett, the company will give an additional performance to benefit "Equity Fights AIDS."

When A CHORUS LINE closes on April 28th, it will have played 6137 performance at the Shubert Theatre.

far as performance, it made the show incredibly real.

The line "Nothing runs forever" became "Nothing runs forever, not even A CHORUS LINE." Standing on that line, you knew in a couple of months you were going to be out of work again. It made the show vital, and every moment on stage became important. I felt like we were a big part of history. If we couldn't be the original company of A CHORUS LINE, hallelujah we're the last company. The houses became magnetic. You'd walk on stage in the black and feel it buzzing. It became the hottest ticket on Broadway. Gifts kept pouring into the theatre.

Everyone who had done the show was coming back. I met more Don Kerrs! The greatest gift I got was from Ron Kuhlman — although it didn't seem like anyone else got gifts from their original counterparts. I'll never forget his letter, "To Keith: It's not how you start … it's how you finish. Here's to Don Kerr, the first, the last, all those in between, and all those yet to come. All the best, Ron Kuhlman." It was such a beautiful letter, with a bottle of champagne, just waiting for me at the theatre. By that point we were opening twenty letters or gifts a performance. We prepped ourselves for the last performance, and then the four week extension went up, and we thought this is going to happen for a year and a half — they're going to keep extending and extending.

But the next extension didn't go up. A week before that last performance, we knew it was closing. One of the last get-togethers we had, management mentioned the Original Cast was coming for a book signing. I had mixed feelings about that, thinking, "I hope this doesn't turn into the Original Cast-fest, because while it certainly was their show then, it's *our* show now." There were instances when I felt like I didn't want to invade their space, but at the same time I didn't want to have my space invaded either. There was a little of that happening that final day. But, overriding all else was always the feeling of we're closing and they get to be a part of it too. It was thrilling. At the last performance, Joe Papp called us out one by one and we got our own bow in the middle of the Shubert stage, then he called the Original Company up on stage, and that was a very joining experience. At the end, no one ever felt shoved aside.

"We prepped ourselves for the last performance, and then the four week extension went up, and we thought this is going to happen for a year and a half — they're going to keep extending and extending. But the next extension didn't go up." — KEITH BERNARDO

Final Performances

LAURIE GAMACHE [Final Cassie]: When people started coming back, the audiences were really enthusiastic, and I realized what we had been missing all that time. It had so slowly petered down that I really wasn't conscious of it, but after they announced the closing, everybody started cheering and jumping up and down.

MICHAEL GRUBER [Final Mike]: You started to see the effect the show had on people. The final matinee was really the last performance where the show was intact. The evening show became about something else, but we were still thrilled they chose to have the last show be the show, and not something like what they did for the Gala. They did that lovely thing at the end where the Original Company came on stage, but it was really nice we could just play the show and not be concerned about where the focus was. Not to say the past doesn't have importance, but ultimately, we got the gift of the final show.

Unfortunately feelings were not necessarily warm towards us from the Originals; there were those who would have nothing to do with us. There was no individual contact between Original and Final Company members. Whatever the reason may be, we were on one side of the room at the party at Mamma Leone's and

they were on the other, like oil and water. They were coming from a different place, a different generation. They had the fantastic opening experience and we had it at the end.

KAY COLE [Original Maggie]: We were given the opening, and they the closing. They were our age when *we* did it, so I was thinking, "The rest of your life you're going to have so much to hang on to because this experience will color everything you do." I was able to appreciate that; it did and continues to color my life.

KEVIN McCREADY: When they brought the Original Company on, you could have split the stage with a knife, we were on one side, they were on another. Some of them were gracious, but others were very cold with an attitude like, "You don't know what it was like, you don't know what you're doing. You're all amateurs." That's how they made us feel.

ROBIN LYON [Final Company Understudy]: There was animosity within the Company because the understudies were treated like they didn't exist; we were left out of everything. And with the Original Company, it was them and us. There was always a separation between the two.

MURPHY CROSS [Judy]: I loved the last show, it was incredible. It was almost too powerful to deal with. There is not enough room in your body and heart and mind to contain all what you feel for a show like that.

JACK NOSEWORTHY: Generally, people were very pleased the show was getting media attention, and, being the final cast member hired, I happened to be somewhat of a focus for that. It was really about the fact this terrific show was not going to be on Broadway anymore. I don't think there was bitter chorus jealousy about someone getting a little more press than another person. Closing night was

Orchestra pit, the last day

very exciting. I remember people being disappointed the orchestra section was sold out to raise money, and the cheering section was upstairs.

I remember watching Laurie Gamache do *The Music and the Mirror.* When she finished the number, which was absolutely brilliant, she stood and held her final position and the audience went fucking wild. She waited for them to stop, but they wouldn't stop clapping, then the applause started to die down just a little bit and she was very emotional, obviously, and started to cry, wiping a tear from her eye and the applause started to rise. They got more excited because she started to cry a little bit, which was a really warm and special moment for her. They understood somehow what this woman was going through, not only Cassie, but what Laurie was really going through in her experience with this show. It was just such a wonderful connection between the audience and the actor.

PAM SOUSA [Cassie]: No matter what else I was doing, I could always stop in and say hello. A CHORUS LINE was always there, and all of a sudden it was closing. I thought we are really ending an era, a time in our lives. This chapter is over. That was hard. And Michael was gone.

FRASER ELLIS [Final Company Understudy; Assistant Stage Manager]: I stayed

until the show closed, over seven and a half years. I kept staying because I always thought it was definitely going to close the next year. It was a great job, and you keep thinking, "Another year — how long can it last?" But eventually, it made the decision for me, which was fine. The Company was in shock when they announced the closing. I really wasn't surprised. As a stage manager, I looked out at those empty seats and knew it was only a matter of time. It seemed like a natural thing to close.

I think Joe Papp could have squeezed another year out of it, had he announced "Last Weeks." But he knew he was dying, and all these other people had died. There was a quote in the mirror over the stage door that said "It may outlive all of us," and I don't think Joe wanted that to happen. I think he still wanted to have the control, he wanted to close it, he wanted to have a clean break with the show before he died.

JOE McLAUGHLIN [Box Office]: The last night when we were closing down the box office window, we opened up a bottle of champagne, said goodbye to everyone and pulled the shade down. And they made us do it twenty times, because television cameras started running in: "Do it again, do it again."

KEITH BERNARDO: Before we went on stage for the last time, the Company had a

little meeting like a football huddle. This was the last time it was going to be done on Broadway, and we wanted to do it right. We got into our lines, holding hands, and the lights went to black. There's something about entering the stage for A CHORUS LINE, holding hands. It couldn't have been a better entrance for us. When we got out there, dropped hands, and found our places, we heard the first notes of the piano, and then the screams from the audience. They were so loud and powerful — we knew we were in for a night!

EMANUEL AZENBERG [General Manager: Original Road Companies]: As time passes and specific memories fade, there is an overall gratification to have, in a small way, been a part of A CHORUS LINE.

BOB REILLY: I watched the final Finale in the wings with Tom Porter and Ron Stafford, the three of us holding on to one

SHUBERT THEATRE
FINAL PERFORMANCE
A CHORUS LINE
8:00P SAT APR 28 1990

$80.00
BALC40
CEN
02
8:00P
A 105

The Shubert Organization

SHUBERT
FINAL PERFORM
A CHORUS LINE
8:00P SAT APR 28 1990

The Shubert Organization

Photo by Maryann Chach/ Courtesy The Shubert Archive

*Taking down Broadway's
most famous marquee, June 6, 1990*

another crying. As soon as we went to black, we turned around and walked offstage together. It was so sad.

RICHARD BERG [Assistant General Manager]: A CHORUS LINE had a tremendous effect on a generation of dancers. It also had a tremendous effect on gay rights in America. I think Paul's monologue probably did more good for gay rights than all the marches put together have achieved because it played everywhere in America. If there was ever a moment in the show that people talk about being the most moving, it's that monologue.

BETTY JACOBS [Mrs. Bernard Jacobs]: It's a show I've seen more than any other show in my lifetime, and I've seen a lot of shows. But with A CHORUS LINE, there was always something else to look at, some little thing you hadn't spotted the first time. It was truly an exciting show, and it took over our life for a long time.

BOB ULLMAN [Press Agent]: The show was a ray of hope for the theatre. It encouraged young people who used to buy standing room that you could still get a break in the theatre and there was still exciting theatre going on Broadway. I never, never lost interest in A CHORUS LINE. I used to stand in the back of the

Shubert at least three times a week and be constantly amazed at the tingle at the back of my neck when I watched moments of that show, how brilliantly it was put together. It never failed to recharge my enthusiasm and make me realize how lucky I was to be associated with that show.

TRISH GARLAND [Original Judy]: When I heard it was closing, I remembered Michael telling me long ago that A CHORUS LINE was never going to end. If it wasn't on Broadway, Michael was going to house it at 890, and it would just run. Michael's dream had changed.

THEONI ALDREDGE [Costume Designer]: Sometimes you get so depressed in this business, the heartache is more than the rewards in the end. I'd go and watch *What I Did For Love* and feel better. I miss the show. I don't go to Shubert Alley anymore. Something is missing — the kids coming in and out of the stage door. A CHORUS LINE was a huge part of our lives and touched all of us. In my life, nothing will ever be like it. It's not a question of being my favorite show, it's like somebody telling me why I am in this business and I have to do what I'm doing and stop bellyaching about it. The gift was ours to borrow.

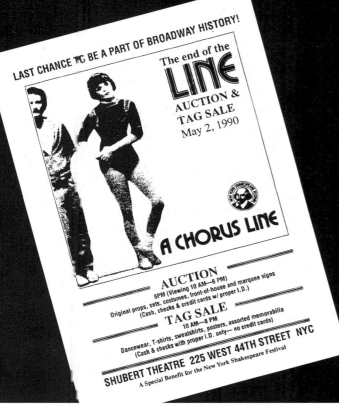

LAST CHANCE TO BE A PART OF BROADWAY HISTORY!

The end of the LINE

AUCTION & TAG SALE
May 2, 1990

A CHORUS LINE

AUCTION
6PM (Viewing 10 AM—6 PM)
Original props, sets, costumes, front-of-house and marquee signs
(Cash, checks & credit cards w/ proper I.D.)

TAG SALE
10 AM—8 PM
Dancewear, T-shirts, sweatshirts, posters, assorted memorabilia
(Cash & checks with proper I.D. only— no credit cards)

SHUBERT THEATRE 225 WEST 44TH STREET NYC
A Special Benefit for the New York Shakespeare Festival

A CHORUS LINE on sale: everything from costumes to mirrors to 2' sections of the white line were sold at the auction on May 2, 1990

Decorations outside Mamma Leone's restaurant, where the closing party was held

The final family of A CHORUS LINE: cast, crew, musicians, and management

"We Will Remember"

by Robin Lyon

There is so much to say, and not enough time
How can we put in words what it's been like inside A CHORUS LINE?
It's so hard to say good-bye, you can't replace a faithful friend.
We gave our hearts and souls, from beginning to the end

But now it's time to travel on and let go
But we have been a part of the greatest show
It's been a home away from home
For a long, long time

There are memories of friends we've lost and we've gained
We've grown a little older
From the good times and the pains
And no one can take these memories from our minds
As years go on and on
We'll keep them safe inside

But now it's time to travel on and let go
But we have been a part of the greatest show
It's been a home away from home
For a long, long time

We have come so far, and we have so much more than we had before
How lucky we are to have been on the line
Michael allowed us gypsies to SHINE

It's gonna be hard to say goodbye
You can't replace this faithful friend
But we'll hold our heads up high
It's the beginning not the end
For it's just time to travel on and let go
But we have been a part of the GREATEST show
It's been our home away from home
For a long, long
WE WILL REMEMBER
For a long, long time…..

Copyright 1990 Robin Lyon. Dedicated to those who have performed A CHORUS LINE
or have been touched by A CHORUS LINE. With so much love, Robin Lyon. Performed for the Company
on April 28, 1990, before the final show by cast member Robin Lyon.

Fifteen Years
of
Record-Breaking
Success

CHAPTER 13

LINER
NOTES

THE FACTS
& FIGURES

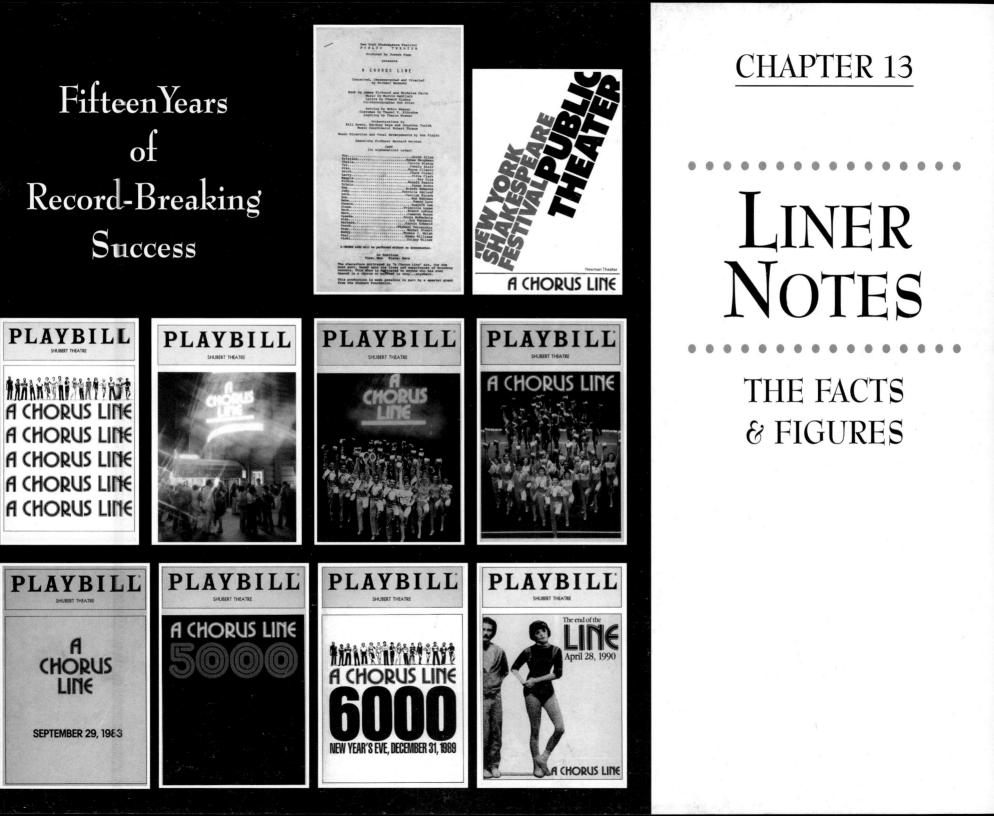

A Chorus Line Broadway Cast Replacement List

Don Kerr	Maggie Winslow	Mike Costa	Connie Wong	Gregory Gardner	Cassie Ferguson	Sheila Bryant	Bobby Mills III	Bebe Benzenheimer
Ron Kuhlman	**Kay Cole**	**Wayne Cilento**	**Baayork Lee**	**Michel Stuart**	**Donna McKechnie**	**Kelly (Carole) Bishop**	**Thommie Walsh**	**Nancy Lane**
David Thomé	Lauree Berger	Don Correia	Lauren Kayahara	Justin Ross	Ann Reinking	Kathrynann Wright	Christopher Chadman	Gillian Scalici
Dennis Edenfield	Donna Drake	Jim Litten	Janet Wong	Danny Weathers	Vicki Frederick	Bebe Neuwirth	Ron Kurowski	Karen Meister
Michael Weir	Christina Saffran	Jeff Hyslop	Cynthia Onrubia	Ronald A. Navarre	Pamela Sousa	Susan Danielle	Tim Cassidy	Rene Ceballos
Michael Danek	Marcia Lynn Watkins	Buddy Balou'	Lauren Tom	Bradley Jones	Cheryl Clark	Jan Leigh Herndon	Ron Stafford	Pamela Ann Wilson
Randy Clements	Pam Klinger	Cary Scott Lowenstein	Lily-Lee Wong	**Doug Friedman**	Deborah Henry	Jane Summerhays	Michael Gorman	Tracy Shayne
Keith Bernardo	Ann Heinricher	Scott Wise	**Sachi Shimizu**		Wanda Richert	Dana Moore	Matt West	Karen Ziemba
	Dorothy Tancredi	Danny Herman			Angelique Ilo	**Susan Danielle**	**Ron Kurowski**	**Christine Maglione**
	Susan Santoro	J. Richard Hart			**Laurie Gamache**			
		Mark Bove						
		Tommy Re						
		Kelly Paterson						
		Michael Gruber						

Note: Although many actors went back and forth into the same role over the years, this compilation lists only the order in which the actor first acquired the role. **Bold** *names signify Original and Final Company Members.*

Source: 15 years of John Willis' Theatre World, Playbill®, and cast contact sheets.

Judy
<u>Turner</u>

Patricia Garland
Sandahl Bergman
Murphy Cross
Victoria Tabaka
Angelique Ilo
Janet Horsley
  Moranz
Melissa Randel
Cindi Klinger
Angelique Ilo

Richie
<u>Walters</u>

Ronald Dennis
Winston DeWitt
  Helmsley
Edward Love
Wellington Perkins
Larry G. Bailey
Carleton T. Jones
Ralph Glenmore
Kevin Chinn
Reggie Phoenix
Gordon Owens
Bruce Anthony Davis
Gregg Burge
Gordon Owens

Alan
<u>DeLuca</u>

Don Percassi
Bill Nabel
John Mineo
Ben Lokey
Jim Corti
Donn Simione
Buddy Balou'
James Young
Jerry Colker
Mark Bove
Kevin Neil
  McCready
Tommy Re
Charlie Marcus
Stephen Bourneuf
Tommy Re

Kristine
<u>Urich</u>

Renee Baughman
Cookie Vazquez
Deborah Geffner
PJ Mann
Christine Barker
Kerry Casserly
Flynn McMichaels
  (McGrath)
Cynthia Fleming
  (a/k/a Thia Fadel)

Valerie
<u>Clark</u>

Pamela Blair
Barbara Monte-
  Britton
Karen Jablons
Mitzi Hamilton
Lois Englund
Deborah Henry
DeLee Lively
Wanda Richert
Diana Kavilis

Mark
<u>Anthony</u>

Cameron Mason
Paul Charles
Timothy Scott
RJ Peters
Timothy Wahrer
Gregory Brock
Danny Herman
Chris Marshall
Gib Jones
Andrew Grose
Matt Zarley
Jack Noseworthy

Paul
<u>San Marco</u>

Sammy Williams
George Pesaturo
Rene Clemente
Timothy Wahrer
Tommy Aguilar
Wayne Meledandri
Drew Geraci

Diana
<u>Morales</u>

Priscilla Lopez
Barbara Luna
Rebecca York
Carole Schweid
Loida Iglesias Santos
Chris Bocchino
Diane Fratantoni
Dorothy Tancredi
Kay Cole
Roxanne Caballero
Gay Marshall
Mercedes Perez
Denise DiRenzo
Arminae Azarian
**Roxanne Caballero
  Biggs**

Swings & Understudies

*Understudies / Swings are listed alphabetically and have, at one time or another, performed a role on the line. Those in **bold** with asterisks (*) were in the Original Company; those in **bold** were in the Final Company.*

Larry

Clive (Clerk) Wilson
Adam Grammis
Paul Charles
RJ Peters
T. Michael Reed
Michael Day Pitts
Donn Simione
J. Richard Hart
Scott Plank
Brad Jeffries
Jim Litten
Danny Herman
Kevin Neil McCready

Zach

Robert LuPone
Joe Bennett
Eivind Harum
Kurt Johnson
Anthony Inneo
Scott Pearson
Tim Millett
Steve Boockvor
Randy Clements
Eivind Harum

Scott Allen*
Robert Amirante
Kevin Backstrom
Dean Badolato
James Beaumont
Tim Cassidy
Kevin Chinn
Gary Chryst
Chuck Cissel*
Catherine Cooper
Noel Craig
Stephen Crenshaw
Karen Curlee
Patti D'Beck
Michael Pierre Dean
John Dolf
Pi Douglass
Donna Drake*
Rob Draper
Diane Duncan
Brandt Edwards*
Fraser Ellis
Susie Fenner
Gail Mae Ferguson
Fern Fitzgerald
Cynthia Fleming
Mark Fotopoulos
Diane Fratantoni
David Fredericks
Morris Freed
Troy Garza
Roscoe Gilliam
Michael Gorman
Christopher Gregory
Niki Harris

Matthew Inge
Kiel Junius
Brian Kelly
Carolyn Kirsch*
Frank Kliegel
Cindi Klinger
Tom Kosis
Joe Langworth
Paula Leggett
Terry Lombardozzi
Carlos Lopez
Cary Scott Lowenstein
Betty Lynd
Robin Lyon
Carol Marik
Jack McGrady
Flynn McMichaels
William Mead
Tim Millett
John Mineo*
Don Mirault
Kathleen Moore
Dana Moore
Janet Moranz
Kevyn Morrow
Bebe Neuwirth
Mary Ann O'Reilly
Cynthia Onrubia
Evan Pappas
Dennis Parlato
Julie Pars
Peggy Parten
Matt Pederson
Philip C. Perry
Laureen Valuch Piper

Sam Piperato
Michael Day Pitts
Donna M. Pompei
Trish Ramish
Michael Ricardo
Joseph Rich
Jon Michael Richardson
Steve Riley
Ken Rogers
Danny Ruvolo
Chesley Santoro
Ann Louise Schaut
Carole Schweid*
Michael Serrechia*
Tracy Shayne
Laurie Dawn Skinner
Tim Smith
Jo Speros
Dale Stotts
Claude Tessier
Candace Tovar
Glenn Turner
Julie Tussey
Sam Viverito
Crissy Wilzak*
Joanna Zercher

Note: There were 27 in the cast at the Public Theatre. One swing was added to the cast for the transfer to Broadway, and subsequently four more swings were added for a total of 32 cast members.

Chorus Couples ...

(Married before, during or after their association with A CHORUS LINE)

... and Their Chorus Kids

(Mom & Dad both associated with A CHORUS LINE)

Vincent Forchetti (pit) and Fran Liebergall (pit) . . . . Kyle
Vincent Fanuele (pit) & Priscilla Lopez (cast) . . . . Alexandra & Gabriella
Eivind Harum (cast) & Angelique Ilo (cast) . . . . Leif & Sonya
J. Richard Hart (cast) & Susan Danielle (cast) . . . . John Michael
Maryann O'Reilly (cast) & Andy Bew (cast) . . . . Jamie, Candace, Christie, Jesse, Jilaine, Damian, Danielle & Gabrielle
Scott Wise (cast) & Keil Junius (cast) . . . . Savannah
Dorothy Tancredi (cast) & Ken Dybisz (pit) . . . . Rocco
Kathleen Moore (cast) & Brad McDougall (pit) . . . . Michael
Wendy Mansfield (stage manager) & Doug Baker (company manager) . . . . Hillary
Steve Boockvor (cast) & Denise Pence (Al & Kristine characters based on them) . . . . Jolan & Brette
Michael Gorman (cast) & Zoe Vonder Haar (cast) . . . . Travis
Tino Gagliardi (pit) & Yukiko Kinase (translator for Japan tour) . . . . Celia Mika
Chris Chew (European crew) & Yo Yo Ikeda (translator for Japan tour) . . . . Oscar
Steven Tate (London cast) & Vickie Spencer (London cast) . . . . Sam, Ben, Joe and Harry
Doug Besterman (pit) & Marty Simpson (cast) . . . . Max Everett
Steve Benson (European pit) & Shelley Price (European company manager) . . . . Benjamin
Albin Konopka (pit) & Ornella Buttazzo (cast) . . . . Carolyn
Ray Fitzgerald (European pit) & Mary Ann Scott (European pit) . . . . Alice
Brad Moranz (cast) & Janet Moranz (cast)
Denise DiRenzo (cast) & Michael Allen (sound man)
Michael Bennett (director) & Donna McKechnie (cast)
Nancy Wood (cast) & Jonathan Deans (sound man)
Ron Kurowski (cast) & Sachi Shimizu (cast)
Betty Lynd (cast) & Steve Terry (sound man)
Jim Litten (cast) & Julie Pappas (cast)
Scott Allen (cast) & Christine Barker (cast)
Scott Allen (cast) & Cheryl Teague (cast)
Danny Antolick (crew) & Anna Simonelli (cast)
Kevin Marlow (British touring cast) & Taffie Taylor (British touring cast)
Karen Curlee (cast) & Leno Gomez (pit)
David Chase (pit) & Paula Leggett (cast)
Alison Gertner (cast) & Chuck Mann (crew)
Danielle Brunner (Vienna cast) & Niki Bolen (Vienna cast)
Paul Welterlen (Vienna cast) & Patricia Tauden (Vienna cast)

... and Other Family Members

Kerry & Janie Casserly (sisters - cast)
Tony & Todd D'Aiuto, (father & son spotlight operators)
Drew & Paul Geraci (brothers - cast)
Pam & Cindi Klinger (sisters - cast)
Judith & Ilona Papp (twin sisters - cast)
Tony (Alec) & Cheryl Teague (uncle & niece - cast)

The authors respectfully regret any errors or omissions.

In Memoriam

"Gone, love is never gone, as we travel on, love's what we'll remember."

Tommy Aguilar (cast)

Michael Austin (cast)

Frank Bade (Berlin cast)

Steve Bellin (cast)

Michael Bennett (director)

Tim Cassidy (cast)

Christopher Chadman (cast)

Rene Clemente (cast)

Nicholas Dante (co-author)

Michael Pierre Dean (cast)

Pat Drylie (stage manager)

Lauren Eager (cast)

Rick Emery (cast)

Mark Fotopolous (cast)

David Fredericks (cast)

Geraldine Gardner (London cast)

Roscoe Gilliam (cast)

Adam Grammis (cast)

Judy Gridley (London cast)

Tom Hancock (conductor)

Winston DeWitt Helmsley (cast)

Kurt Johnson (cast)

Reed Jones (cast)

Gib Jones (cast)

Carlton T. Jones (cast)

Keith Keen (cast)

Andy Keyser (cast)

James Kirkwood (co-author)

Ed Kleban (lyricist)

Bernd Kleberg (Vienna cast)

Nanette Kramer (pit)

Edward Love (cast)

Cary Scott Lowenstein (cast)

Alex MacKay (dance captain)

Cameron Mason (cast)

CJ McCaffrey (cast)

Calvin McCrae (cast)

LuEsther Mertz (ACL funding)

Tim Millett (cast)

James Morreale (pit)

Joseph Papp (producer)

Kelly Paterson (cast)

George Pesaturo (cast)

Tom Porter (stage manager)

T. Michael Reed (dance captain)

Nolan Rice (cast)

Jimmy Roddy (cast)

Danny Rounds (cast)

Danny Ruvolo (cast)

Timothy Scott (cast)

David Serko (cast)

Greg Sims (Australian cast)

Roy Smith (dance captain)

Michael Staniforth (London cast)

Danny Taylor (cast)

Tony (Alec) Teague (cast)

Claude R. Tessier (cast)

Blaise Turi (pit)

Diana Warner (dresser)

Robert Warner (cast)

Norman Wells (pit)

Larry Wilcox (orchestrator)

Charlie Willard (company manager)

The authors respectfully regret any omissions.

1976 Tony® Awards
Categories in which A CHORUS LINE was nominated and / or won. **Bold** *indicates winner.*

BEST MUSICAL

A CHORUS LINE
BUBBLING BROWN SUGAR
CHICAGO
PACIFIC OVERTURES

BEST MUSICAL BOOK

A CHORUS LINE —
 James Kirkwood & Nicholas Dante
CHICAGO — Fred Ebb & Bob Fosse
PACIFIC OVERTURES — John Weldman
THE ROBBER BRIDEGROOM — Alfred Uhry

BEST MUSICAL SCORE

A CHORUS LINE — music: Marvin Hamlisch;
 lyrics: Edward Kleban
CHICAGO —
 music: John Kander; lyrics: Fred Ebb
PACIFIC OVERTURES —
 music & lyrics: Stephen Sondheim
TREEMONISHA —
 music & lyrics: Scott Joplin

BEST ACTRESS — MUSICAL

Donna McKechnie — A CHORUS LINE
Vivian Reed — BUBBLING BROWN SUGAR
Chita Rivera — CHICAGO
Gwen Verdon — CHICAGO

BEST FEATURED ACTOR — MUSICAL

Robert LuPone — A CHORUS LINE
Charles Repole — VERY GOOD EDDIE
Isao Sato — PACIFIC OVERTURES
Sammy Williams — A CHORUS LINE

BEST FEATURED ACTRESS — MUSICAL

Carole (Kelly) Bishop — A CHORUS LINE
Priscilla Lopez — A CHORUS LINE
Patti LuPone — THE ROBBER BRIDEGROOM
Virginia Seidel — VERY GOOD EDDIE

BEST DIRECTOR — MUSICAL

Michael Bennett — A CHORUS LINE
Bob Fosse — CHICAGO
Bill Gile — VERY GOOD EDDIE
Harold Prince — PACIFIC OVERTURES

BEST COSTUME DESIGN

Theoni V. Aldredge — A CHORUS LINE
Florence Klotz — PACIFIC OVERTURES
Ann Roth — THE ROYAL FAMILY
Patricia Zipprodt — CHICAGO

BEST LIGHTING DESIGN

Ian Calderon — TRELAWNY OF THE WELLS
Jules Fisher — CHICAGO
Tharon Musser — A CHORUS LINE
Tharon Musser — PACIFIC OVERTURES

BEST CHOREOGRAPHY

Michael Bennett & Bob Avian —
 A CHORUS LINE
Patricia Birch — PACIFIC OVERTURES
Bob Fosse — CHICAGO
Billy Wilson — BUBBLING BROWN SUGAR

Notes on the Tonys®:

• A CHORUS LINE was nominated for 12 awards and won 9.

• A CHORUS LINE Tony® losses:
 Robert LuPone —
 Best Supporting Actor — Musical

 Priscilla Lopez —
 Best Supporting Actress — Musical

 Theoni V. Aldredge —
 Best Costume Design

• Robert LuPone and his sister, Patti LuPone (THE ROBBER BRIDEGROOM), were both nominated in the respective Supporting Actor/Actress categories.

• Tharon Musser was a double nominee, winning for A CHORUS LINE, losing for PACIFIC OVERTURES.

235

More Award Highlights

1975 New York Drama Critics Award — Best Musical

1975 Pulitzer Prize for Drama

1975 CLIO Finalist Certificate for the Bob Giraldi Commercial

1975 Hollywood Radio & Television Society International Broadcasting Award for the Bob Giraldi Commercial

1976 Special Theatre World Award to every member of creative staff & Original Cast

1976 Obie Award — Special Citation to the creators and for performance, Priscilla Lopez & Sammy Williams

1976 Drama Desk Awards for:
BEST BOOK
BEST SCORE
BEST DIRECTOR
BEST CHOREOGRAPHER
BEST ACTRESS — tie:
        Donna McKechnie/Kelly Bishop

1976 Los Angeles Drama Critic's Circle Distinguished Achievement Award for BEST PRODUCTION, DIRECTION, BOOK, CHOREOGRAPHY, & LIGHTING

1977 London Evening Standard Award — BEST MUSICAL

1978 Gold Record Award from Columbia Records

1984 A CHORUS LINE receives a Special Tony® as the Longest Running Show in Broadway history. Producer Joseph Papp and creator Michael Bennett are the only people ever to receive this prestigious gold Tony® Award.

As of April 28, 1990*:

- A CHORUS LINE has given 6,137 performances on Broadway.

- Attendance at the Shubert Theatre has been approximately 6,642,400.

- 510 "Chorus Liners" on the Shubert stage, including the Gala.

- The New York Shakespeare Festival's net income to date from all NYSF sponsored companies is $38,750,000. This figure includes ancillary income as well.

- The total box office gross for all A CHORUS LINE companies is $280,583,900, which includes $66,600,000 from International Company, $48,930,000 from National Company, $15,630,000 from Bus & Truck Company.

- The total New York box office gross is $149,035,253.

- The total profit is approximately $50,000,000. Profit split 75%-25% between NYSF and Plum Productions (Michael Bennett). Total includes $24,217,457 from Broadway Company, $8,800,000 from the International Company, $6,524,000 from National Company, $2,084,000 from Bus & Truck Company, $8,780,924 from ancillary income including film sale, original cast album, foreign royalties, domestic stock, and amateur royalties, and merchandising.

- Production capitalization was $1,138,415 ($549,526 as cost of two workshop productions and off-Broadway production; $588,889 as cost of transfer to Broadway).

Additional Companies

- London Company opened July 17, 1976, Drury Lane Theatre; Closed March 31, 1979, after 901 performances.

- National Company opened May 6, 1976, San Francisco, closed September 14, 1980, Montreal.

- International Company opened April 29, 1976, Toronto, closed August 14, 1983, Toronto.

- Bus & Truck Company opened September 18, 1980, Schenectady, NY, closed October 3, 1982, Pittsburgh.

- Productions performed in Puerto Rico, England, France, Australia, Germany, Sweden, Japan, Argentina, Brazil, Mexico, Spain, Austria, Singapore, Netherlands, Switzerland, Italy, Canada, Belgium, Denmark, Norway, South Africa, New Zealand, Hong Kong

Film Sale

Film rights sold in 1975 to Universal Pictures for $5,500,000 plus 20% of distributor's gross rentals above $30,000,000. Rights subsequently sold by Universal to Embassy Pictures.

Film Production Cost

$27,000,000

Film U.S. Domestic Rentals

$9,828,427

Stock & Amateur License

Rights sold for $2,000,000 advance (Broadway record) in spring of 1985 to TamsWitmark, Inc.

Original Cast Album

Released in 1975 by Columbia Records; total sales in excess of 1,250,000 units as of October, 1983

Home Video

Embassy Home Entertainment, released Feb. 1987

source: Merle Debuskey & Associates

A CHORUS LINE Revenue Generated by Theatre Development Fund

Year	Non-Subsidy # Tickets	$ Amount	TKTS Booth # Tickets	$ Amount	TAP # Tickets	$ Amount
1979-80	200	1,374.50	102,564	1,036,999.00		
1980-81			99,128	1,139,480.00	226	4,193.75
1981-82			122,545	1,836,726.00	245	2,334.00
1982-83	15,749	89,830.75	131,954	2,438,965.00	64	997.50
1983-84	8,870	52,381.50	130,205	2,750,472.50	79	1,412.50
1984-85	6,230	42,052.50	137,841	2,952,337.52	65	1,462.50
1985-86	961	7,207.50	128,357	2,767,387.50		
1986-87	2,031	17,263.50	123,182	2,660,652.50	73	1,402.50
1987-88	6,954	59,109.00	128,005	2,776,548.75	40	780.00
1988-89	12,024	108,908.00	130,233	2,959,840.00		
1989-90	16,457	156,341.50	99,145	2,386,808.75		
TOTAL	**69,476**	**$534,468.75**	**1,333,159**	**$25,706,217.52**	**792**	**$12,582.75**

Total Number of Tickets   1,403,427
Total Dollar Amount $26,253,269.02

Actors' Fund Benefit Performances

(Actors' Fund revenue generated by A CHORUS LINE)

Date	Gross Receipts	Location
11/2/75	19,401.00	New York
8/16/76	25,207.00	Los Angeles
4/17/77	21,732.00	New York
2/26/78	18,417.28	Cleveland
11/26/78	21,477.12	New York
1/27/80	23,152.55	New York
2/4/80	23,879.35	San Francisco

Actors' Fund Bread Basket Campaign

(Monies from Audiences)

Year Ending	Take	Location
4/30/76	4,117.77	New York
4/30/77	4,147.00	New York
4/30/78	3,319.93	New York
4/30/79	3,576.04	New York
4/30/79	1,340.00	Forrest Theatre, Philadelphia
4/30/79	5,044.76	Shubert Theatre, Boston
4/30/80	2,601.20	New York

Source: Theatre Development Fund & the Actors' Fund of America

A CHORUS LINE Out-Ran Them All

The 677 Broadway productions that ran during the fifteen years of A CHORUS LINE. Source: John Willis' Theatre World

Already playing on Broadway when A CHORUS LINE moved to the Shubert Theater, July 25, 1975

Grease
Pippin
Raisin
Candide
The Magic Show
Absurd Person Singular
Equus
The Wiz
Shenandoah
Sherlock Holmes
The Ritz
Same Time Next Year
Rodgers & Hart
Chicago
Death of a Salesman

1975/1976

The Skin of Our Teeth
Ah, Wilderness!
Lampost Reunion
The Leaf People
Treemonisha
Me and Bessie
Yentl
Summer Brave
Travesties
Kennedy's Children
Hello, Dolly! - Pearl Bailey
A Musical Jubilee
Boccacio
The Norman Conquests

Habeas Corpus
The Glass Menagerie
Very Good Eddie
Angel Street
Murder Among Friends
Sweet Bird of Youth
The Royal Family
Home Sweet Homer
The Poison Tree
Pacific Overtures
A Matter of Gravity
Rockabye Hamlet
Knock Knock
Bubbling Brown Sugar
Songs of the Street
Me Jack, You Jill
Zalman or the Madness of God
The Lady from the Sea
My Fair Lady
Who's Afraid of Virginia Woolf?
Shirley MacLaine
The Heiress
Rex
So Long 174th Street
The Belle of Amherst
1600 Pennsylvania Avenue
Days in the Trees
Legend
The Runner Stumbles
Something's Afoot

1976/1977

Knock Knock
Al Green / Ashford & Simpson
California Suite
An Evening with Diana Ross

Godspell
Pal Joey
Let My People Come
Shirley MacLaine
Guys and Dolls
Checking Out
For Colored Girls...
The Debbie Reynolds Show
Going Up
I Have a Dream
A Texas Trilogy
Oh! Calcutta!
Porgy and Bess
Days in the Trees
Siamsa
Kings
Equus
The Robber Bridegroom
Wheelbarrow Closers
Best Friend
Poor Murderer
The Innocents
No Man's Land
The Chinese Acrobats of Taiwan
The Eccentricities of a
   Nightingale
Natalie Cole
Comedians
Herzl
Bing Crosby on Broadway
Sly Fox
The Night of the Iguana
Music Is
Barry Manilow on Broadway
Your Arms Too Short...
Fiddler on the Roof

Something Old, Something New
The Trip Back Down
Dirty Linen and New-Found
   Land
Ipi-Tombi
Otherwise Engaged
A Party with Betty Comden &
   Adolph Green
American Buffalo
Caesar and Cleopatra
Unexpected Guests
Mark Twain Tonight
Romeo and Juliet
Lily Tomlin: Appearing Nitely
Mummenschanz
The Shadow Box
Ladies at the Alamo
Anna Christie
I Love My Wife
Side By Side by Sondheim
Annie
The Basic Training of Pavlo
   Hummel
Nana Mouskouri on Broadway
The King and I
Happy End
Vieux Carre
Toller Cranston's The Ice Show
Gemini

1977/78

The Importance of Being Earnest
Beatlemania
Man of La Mancha
Tartuffe
Estrada

Miss Margarida's Way
Victor Borge in Comedy with
   Music
Cleo on Broadway
Hair
The Gin Game
The Night of the Tribades
Dracula
Some of My Best Friends
An Almost Perfect Person
The Act
Golda
The Merchant
Bully
Jesus Christ Superstar
Lou Rawls on Broadway
Chapter Two
Saint Joan
A Touch of the Poet
Cold Storage
Do You Turn Somersaults?
The November People
Cheaters
Paul Robeson
Elvis: The Legend Lives!
On the Twentieth Century
Deathtrap
Timbuktu!
Hello, Dolly! - Carol Channing
The Water Engine and Mr.
   Happiness
The Effect of Gamma Rays...
13 Rue de L'Amour
Stages
Dancin'
A History of the American Film

Diversions and Delights
The Mighty Gents
Da
Ain't Misbehavin'
Angel
Runaways
Working

1978/1979

Tribute
Once in a Lifetime
The Best Little Whorehouse in
    Texas
Players
Eubie!
The Inspector General
The Crucifer of Blood
First Monday in October
King of Hearts
Gorey Stories
Platinum
The Kingfisher
Ballroom
Man and Superman
A Broadway Musical
Icedancing
Monteith and Rand
The Grand Tour
Wings
They're Playing Our Song
Whoopee!
Sarava
On Golden Pond
Sweeney Todd
Strangers
Spokesong
Zoot Suit
Bedroom Farce
A Meeting by the River
Faith Healer

Carmelina
Whose Life is it Anyway? -
    Tom Conti
The Elephant Man
Break a Leg
The Goodbye People
Bosoms and Neglect
Knockout
The Utter Glory of Morrisey Hall
Murder at the Howard Johnson's
Peter Allen Up in One
I Remember Mama

1979/1980

Loose Ends
Bruce Forsyth on Broadway!
The Madwoman of CPW
Richard III
Got tu go Disco
Broadway Opry '79
Gilda Radner Live from NY
But Never Jam Today
Peter Pan
On Golden Pond
Evita
Dogg's Hamlet, Cahoot's Macbeth
The 1940's Radio Hour
Sugar Babies
Once a Catholic
The Most Happy Fella
A Kurt Weill Cabaret
Engelbert on Broadway
Devour the Snow
Romantic Comedy
Strider
Last Licks
Night and Day
Bent
Bette! Divine Madness

Chinese Acrobats and Magicians
    of Taiwan
Oklahoma!
Teibele and Her Demon
Comin' Uptown
Watch on the Rhine
Betrayal
The Lady from Dubuque
Harold and Maude
Filumena
Canterbury Tales
West Side Story
Talley's Folly
Charlotte
Mister Lincoln
Whose Life is it Anyway? - Mary
    Tyler Moore
Major Barbara
Censored Scenes from King Kong
Heartaches of a Pussycat
Clothes for a Summer Hotel
Reggae
Children of a Lesser God
Horowitz and Mrs. Washington
I Ought to be in Pictures
Morning's at Seven
Goodbye Fidel
Past Tense
Happy New Year
Nuts
Barnum
A Day in Hollywood / A Night in
    the Ukraine
Hide and Seek
Home
The Roast
Musical Chairs
Blackstone
Of the Fields, Lately
Billy Bishop Goes to War

1980/1981

Your Arms Too Short...
It's So Nice to be Civilized
The Music Man
Fearless Frank
The Man Who Came to Dinner
Camelot
42nd Street
Charlie and Algernon
Passione
Insideoutsideandallaround
    with Shelley Berman
The Bacchae
Division Street
The Suicide
Brigadoon
Banjo Dancing
Tintypes
Quick Change
A Life
Fifth of July
Tricks of the Trade
Lunch Hour
The Philadelphia Story
A Lesson from Aloes
The American Clock
Perfectly Frank
Onward Victoria
Amadeus
John Gabriel Borkman
Mixed Couples
Frankenstein
Emlyn Williams as Charles
    Dickens
The Pirates of Penzance
To Grandmother's House
    We Go
Shakespeare's Cabaret
Macbeth
The Five O'Clock Girl

Piaf
Heartland
The Survivor
Sophisticated Ladies
Bring Back Birdie
Broadway Follies
Lolita
Rose
Woman of the Year
The Father
Fools
Copperfield
Aaah Oui Genty!
Animals
The Floating Lightbulb
Can-Can
The Moony Shapiro Songbook
Passionate Ladies
Inacent Black
The Little Foxes
I Won't Dance
It Had To BeYou
Lena Horne: The Lady and Her
    Music

1981/1982

Wally's Cafe
This Was Burlesque
Scenes and Revelations
A Taste of Honey
Fiddler on the Roof
The Supporting Cast
My Fair Lady
An Evening with Dave Allen
A Talent for Murder
Marlowe
The Life and Adventures of
    Nicholas Nickleby
Candida
Einstein and the Polar Bear

Crimes of the Heart
Ned and Jack
The Dresser
Oh, Brother!
Mass Appeal
Camelot
Merrily We Roll Along
The First
The West Side Waltz
Grownups
Kingdoms
Duet for One
Dreamgirls
The Little Prince and the Aviator
Waltz of the Stork
Little Me
The Curse of an Aching Heart
Joseph and the Amazing...
Macbeth
Othello
Pump Boys and Dinettes
The World of Sholom Aleichem
Special Occasions
Come Back to the Five and Dime...
Little Johnny Jones
Eminent Domain
Agnes of God
Solomon's Child
Medea
Master Harold...and the Boys
The Hothouse
Is There Life After High School?
Nine
Beyond Therapy
Do Black Patent Leather Shoes...?
The Best Little Whorehouse in
    Texas

1982/1983

Blues in the Night
Torch Song Trilogy
Cleavage
Play Me a Country Song
Seven Brides for Seven Brothers
Present Laughter
Ghosts
Your Arms Too Short...
A Doll's Life
The Queen and the Rebels
Cats*
Good
The Wake of Jamey Foster
Rock 'n' Roll! The First 5,000
    Years
Twice Around the Park
Foxfire
84 Charing Cross Road
Herman Van Veen: All of Him
Steaming
Monday After the Miracle
A Little Family Business
Almost and Eagle
Alice in Wonderland
Whodunnit
Plenty
Angels Fall
The Misanthrope
A View From the Bridge
Merlin
Moose Murders
On Your Toes
Slab Boys
Marcel Marceau
Charles Aznavour
Brighton Beach Memoirs
K2
'night Mother
You Can't Take it With You

The Man Who Had Three Arms
All's Well That Ends Well
Teaneck Tanzi: The Venus Flytrap
Show Boat
Total Abandon
My One and Only
The Ritz
The Caine Mutiny Court-Martial
Private Lives
The Flying Karamazov Brothers
Dance a Little Closer
Passion

1983/1984

The Guys in the Truck
Mame
The Corn Is Green
La Cage Aux Folles
Edmund Kean
Zorba
American Buffalo
Brothers
Amen Corner
La Tragedie de Carmen
Marilyn: An American Fable
Doonesbury
The Glass Menagerie
Baby
Heartbreak House
Noises Off
Peg
The Tap Dance Kid
The Real Thing
Ian McKellen Acting
    Shakespeare
Open Admissions
The Rink
Awake and Sing!
Glengarry Glen Ross
Death of a Salesman

The Human Comedy
Shirley MacLaine on Broadway
Beethoven's Tenth
Play Memory
Oliver!
A Moon for the Misbegotten
Sunday in the Park with George
A Woman of Independent Means
End of the World
The Babe
The Wiz

1984/1985

Design for Living
Hurlyburly
Death of a Salesman
Kipling
Ma Rainey's Black Bottom
Much Ado About Nothing
Cyrano de Bergerac
Alone Together
Whoopi Goldberg
The Three Musketeers
Accidental Death of an Anarchist
Haarlem Nocturne
Doug Henning and His World of
    Magic
Home Front
Dancing in the End Zone
The King and I
Harrigan 'n Hart
Pack of Lies
Strange Interlude
The Octette Bridge Club
The Loves of Anatol
Requiem for a Heavyweight
Joe Egg
Biloxi Blues
Leader of the Pack
Take Me Along

Grind
Aren't We All?
Big River
As Is
Doubles
Arms and the Man

1985/1986

The Odd Couple
Singin' in the Rain
The Search for Signs...
Song and Dance
The Iceman Cometh
Tango Argentino
The Marriage of Figaro
Mayor
The News
The Boys of Winter
I'm Not Rappaport
The Mystery of Edwin Drood
Blood Knot
Hay Fever
Jerry's Girls
The Robert Klein Show!
Wind in the Willows
Benefactors
The Caretaker
Corpse!
Lillian
Jerome Kern Goes to Hollywood
Uptown...It's Hot!
Execution of Justice
Precious Sons
The Flying Karamazov Brothers
Loot
Big Deal
Social Security
The Petition
Sweet Charity
Long Day's Journey Into Night

The House of Blue Leaves
The Boys in Autumn

1986/1987

Mummenschanz The New Show
Arsenic and Old Lace
Honky Tonk Nights
Me and My Girl
Rags
The Life and Adventures of
    Nicholas Nickleby
Cuba and His Teddy Bear
You Never Can Tell
Rowan Atkinson at the Atkinson
Raggedy Ann
Flamenco Puro
Into the Light
A Little Like Magic
Oh Coward!
Smile
The Front Page
Broadway Bound
Wild Honey
The World According to Me
Sweet Sue
Stepping Out
Stardust
South Pacific
Death and King's Horseman
Coastal Disturbances
Starlight Express
Les Miserables*
The Nerd
Fences
Blithe Spirit
The Mikado
Safe Sex
The Musical Comedy Murders of
    1940
The Regard of Flight

Barbara Cook: A Concert for the
    Theater
A Month of Sundays
All My Sons
Asinamali!
Pygmalion
Les Liaisons Dangereuses
Sleight of Hand
The Comedy of Errors

1987/1988

Broadway
Dreamgirls
Sherlock's Last Case
Roza
Mort Sahl on Broadway!
Italy on Stage
Burn This
Late Nite Comic
Cabaret
Don't Get God Started
Into the Woods
Teddy & Alice
Breaking the Code
Sally (in concert)
Penn & Teller
The Phantom of the Opera*
Sarafina!
Serious Money
A Walk in the Woods
A Streetcar Named Desire
M. Butterfly
The Gospel at Colonus
Joe Turner's Come and Gone
Oba Oba
Mail
Michael Feinstein in Concert
The World According to Me
Macbeth
Chess

Romance/Romance
Carrie

1988/1989

Long Day's Journey into Night
Ah, Wilderness
An Evening with Robert Klein
Canciones de mi Padre
The Night of the Iguana
Juno and the Paycock
Checkmates
Ain't Misbehavin'
Georgian State Dancers
Paul Robeson
Michael Feinstein in Concert
Cafe Crown
Kenny Loggins on Broadway
Spoils of War
The Devil's Disciple
Rumors
Our Town
Legs Diamond
Eastern Standard
Black and Blue*
Born Yesterday
Shirley Valentine
Jerome Robbins' Broadway*
Lend Me a Tenor
The Pajama Game
Metamorphosis
Run For Your Wife!
The Heidi Chronicles*
Chu Chem
Welcome to the Club
Barry Manilow at the Gershwin
Starmites
Ghetto
Largely New York

1989/1990

Shenandoah
Mandy Patinkin in concert: Dress
    Casual
Sweeney Todd
Orpheus Descending
Mastergate
Dangerous Games
Love Letters
The Secret Rapture
Sid Caesar & Company
Meet Me in St. Louis*
3 Penny Opera
Prince of Central Park
Grand Hotel*
A Few Good Men*
Gypsy*
The Circle*
Artist Descending a Staircase
The Victor Borge Holiday Show
Peter, Paul & Mary A Holiday
    Celebration
Tru*
City of Angels*
The Merchant of Venice
Don Cossacks
Miss Margarida's Way
The Sound of Music
Oba Oba '90
Cat on a Hot Tin Roof*
The Grapes of Wrath*
Lettice & Lovage*
Aspects of Love*
The Piano Lesson*
Truly Blessed*
Accomplice*
A Change In The Heir**
Prelude to A Kiss**
Some American Abroad**
Zoya's Apartment**
A CHORUS LINE CLOSED

* still playing on Broadway when
    A CHORUS LINE closed
**previewing when A CHORUS
    LINE closed

The Numbers and Historical Data

Source: Variety *Weekly Broadway Grosses and The Shubert Organization*

Seats	Ticket Price/ Potential	Week Ending	Net Receipts	% Capacity

1975

Seats	Ticket Price/ Potential	Week Ending	Net Receipts	% Capacity
1466	$15/$140,000			
33 standees		Week 1: July 27	49,250.00	N/A
		3 performances		
		Week 2: August 3	133,474.00	N/A
		Week 3: August 10	134,887.00	N/A
		Week 4: August 17	136,476.00	N/A
		Week 5: August 24	139,178.00	N/A
		Week 6: August 31	140,340.00	N/A
		Week 7: September 7	139,564.00	N/A
		Week 8: September 14	138,602.00	N/A
		Week 9: September 21	66,747.00	N/A
		Sep. 18 — Musicians strike closes all musicals on Broadway		
		Music Strike: September 28	0.00	Dark
		Music Strike: October 5	0.00	Dark
		Music Strike: October 12	0.00	Dark
		Week 10: October 19	137,483.00	N/A
		Oct. 13 — Strike settled, performances resumed. Oct. 19 — Press Opening		
		Week 11: October 26	137,880.00	N/A
		Week 12: November 2	135,828.00	N/A
		Nov. 2 — ACL plays first Actors' Fund performance		
		Week 13: November 9	138,501.00	N/A
		Week 14: November 16	139,163.00	N/A
		Nov. 11 — Sir Laurence Olivier sees show and poses with cast		
		Week 15: November 23	139,191.00	N/A
		Week 16: November 30	140,456.00	N/A
		Week 17: December 7	139,490.00	N/A
		Week 18: December 14	139,391.00	103.00
		Week 19: December 21	139,586.00	103.00
		Week 20: December 28	141,486.00	103.00
		Week 21: January 4	154,072.00	102.02
		House Record ($25 New Year's Eve)		
		Year End Total	**$2,761,045.00**	**102.76**

1976

Seats	Ticket Price/ Potential	Week Ending	Net Receipts	% Capacity
		Week 22: January 11	140,047.00	101.90
		Week 23: January 18	139,009.00	102.00
		Week 24: January 25	140,593.00	102.00
		Week 25: February 1	141,614.00	102.00
		Jan. 31 performance — No Sheila role		
		Week 26: February 8	137,758.00	102.00
		Week 27: February 15	141,141.00	102.00
		Week 28: February 22	141,302.00	102.00
		Week 29: February 29	140,535.00	102.00
		Week 30: March 7	140,500.00	102.00
		Week 31: March 14	139,003.00	102.00
		Week 32: March 21	139,081.00	102.00
		Mar. 19 — Betty Ford sees show and meets cast		
		Week 33: March 28	140,319.00	102.00
		Mar. 23 — ACL nominated for 12 Tony® Awards		
		Week 34: April 4	140,298.00	103.00
		Week 35: April 11	140,276.00	103.00
		Apr. 10 — Elizabeth Taylor and Audrey Hepburn in audience		
		Week 36: April 18	141,294.00	103.00
		Apr. 18 — ACL wins 9 Tony® Awards including Best Musical		
		Week 37: April 25	141,245.00	N/A
		Week 38: May 2	141,319.00	103.00
		May 3 — ACL receives Pulitzer Prize for Drama		
		Week 39: May 9	139,822.00	103.00
		May 6 — National Co. opens in San Francisco & International Co. opens in Toronto		
		Week 40: May 16	140,938.00	103.00
		Week 41: May 23	140,591.00	103.00
		Week 42: May 30	142,379.00	103.00
		Week 43: June 6	141,879.00	90.00
		Week 44: June 13	142,421.00	103.20
		Week 45: June 20	142,163.00	103.00
		Week 46: June 27	141,525.00	99.98
		Week 47: July 4	142,255.00	101.00
		Jul. 1 — ACL opens in L.A. with largest advance sale in L.A. history: $1,400,000		

Seats	Ticket Price/ Potential	Week Ending	Net Receipts	% Capacity		Seats	Ticket Price/ Potential	Week Ending	Net Receipts	% Capacity
		Week 48: July 11	142,561.00	101.00				Week 81: February 27	158,348.00	102.20
		Week 49: July 18	142,418.00	101.00				Week 82: March 6	157,034.00	102.20
		Week 50: July 25	141,832.00	101.00				Week 83: March 13	158,699.00	101.80
		Jul. 22 — ACL opens in London;						Week 84: March 20	157,726.00	102.20
		Jul. 25 — ACL begins 2nd year						Week 85: March 27	157,740.00	102.10
		Week 51: August 1	141,390.00	101.00				*Mar. 21 — Gerald & Betty Ford see show*		
		Week 52: August 8	142,355.00	101.00				*(her second time)*		
		Week 53: August 15	142,131.00	101.00				Week 86: April 3	158,117.00	102.20
		Week 54: August 22	142,447.00	101.00				Week 87: April 10	158,076.00	102.20
		Week 55: August 29	142,279.00	101.00				*Apr. 7 — ACL wins five L.A. Drama Critics*		
		Week 56: September 5	142,593.00	101.00				*awards including Best Musical*		
1466	$16.50/$157,280.86	Week 57: September 12	153,815.00	101.00				Week 88: April 17	157,217.00	102.10
33 standees		Week 58: September 19	153,036.00	101.00				Week 89: April 24	155,206.00	102.00
		Week 59: September 26	153,579.00	101.00				Week 90: May 1	155,928.00	101.90
		Week 60: October 3	153,871.00	101.00				Week 91: May 8	157,332.00	102.10
		Week 61: October 10	153,552.00	101.00				Week 92: May 15	156,585.00	101.90
		Week 62: October 17	153,849.00	101.00				Week 93: May 22	157,537.00	102.20
		Week 63: October 24	152,846.00	101.00				Week 94: May 29	157,511.00	102.20
		Week 64: October 31	153,155.00	101.00				*May 24 — Australian production opens*		
		Week 65: November 7	154,345.00	101.00				*at Sydney's Her Majesty's Theatre*		
		Week 66: November 14	154,245.00	101.00				Week 95: June 5	158,377.00	102.20
		Week 67: November 21	154,496.00	101.00				Week 96: June 12	158,570.00	101.80
		Week 68: November 28	154,125.00	100.80				Week 97: June 19	158,150.00	101.80
	$16,50/$161,144.80	Week 69: December 5	153,853.00	100.50				*Jun. 13 — The Stuttgart Ballet sees show*		
		Week 70: December 12	155,542.00	101.20				Week 98: June 26	158,943.00	101.80
		Week 71: December 19	154,988.00	100.80				Week 99: July 3	158,737.00	101.80
		Week 72: December 26	154,967.00	100.80				Week 100: July 10	159,693.00	99.98
		Week 73: January 2	165,555.00	101.20			$17.50/$164,868.30	Week 101: July 17	156,423.00	99.97
		House Record Gross						*Jul. 13 — ConEd blackout interrupts Paul's monologue*		
		Year End Total	**$7,569,132.00**	**99.43**				Week 102: July 24	155,452.00	102.20
								Week 103: July 31	154,764.00	102.10
								Jul. 25 — ACL begins 3rd year on Broadway		

1977

Seats	Ticket Price/ Potential	Week Ending	Net Receipts	% Capacity
		Week 74: January 9	156,924.00	100.80
		Week 75: January 16	155,586.00	101.20
		Week 76: January 23	157,072.00	102.20
		Week 77: January 30	157,256.00	102.20
		Feb. 2 — International Co. returns from London,		
		opens in Baltimore Feb. 13		
		Week 78: February 6	157,705.00	102.20
		Feb. 12 — ACL wins London Evening Standard		
		award for Best Musical		
		Week 79: February 13	158,382.00	102.20
		Week 80: February 20	157,835.00	101.80

Week Ending	Net Receipts	% Capacity
Week 104: August 7	159,940.00	102.20
Week 105: August 14	160,201.00	102.10
Week 106: August 21	160,780.00	102.20
Week 107: August 28	160,715.00	102.20
Week 108: September 4	162,034.00	102.10
Week 109: September 11	160,521.00	102.20
Week 110: September 18	161,232.00	102.20
Week 111: September 25	160,487.00	100.50
Week 112: October 2	161,631.00	101.90
Week 113: October 9	162,251.00	101.90
Week 114: October 16	161,515.00	102.20
Week 115: October 23	162,578.00	102.20

Seats	Ticket Price/Potential	Week Ending	Net Receipts	% Capacity
		Week 116: October 30	161,904.00	102.20
		Week 117: November 6	158,579.00	100.60
		Week 118: November 13	161,989.00	100.60
		Week 119: November 20	161,150.00	101.50
		Nov. 15 — Greer Garson sees show and poses with cast		
		Week 120: November 27	161,615.00	102.20
		Week 121: December 4	158,196.00	100.10
		Week 122: December 11	156,839.00	99.96
		Week 123: December 18	154,390.00	97.00
		Week 124: December 25	160,848.00	85.70
		Week 125: January 1	172,388.00	102.00
		Year End Total	**$8,264,708.00**	**101.37**

1978

Seats	Ticket Price/Potential	Week Ending	Net Receipts	% Capacity
		Week 126: January 8	162,682.00	102.00
		Jan. 7 — ACL closes in L.A. after 18 months and opens in Chicago		
		Week 127: January 15	161,153.00	102.20
		Jan. 9 — ACL plays its 1,000th performance		
		Week 128: January 22	160,021.00	101.30
		Jan. 17 — ACL wins Gold Record award from Columbia Records		
		Week 129: January 29	153,241.00	95.40
		Week 130: February 5	143,304.00	92.60
		Week 131: February 12	140,475.00	91.80
		Week 132: February 19	138,617.00	95.40
		Week 133: February 26	161,587.00	100.50
		Week 134: March 5	146,749.00	93.40
1472	$18.50/$174,042.98	Week 135: March 12	156,756.00	95.60
33 standees		Week 136: March 19	161,385.00	100.60
		Week 137: March 26	164,365.00	102.20
		Week 138: April 2	162,561.00	102.20
		Week 139: April 9	161,393.00	99.50
		Week 140: April 16	162,104.00	100.30
		Week 141: April 23	165,242.00	102.00
		Week 142: April 30	166,074.00	102.00
		Week 143: May 7	165,220.00	101.20
		Week 144: May 14	165,228.00	100.90
		Week 145: May 21	167,828.00	102.10
		Week 146: May 28	166,180.00	102.10
		Week 147: June 4	163,980.00	98.90
		Week 148: June 11	167,868.00	102.00

Seats	Ticket Price/Potential	Week Ending	Net Receipts	% Capacity
		Week 149: June 18	168,035.00	101.50
		Week 150: June 25	168,579.00	101.40
		Week 151: July 2	166,758.00	100.00
		Week 152: July 9	161,673.00	96.70
		Week 153: July 16	169,950.00	93.70
		Week 154: July 23	169,533.00	102.00
		Week 155: July 30	170,406.00	102.20
		Jul. 25 — ACL begins 4th year on Broadway		
	$19.50/$179,754.63	Week 156: August 6	174,956.00	102.10
		Week 157: August 13	175,864.00	102.20
		Week 158: August 20	175,970.00	102.20
		Newspaper strike — 3 daily papers		
	$21.50/$203,105.79	Week 159: August 27	190,947.00	101.20
		Newspaper strike — 3 daily papers		
		Week 160: September 3	185,843.00	98.00
		Newspaper strike — 3 daily papers		
		Week 161: September 10	154,449.00	80.40
		Newspaper strike — 3 daily papers		
		Week 162: September 17	171,799.00	88.70
		Newspaper strike — 3 daily papers		
		Week 163: September 24	168,558.00	86.30
		Newspaper strike — 3 daily papers		
		Week 164: October 1	166,371.00	85.50
		Week 165: October 8	163,871.00	90.20
		Week 166: October 15	177,434.00	97.40
		Week 167: October 22	180,766.00	99.20
		Week 168: October 29	176,281.00	97.50
		Week 169: November 5	162,957.00	91.70
		Week 170: November 12	170,635.00	94.20
		Week 171: November 19	172,142.00	98.80
		Week 172: November 26	176,484.00	95.60
		Week 173: December 3	151,669.00	84.10
		Dec. 2 — ACL closes in Chicago after 11 months and begins road tour		
		Week 174: December 10	163,287.00	90.00
		Week 175: December 17	158,568.00	88.20
		Week 176: December 24	158,622.00	89.20
	$24.00/$219,212.35	Week 177: December 31	221,712.00	102.20
		New Year's Eve — $27.50		
		Total Year End	**$8,638,132.00**	**97.09**

Seats	Ticket Price/ Potential	Week Ending	Net Receipts	% Capacity

1979

Seats	Ticket Price/ Potential	Week Ending	Net Receipts	% Capacity
		Week 178: January 7	196,312.00	98.90
		Week 179: January 14	192,922.00	99.00
		Week 180: January 21	188,843.00	98.10
		Week 181: January 28	178,491.00	93.90
		Week 182: February 4	180,711.00	94.90
		Week 183: February 11	165,285.00	83.70
		Week 184: February 18	185,028.00	101.70
		Week 185: February 25	204,175.00	100.40
		Week 186: March 4	175,459.00	93.10
		Week 187: March 11	182,853.00	93.50
		Week 188: March 18	193,736.00	99.40
		Week 189: March 25	208,227.00	100.70
		Week 190: April 1	198,273.00	99.80
		Week 191: April 8	187,894.00	101.00
		Week 192: April 15	203,799.00	100.90
		Week 193: April 22	215,530.00	101.40
		Week 194: April 29	196,969.00	93.30
		Week 195: May 6	191,042.00	96.40
		Week 196: May 13	187,259.00	96.10
	$25.00/$222,185.38	Week 197: May 20	194,147.00	99.40
		Week 198: May 27	202,669.00	101.40
		Week 199: June 3	194,259.00	99.70
		Week 200: June 10	199,466.00	83.30
		Week 201: June 17	194,223.00	91.50
		Week 202: June 24	201,091.00	96.60
		Week 203: July 1	198,660.00	101.25
		Week 204: July 8	172,137.00	93.90
		Week 205: July 15	189,945.00	97.30
		Week 206: July 22	192,170.00	99.98

Jul. 17 — Peking Dance Company & National Dance Theatre of China attend show

Seats	Ticket Price/ Potential	Week Ending	Net Receipts	% Capacity
		Week 207: July 29	188,291.00	103.40

Jul. 25 — ACL begins 5th year on Broadway

Seats	Ticket Price/ Potential	Week Ending	Net Receipts	% Capacity
		Week 208: August 5	191,847.00	89.20
		Week 209: August 12	199,941.00	101.40
		Week 210: August 19	207,034.00	101.66
		Week 211: August 26	200,767.00	101.77
		Week 212: September 2	194,106.00	99.00
		Week 213: September 9	179,307.00	85.40
		Week 214: September 16	179,647.00	94.20
		Week 215: September 23	182,395.00	99.80
		Week 216: September 30	182,814.00	95.10
		Week 217: October 7	176,602.00	82.30
		Week 218: October 14	191,474.00	97.50
		Week 219: October 21	200,017.00	100.40
		Week 220: October 28	193,475.00	92.10
		Week 221: November 4	174,334.00	87.50
		Week 222: November 11	190,153.00	99.10
		Week 223: November 18	187,496.00	96.80
		Week 224: November 25	197,629.00	100.67
	$25.00/$227,182.78	Week 225: December 2	175,330.00	80.30
		Week 226: December 9	173,957.00	87.70
		Week 227: December 16	167,329.00	84.90
		Week 228: December 23	149,727.00	79.90
		Week 229: December 30	219,468.00	102.22
		Total Year End	**$9,874,715.00**	**95.63**

1980

Seats	Ticket Price/ Potential	Week Ending	Net Receipts	% Capacity
		Week 230: January 6	214,910.00	93.90
		Week 231: January 13	195,993.00	90.90
		Week 232: Janurary 20	188,882.00	97.50
		Week 233: January 27	181,059.00	93.70
		Week 234: February 3	164,150.00	83.40
		Week 235: February 10	159,729.00	66.70
		Week 236: February 17	183,664.00	90.20
		Week 237: February 24	206,337.00	100.45
		Week 238: March 2	170,761.00	85.00
		Week 239: March 9	169,118.00	77.30
		Week 240: March 16	182,454.00	94.10
		Week 241: March 23	197,572.00	99.97
		Week 242: March 30	188,844.00	96.60
		Week 243: April 6	195,425.00	97.70
		Week 244: April 13	177,335.00	90.90
		Week 245: April 20	173,540.00	87.70
		Week 246: April 27	194,514.00	98.20

Apr. 24 — Mikhail Baryshnikov joins the ACL cast in ONE for the finale of "Baryshnikov on Broadway"

Seats	Ticket Price/ Potential	Week Ending	Net Receipts	% Capacity
	$27.50/$240,946.24	Week 247: May 4	176,820.00	89.00
		Week 248: May 11	184,695.00	90.30
		Week 249: May 18	193,171.00	95.80
		Week 250: May 25	197,560.00	98.00

Seats	Ticket Price/ Potential	Week Ending	Net Receipts	% Capacity		Seats	Ticket Price/ Potential	Week Ending	Net Receipts	% Capacity
		Week 251: June 1	191,644.00	94.20						
		Week 252: June 8	195,966.00	95.40				**1981**		
		Week 253: June 15	202,463.00	97.70				Week 283 : January 11	193,484.00	85.50
		Jun. 11 — ACL plays 2,000 performance						Week 284: January 18	182,087.00	79.50
		Week 254: June 22	209,846.00	96.50				Week 285: January 25	171,772.00	95.20
		Week 255: June 29	216,447.00	98.90				Week 286: February 1	174,604.00	76.30
		Week 256: July 6	197,626.00	98.00				*Jan. 30 — Iranian hostages attend show*		
		Week 257: July 13	202,636.00	97.20				Week 287: February 8	148,959.00	64.20
	$30.00/$254,048.84	Week 258: July 20	214,637.00	97.10				Week 288: February 15	175,803.00	76.50
		Week 259: July 27	219,509.00	100.54				Week 289: February 22	219,056.00	95.40
		Jul. 25 — ACL begins 6th year on Broadway						Week 290: March 1	190,762.00	87.70
		Week 260: August 3	225,372.00	99.70				*Feb. 24 — ACL entertains President & Mrs. Reagan*		
	$30.00/$275,267.08	Week 261: August 10	232,518.00	99.20				*and the nation's governors at the first official*		
		Week 262: August 17	226,194.00	99.40				*White House dinner*		
		Week 263: August 24	245,530.00	101.37				Week 291: March 8	166,840.00	75.90
		Week 264: August 31	244,642.00	99.40				Week 292: March 15	187,455.00	97.60
		Week 265: September 7	202,235.00	92.60				Week 293: March 22	208,922.00	96.00
		Week 266: September 14	213,211.00	94.00				Week 294: March 29	214,010.00	97.60
		Sep. 14 — National Tour closes in Montreal,					$30.00/$273,454.44	Week 295: April 5	181,416.00	83.60
		becomes the Bus & Truck Tour						Week 296: April 12	182,466.00	82.00
		Week 267: September 21	211,147.00	91.90				Week 297: April 19	218,882.00	96.40
		Week 268: September 28	211,146.00	89.90				Week 298: April 26	230,547.00	99.90
		Week 269: October 5	209,816.00	92.00				Week 299: May 3	185,286.00	80.50
		Week 270: October 12	216,634.00	94.50				Week 300: May 10	182,419.00	86.70
		Week 271: October 19	222,739.00	95.30				Week 301: May 17	199,833.00	84.30
		Week 272: October 26	220,795.00	95.60				Week 302: May 24	210,080.00	93.60
		Week 273: November 2	207,790.00	92.80				Week 303: May 31	186,487.00	84.20
		Week 274: November 9	202,913.00	89.20				*May 27 — ACL chosen as first musical to be given a*		
		Week 275: November 16	216,077.00	94.30				*sign-interpreted performance*		
		Week 276: November 23	191,804.00	85.70				Week 304: June 7	187,409.00	82.90
		Week 277: November 30	219,106.00	96.00				Week 305: June 14	199,810.00	87.70
		Week 278: December 7	200,174.00	89.20				Week 306: June 21	198,540.00	72.40
		Week 279: December 14	195,171.00	86.10				Week 307: June 28	215,754.00	94.80
		Week 280: December 21	165,088.00	76.10				*Jun. 23 — Second sign-interpreted performance given*		
		Week 281: December 28	211,982.00	85.60				Week 308: July 5	170,736.00	78.90
		Week 282: January 4	258,431.00	99.90				Week 309: July 12	183,504.00	82.90
		Total Year End	**$10,697,822.00**	**93.07**				Week 310: July 19	192,530.00	87.10
								Week 311: July 26	203,277.00	91.70
								Jul. 25 — ACL begins 7th year on Broadway		
		•						Week 312: August 2	203,387.00	90.80
								Week 313: August 9	214,326.00	94.90
							$35.00/$310,214.30	Week 314: August 16	222,392.00	97.40
								Week 315: August 23	229,518.00	96.10
								Week 316: August 30	221,392.00	92.40

Seats	Ticket Price/ Potential	Week Ending	Net Receipts	% Capacity
		Week 317: September 6	199,984.00	82.10
		Week 318: September 13	176,980.00	70.00
		Week 319: September 20	192,961.00	74.30
		Week 320: September 27	194,651.00	74.20
		Week 321: October 4	190,490.00	74.30
		Week 322: October 11	196,689.00	73.80
		Week 323: October 18	218,520.00	81.90
		Week 324: October 25	206,605.00	78.90
		Week 325: November 1	180,866.00	69.40
		Week 326: November 8	182,989.00	70.20
		Week 327: November 15	215,406.00	85.30
		Week 328: November 22	170,387.00	68.30
		Week 329: November 29	214,601.00	77.40
		Week 330: December 6	169,021.00	66.30
		Week 331: December 13	171,671.00	66.80
		Week 332: December 20	128,517.00	51.40
		Week 333: December 27	197,059.00	61.50
		Week 334: January 3	284,058.00	98.50
		Year End Total	**$10,145,200.00**	**82.56**

1982

Seats	Ticket Price/ Potential	Week Ending	Net Receipts	% Capacity
	$40.00/$361,803.40	Week 335: January 10	194,297.00	73.60
		ACL begins using Twofers		
		Week 336: January 17	161,909.00	57.70
		Week 337: January 24	148,174.00	52.40
		Week 338: January 31	161,363.00	58.10
		Eliminates Monday evenings — begins Sunday matinees		
		Week 339: February 7	175,047.00	63.90
		Week 340: February 14	217,983.00	76.60
		Week 341: February 21	239,399.00	87.90
		Week 342: February 28	214,258.00	80.20
		Feb. 26 — ACL passes record run of MY FAIR LADY		
		Week 343: March 7	191,044.00	72.80
		Week 344: March 14	216,851.00	83.00
		Week 345: March 21	222,556.00	81.70
		Week 346: March 28	253,196.00	93.60
		Week 347: April 4	203,899.00	78.60
		Week 348: April 11	224,340.00	82.50
		Week 349: April 18	252,166.00	91.50
		Week 350: April 25	231,977.00	83.70
		Apr. 24 — Mexico City production opens		
		Week 351: May 2	202,983.00	75.10

Seats	Ticket Price/ Potential	Week Ending	Net Receipts	% Capacity
		Week 352: May 9	206,716.00	76.50
		Week 353: May 16	200,801.00	74.30
		Week 354: May 23	233,843.00	86.20
		Week 355: May 30	207,790.00	79.30
		Week 356: June 6	174,957.00	65.30
		Week 357: June 13	205,671.00	75.80
		Week 358: June 20	194,989.00	73.60
		Jun. 17 — ACL passes HELLO,DOLLY! and becomes 3rd longest running musical in Broadway history & 5th longest running show		
		Week 359: June 37	206,111.00	75.50
		Week 360: July 4	175,801.00	66.60
		Week 361: July 11	177,848.00	66.90
		Week 362: July 18	186,207.00	71.30
		Week 363: July 25	192,036.00	73.30
		Jul. 25 — ACL begins 8th year on Broadway		
		Week 364: August 1	212,656.00	82.50
		Week 365: August 8	212,318.00	81.20
		Week 366: August 15	231,491.00	89.50
		Week 367: August 22	232,855.00	90.10
		Week 368: August 29	218,838.00	85.10
		Week 369: September 5	207,696.00	83.50
	$40.00/$378,114.80	Week 370: September 12	177,478.00	65.80
		Week 371: September 19	193,353.00	72.50
		Week 372: September 26	211,914.00	76.10
		Week 373: October 3	234,490.00	84.10
		Oct .3 — Bus & Truck tour closes in Pittsburgh		
		Week 374: October 11	238,711.00	79.10
		Week 375: October 17	236,183.00	81.10
		Week 376: October 24	228,438.00	78.80
		Oct. 24 — ACL plays its 3,000th performance		
		Week 377: October 31	205,914.00	73.80
		Week 378: November 7	211,214.00	72.60
		Week 379: November 14	240,460.00	84.70
	$45.00/$423,954.80	Week 380: November 21	193,828.00	65.10
		Week 381: November 28	254,295.00	76.00
		Week 382: December 5	228,185.00	77.50
		Week 383: December 12	211,248.00	69.40
		Week 384: December 19	163,145.00	56.00
		Week 385: December 26	157,335.00	56.00
		Week 386: January 2	296,544.00	88.20
		Total Year End	**$10,872,801.00**	**75.89**

Seats	Ticket Price/ Potential	Week Ending	Net Receipts	% Capacity

1983

Seats	Ticket Price/ Potential	Week Ending	Net Receipts	% Capacity
		Week 387: January 9	229,991.00	76.10
		Week 388: January 16	181,058.00	71.20
		Week 389: January 23	184,328.00	60.20
		Week 390: January 30	176,746.00	59.70
		Week 391: February 6	156,895.00	50.80
		Week 392: February 13	140,357.00	48.10
		Week 393: February 20	191,810.00	69.40
		Week 394: February 27	190,439.00	69.50
		Week 395: March 6	159,367.00	51.80
		Week 396: March 13	181,461.00	61.80
		Week 397: March 20	229,811.00	79.70
		Week 398: March 27	237,161.00	83.10
		Week 399: April 3	266,685.00	92.10

Apr. 2 — ACL passes TOBACCO ROAD run

Seats	Ticket Price/ Potential	Week Ending	Net Receipts	% Capacity
		Week 400: April 10	232,868.00	80.30
		Week 401: April 17	194,821.00	63.50

Apr. 15 — Sao Paulo production opens

Seats	Ticket Price/ Potential	Week Ending	Net Receipts	% Capacity
		Week 402: April 24	224,375.00	70.20
		Week 403: May 1	207,458.00	70.60
		Week 404: May 8	179,637.00	63.90
		Week 405: May 15	211,009.00	67.20

May 9 — ACL passes LIFE WITH FATHER run

Seats	Ticket Price/ Potential	Week Ending	Net Receipts	% Capacity
		Week 406: May 22	244,722.00	83.40
		Week 407: May 29	214,921.00	74.10

May 25 — ACL passes FIDDLER ON THE ROOF to become 2nd longest running show in Broadway history

Seats	Ticket Price/ Potential	Week Ending	Net Receipts	% Capacity
		Week 408: June 5	179,426.00	59.70

May 29 — International Co. closes in Chicago

Seats	Ticket Price/ Potential	Week Ending	Net Receipts	% Capacity
		Week 409: June 12	195,281.00	65.10
		Week 410: June 19	176,598.00	58.30
		Week 411: June 26	197,657.00	63.90
		Week 412: July 3	177,676.00	59.80
		Week 413: July 10	161,237.00	53.40
		Week 414: July 17	189,104.00	62.80
		Week 415: July 24	192,191.00	62.90
		Week 416: July 31	211,099.00	71.20

Jul. 25 — ACL begins 9th year on Broadway

Seats	Ticket Price/ Potential	Week Ending	Net Receipts	% Capacity
		Week 417: August 7	210,402.00	70.70
	$45.00/$463,071.60	Week 418: August 14	240,499.00	77.90
		Week 419: August 21	233,949.00	73.30
		Week 420: August 28	233,650.00	73.80

Seats	Ticket Price/ Potential	Week Ending	Net Receipts	% Capacity
		Week 421: September 4	207,740.00	64.00
		Week 422: September 11	180,139.00	58.30
		Week 423: September 18	196,995.00	62.40
		Week 424: September 25	217,364.00	55.90
		Week 425: October 2	225,147.00	66.90

Sep. 29 — Performance #3389. ACL passes GREASE to become the longest running show in Broadway history — no charge for Gala, invitation only

Seats	Ticket Price/ Potential	Week Ending	Net Receipts	% Capacity
		Week 426: October 9	326,158.00	94.00
		Week 427: October 16	305,796.00	89.10
		Week 428: October 23	321,221.00	89.80
		Week 429: October 30	310,350.00	89.90
		Week 430: November 6	264,505.00	71.00
		Week 431: November 13	297,221.00	83.60
		Week 432: November 20	283,430.00	79.80
		Week 433: November 27	319,964.00	86.30
		Week 434: December 4	258,716.00	77.20
		Week 435: December 11	265,392.00	74.30
		Week 436: December 18	242,441.00	69.00
		Week 437: December 25	169,414.00	46.40
		Week 438: January 1	387,762.00	97.20
		Total Year End	**$11,614,444.00**	**70.28**

1984

Seats	Ticket Price/ Potential	Week Ending	Net Receipts	% Capacity
		Week 439: January 8	226,073.00	67.20
		Week 440: January 15	211,886.00	63.10
		Week 441: January 23	178,729.00	52.30
		Week 442: January 30	178,683.00	53.00
		Week 443: February 5	150,349.00	45.50
		Week 444: February 12	160,973.00	45.80
		Week 445: February 19	206,633.00	58.80
		Week 446: February 26	255,641.00	62.80
		Week 447: March 4	192,071.00	58.50
		Week 448: March 11	208,492.00	65.80
		Week 449: March 18	256,027.00	80.20
		Week 450: March 25	267,670.00	80.60
		Week 451: April 1	227,582.00	69.50
		Week 452: April 8	225,089.00	68.20
		Week 453: April 15	239,245.00	74.40
		Week 454: April 22	308,708.00	92.00
		Week 455: April 29	275,710.00	84.80
		Week 456: May 6	245,310.00	76.50

Seats	Ticket Price/ Potential	Week Ending	Net Receipts	% Capacity		Seats	Ticket Price/ Potential	Week Ending	Net Receipts	% Capacity
		Week 457: May 13	228,960.00	71.40						
		Week 458: May 20	255,060.00	76.80				**1985**		
		Week 459: May 27	257,516.00	77.50				Week 491: January 6	242,501.00	68.20
		Week 460: June 3	211,766.00	64.40				Week 492: January 13	179,428.00	50.60
		Week 461: June 10	245,064.00	74.90				Week 493: January 20	183,704.00	54.70
		Week 462: June 17	234,488.00	67.80				Week 494: January 27	148,124.00	43.10
		Week 463: June 24	253,251.00	74.50				Week 495: February 3	128,259.00	40.30
		Week 464: July 1	239,115.00	71.30				Week 496: February 10	128,677.00	36.50
		Week 465: July 8	212,342.00	69.30				Week 497: February 17	187,398.00	49.70
		Week 466: July 15	244,270.00	81.00				Week 498: February 24	223,251.00	66.90
		Week 467: July 22	243,312.00	80.20				Week 499: March 3	160,270.00	46.80
		Week 468: July 29	242,007.00	77.30				Week 500: March 10	180,457.00	51.60
		Jul. 25 — ACL begins 10th year on Broadway						Week 501: March 17	236,899.00	73.00
		Week 469: August 5	230,243.00	71.90				*Mar. 16 — ACL plays 4,000 performance*		
		Week 470: August 12	257,443.00	77.70				Week 502: March 24	264,415.00	83.20
		Week 471: August 19	266,559.00	79.40				Week 503: March 31	230,432.00	73.80
		Week 472: August 26	260,704.00	77.50				Week 504: April 7	266,690.00	84.50
		Week 473: September 2	242,003.00	71.80				Week 505: April 14	282,880.00	86.70
		Week 474: September 9	194,559.00	55.90				Week 506: April 21	246,400.00	75.80
		Week 475: September 16	223,483.00	64.40				Week 507 :April 28	254,678.00	79.60
		Week 476: September 23	235,318.00	65.10				Week 508: May 5	236,483.00	75.80
		Week 477: September 30	241,364.00	68.90				Week 509: May 12	226,424.00	70.80
		Week 478: October 7	235,820.00	65.40				Week 510: May 19	258,414.00	78.10
		Week 479: October 14	270,535.00	76.60				Week 511: May 26	246,925.00	75.40
		Week 480: October 21	269,091.00	76.70				Week 512: June 2	194,341.00	62.50
		Week 481: October 28	275,169.00	77.60				Week 513: June 9	222,584.00	69.40
		Week 482: November 4	230,247.00	64.50				Week 514: June 16	219,204.00	67.20
		Week 483: November 11	234,148.00	68.10				Week 515: June 23	228,426.00	68.80
		Week 484: November 18	237,532.00	65.80				Week 516 :June 30	230,472.00	66.60
		Week 485: November 25	302,189.00	80.40				Week 517: July 7	183,355.00	52.50
		Week 486: December 2	223,278.00	63.70				Week 518: July 14	192,005.00	55.60
		Week 487: December 9	247,561.00	71.00				Week 519: July 21	221,613.00	67.30
		Week 488: December 16	207,242.00	58.70				Week 520: July 28	221,924.00	66.40
		Week 489: December 23	181,870.00	50.80				*Jul. 25 — ACL begins 11th year on Broadway*		
		Week 490: December 30	395,627.00	99.50				Week 521: August 4	221,873.00	65.70
		New House Record and new high gross for the show						Week 522 :August 11	248,522.00	74.30
		Total Year End	**$12,344,007.00**	**69.94**				Week 523: August 18	285,858.00	85.10
								Week 524 :August 25	275,565.00	84.20
								Week 525: September 1	254,608.00	75.50
								Week 526: September 8	172,328.00	49.80
								Week 527: September 15	190,672.00	56.50
								Week 528: September 22	189,860.00	54.40

Seats	Ticket Price/ Potential	Week Ending	Net Receipts	% Capacity
		Week 529: September 29	174,957.00	50.00
		Week 530: October 6	192,262.00	53.00
		Week 531: October 13	231,773.00	64.70
		Week 532: October 20	249,316.00	69.90
		Week 533: October 27	225,653.00	64.70
		Week 534: November 3	199,286.00	55.90
		Week 535: November 10	218,474.00	64.30
		Week 536: November 17	209,932.00	62.60
		Week 537: Novemebr 24	189,451.00	55.00
		Week 538: December 1	282,963.00	74.60
		Week 539: December 8	242,153.00	71.10
		Week 540: December 15	241,312.00	68.50

Dec. 9 — A CHORUS LINE — THE MOVIE opens

Seats	Ticket Price/ Potential	Week Ending	Net Receipts	% Capacity
		Week 541: December 22	189,661.00	55.90
		Week 542: December 29	380,075.00	95.70
		Total Year End	**$11,303,327.00**	**65.25**

1986

Seats	Ticket Price/ Potential	Week Ending	Net Receipts	% Capacity
		Week 543: January 5	309,586.00	84.60
		Week 544: January 12	200,685.00	55.30
		Week 545: January 19	201,209.00	54.00
		Week 546: January 26	163,872.00	43.50
		Week 547: February 2	152,050.00	42.30
		Week 548: February 9	150,029.00	41.30
		Week 549: February 16	210,343.00	56.40
		Week 550: February 23	207,716.00	57.30
		Week 551: March 2	178,695.00	51.10
		Week 552: March 9	178,880.00	50.70
		Week 553: March 16	223,335.00	65.10
		Week 554: March 23	222,512.00	63.80
		Week 555: March 30	285,565.00	83.40
		Week 556: April 6	236,833.00	71.60
		Week 557: April 13	208,001.00	64.50
		Week 558: April 20	209,041.00	65.00
		Week 559: April 27	234,722.00	69.30
		Week 560: May 4	226,166.00	70.10
		Week 561: May 11	218,967.00	67.20
		Week 562: May 18	225,179.00	67.10
		Week 563: May 25	239,299.00	72.40
		Week 564: June 1	190,226.00	57.60

Amateur and stock rights released for the first time

Seats	Ticket Price/ Potential	Week Ending	Net Receipts	% Capacity
		Week 565: June 8	187,722.00	57.50
		Week 566: June 15	199,711.00	61.70
		Week 567: June 22	204,633.00	60.70
		Week 568: June 29	202,416.00	59.90
		Week 569: July 6	242,576.00	58.10
		Week 570: July 13	236,808.00	70.00
		Week 571: July 20	253,030.00	80.10
		Week 572: July 27	252,008.00	77.90

Jul. 25 — ACL begins 12th year on Broadway

Seats	Ticket Price/ Potential	Week Ending	Net Receipts	% Capacity
		Week 573: August 3	251,698.00	76.50
		Week 574: August 10	265,593.00	77.00
		Week 575: August 17	277,699.00	80.70
		Week 576: August 24	273,384.00	81.00
		Week 577: August 31	242,645.00	69.10
		Week 578: September 7	151,569.00	42.10

Sep. 1 — Donna McKechnie returns to Broadway as Cassie

Seats	Ticket Price/ Potential	Week Ending	Net Receipts	% Capacity
		Week 579: September 14	186,211.00	55.30
		Week 580: September 21	204,637.00	58.60
		Week 581: September 28	201,947.00	56.80
		Week 582: October 5	182,657.00	50.60
		Week 583: October 12	219,857.00	60.00
		Week 584: October 19	217,052.00	63.00
		Week 585: October 26	217,158.00	61.80
		Week 586: November 2	182,432.00	52.60
		Week 587: November 9	233,307.00	68.20
		Week 588: November 16	220,383.00	61.60
		Week 589: November 23	189,810.00	55.20
		Week 590: November 30	258,123.00	69.30
		Week 591: December 7	206,834.00	59.80
		Week 592: December 14	200,307.00	54.40
		Week 593: December 21	143,065.00	41.30
		Week 594: December 28	270,351.00	71.30
		Week 595: January 4	288,258.00	77.60
		Total Year End	**$11,536,792.00**	**62.70**

Seats	Ticket Price/ Potential	Week Ending	Net Receipts	% Capacity
1987				
		Week 596: January 11	154,854.00	42.60
		Week 597: January 18	156,170.00	41.70
		Week 598: January 25	127,492.00	33.60
		Week 599: February 1	109,185.00	30.00
		Week 600: February 8	120,255.00	35.10
		Week 601: February 15	162,161.00	46.20
		Week 602: February 22	187,139.00	58.10
		Week 603: March 1	144,240.00	46.20
		Week 604: March 8	146,694.00	45.40
		Week 605: March 15	176,982.00	55.50
		Week 606: March 22	205,955.00	60.60
		Week 607: March 29	217,665.00	64.80
		Week 608: April 5	175,255.00	51.00
		Week 609: April 12	196,883.00	57.80
		Week 610: April 19	277,880.00	80.10
		Week 611: April 26	233,519.00	70.90
		Week 612: May 3	221,566.00	67.80
		Week 613: May 10	199,324.00	59.90
		Week 614: May 17	196,186.00	57.00
		May 16 — Donna McKechnie's last performance on Broadway		
		Week 615: May 24	218,034.00	65.80
		Week 616: May 31	193,449.00	58.70
		Week 617: June 7	177,759.00	54.00
		Week 618: June 14	202,066.00	59.30
		Week 619: June 21	194,192.00	55.30
		Week 620: June 28	212,682.00	61.90
		Week 621: July 5	163,548.00	48.20
		Jul. 2 — Michael Bennett dies		
		Week 622: July 12	209,619.00	63.10
		Week 623: July 19	234,330.00	74.30
		Week 624: July 27	224,869.00	66.10
		Jul. 25 — ACL begins 13th year on Broadway		
		Week 625: August 2	238,699.00	73.10
		Week 626: August 9	264,376.00	77.80
		Week 627: August 16	298,376.00	84.60
		Aug. 10 — ACL plays 5,000 performances (Chance to Dance contest)		
		Week 628: August 23	297,554.00	86.70
		Week 629: August 30	292,756.00	85.70
		Week 630: September 6	214,242.00	62.60

Seats	Ticket Price/ Potential	Week Ending	Net Receipts	% Capacity
		Week 631: September 13	206,929.00	58.10
		Week 632: September 20	231,890.00	64.30
		Week 633: September 27	205,154.00	58.90
1472	$47.50/$467,159.00	Week 634: October 4	196,513.00	54.00
24 standees		Week 635: October 11	240,755.00	65.10
		Week 636: October 18	234,334.00	63.80
		Week 637: October 25	212,437.00	57.60
		Week 638: November 1	165,664.00	45.80
		Week 639: November 8	192,296.00	53.70
		Week 640: November 15	187,064.00	51.20
		Week 641: November 22	165,211.00	45.90
		Week 642: November 29	240,973.00	65.60
		Week 643: December 6	192,370.00	58.80
		Week 644: December 13	206,052.00	61.90
		Week 645: December 20	132,889.00	42.00
		Week 646: December 27	202,077.00	58.80
		Week 647: January 3	342,520.00	91.30
		Total Year End	**$10,601,084.00**	**59.20**
1988				
		Week 648 January 10	138,781.00	40.70
		Week 649: January 17	143,802.00	43.30
		Week 650: January 24	125,271.00	38.40
		Week 651: January 31	116,577.00	35.40
		Week 652: February 7	115,504.00	34.20
		Week 653: February 14	160,773.00	46.00
		Week 654: February 21	183,341.00	57.40
		Week 655: February 28	134,353.00	41.40
		Week 656: March 6	147,072.00	42.70
		Week 657: March 13	154,123.00	46.60
		Week 658: March 20	191,043.00	56.30
		Week 659: March 27	190,105.00	56.80
		Week 660: April 3	235,290.00	72.20
		Week 661: April 10	248,694.00	76.80
		Week 662: April 17	172,617.00	50.80
		Week 663: April 24	184,905.00	55.10
		Week 664: May 1	167,274.00	51.30
		Week 665: May 8	198,237.00	58.10
		Week 666: May 15	189,945.00	58.40
		Week 667: May 22	208,496.00	60.40
		Week 668: May 29	190,856.00	56.80

Seats	Ticket Price/ Potential	Week Ending	Net Receipts	% Capacity
		Week 669: June 5	152,535.00	44.20
		Week 670: June 12	203,510.00	59.30
		Week 671 June 19	194,871.00	54.20
		Week 672: June 26	207,481.00	58.00
		Week 673: July 3	187,781.00	55.20
		Week 674: July 10	160,947.00	46.50
		Week 675: July 17	198,667.00	59.20
		Week 676: July 24	229,067.00	73.00
		Week 677: July 31	224,645.00	69.00
		Jul. 25 — ACL begins 14th year on Broadway		
		Week 678: August 7	228,515.00	67.40
		Week 679: August 14	248,216.00	72.10
		Week 680: August 21	274,433.00	78.80
		Week 681: August 28	237,182.00	68.00
		Week 682: September 4	188,784.00	57.00
		Week 683: September 11	156,410.00	44.00
		Week 684: September 18	176,346.00	49.00
		Week 685: September 25	170,145.00	48.00
		Week 686: October 2	186,944.00	52.00
		Week 687: October 9	195,395.00	54.10
1472	$47.50/$499,820	Week 688: October 16	215,068.00	57.80
28 standees		Week 689: October 23	203,974.00	55.90
		Week 690: October 30	168,465.00	46.20
		Week 691: November 6	148,758.00	40.60
		Week 692: November 13	185,267.00	50.20
		Week 693: November 20	151,724.00	40.40
		Week 694: November 27	219,746.00	56.90
		Week 695: December 4	173,302.00	52.20
		Week 696: December 11	191,435.00	55.50
		Week 697: December 18	137,139.00	44.50
		Week 698: December 25	107,799.00	42.90
		Week 699: January 1	344,726.00	86.10
		Total Year End	**$9,666,336.00**	**54.18**

1989

Seats	Ticket Price/ Potential	Week Ending	Net Receipts	% Capacity
		Week 700: January 8		
		Week 701: January 15	152,582.00	43.30
		Week 702: January 22	142,499.00	40.50
		Week 703: January 29	140,114.00	40.00
		Week 704: February 5	115,636.00	37.00
		Week 705 February 12	132,092.00	45.00

Seats	Ticket Price/ Potential	Week Ending	Net Receipts	% Capacity
		Week 706: February 19	179,071.00	53.40
		Week 707: February 26	181,098.00	53.20
		Week 708: March 5	150,803.00	46.10
		Week 709: March 12	185,159.00	60.30
		Week 710: March 19	207,060.00	63.20
		Week 711: March 26	248,518.00	68.90
		Week 712: April 2	220,901.00	64.10
		Week 713: April 9	164,481.00	48.60
		Week 714: April 16	160,881.00	47.30
		Week 715: April 23	204,269.00	60.70
		Week 716: April 30	188,749.00	56.30
		Week 717: May 7	251,746.00	70.70
		Week 718: May 14	168,265.00	49.70
		Week 719: May 21	197,598.00	54.60
		Week 720: May 28	176,304.00	49.70
		Week 721: June 4	124,123.00	35.90
		Week 722: June 11	177,674.00	49.30
		Week 723: June 18	181,244.00	50.70
		Week 724: June 25	183,509.00	51.40
		Week 725: July 2	149,973.00	42.30
		Week 726: July 9	149,126.00	41.60
		Week 727 July 16	173,037.00	50.40
		Week 728: July 23	197,576.00	56.40
		Week 729: July 30	193,058.00	55.00
		Jul. 25 — ACL begins 15th year on Broadway		
		Week 730: August 6	193,229.00	54.40
		Week 731: August 13	248,135.00	68.40
	$50/$532,366.40	Week 732: August 20	258,544.00	69.50
	Last ticket price increase			
		Week 733: August 27	231,261.00	62.10
		Week 734: September 3	181,343.00	48.50
		Week 735: September 10	153,850.00	40.10
		Week 736: September 17	179,958.00	46.00
		Week 737: September 24	178,187.00	45.90
		Week 738: October 1	154,806.00	40.10
		Week 739: October 8	184,074.00	46.60
		Week 740: October 15	198,670.00	51.50
		Week 741: October 22	199,618.00	51.10
		Week 742: October 29	158,962.00	39.30
		Week 743: November 5	148,968.00	37.10
		Week 744: November 12	170,660.00	44.60
		Week 745: November 19	137,119.00	36.90

Seats	Ticket Price/ Potential	Week Ending	Net Receipts	% Capacity
		Week 746: November 26	209,890.00	54.50
		Week 747: December 3	136,412.00	34.40
		Week 748: December 10	178,876.00	49.50
		Week 749: December 17	119,234.00	39.30
		Dec. 11 — Joe Papp gives 500 free tickets for New Year's Eve performance		
		Week 750: December 24	92,121.00	32.20
		Week 751: December 31	322,051.00	83.00
		Dec. 31 — ACL plays 6,000th performance		
		Total Year End	**$9,133,114.00**	**50.21**

1990

Seats	Ticket Price/ Potential	Week Ending	Net Receipts	% Capacity
		Week 752: January 7	146,322.00	50.30
		Jan. 7 — All Mezzanine Seats reduced to $15 for the entire month		
		Week 753: January 14	131,921.00	47.00
		Week 754: January 21	108,451.00	38.30
		Week 755: January 28	108,400.00	38.00
		Week 756: February 4	96,116.00	35.40
		Week 757: February 11	104,711.00	33.40
		Week 758: February 18	163,854.00	52.80

Seats	Ticket Price/ Potential	Week Ending	Net Receipts	% Capacity
		Week 759: February 25	228,718.00	75.40
		Feb. 21, 12:15 p.m. — Joe Papp announces closing		
		Week 760: March 4	218,872.00	61.90
		Week 761: March 11	311,504.00	76.50
		Week 762: March 18	346,914.00	85.60
		Week 763: March 25	390,443.00	93.00
		Highest gross for ACL ever		
		Week 764: April 1	396,049.00	95.20
		New highest gross for ACL ever / ACL originally supposed to close Mar. 31		
		Week 765: April 8	276,741.00	69.30
		First week of 4 week extension beyond announced closing / Final Actors' Fund Performance Apr. 8		
		Week 766: April 15	399,265.00	93.50
		New highest gross for ACL ever		
		Week 767: April 22	406,407.00	94.50
		Week 768: April 29	420,407.00	94.30
		Highest gross ever — ACL closes Apr. 28 after 6137 performances		
		Total Year End	**$4,255,095.00**	**66.73**
		TOTAL 15 YEARS	**$149,277,754.00**	**77.91%**

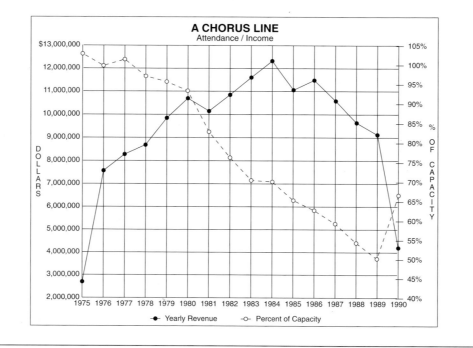

A CHORUS LINE
Attendance / Income

—●— Yearly Revenue   —○— Percent of Capacity

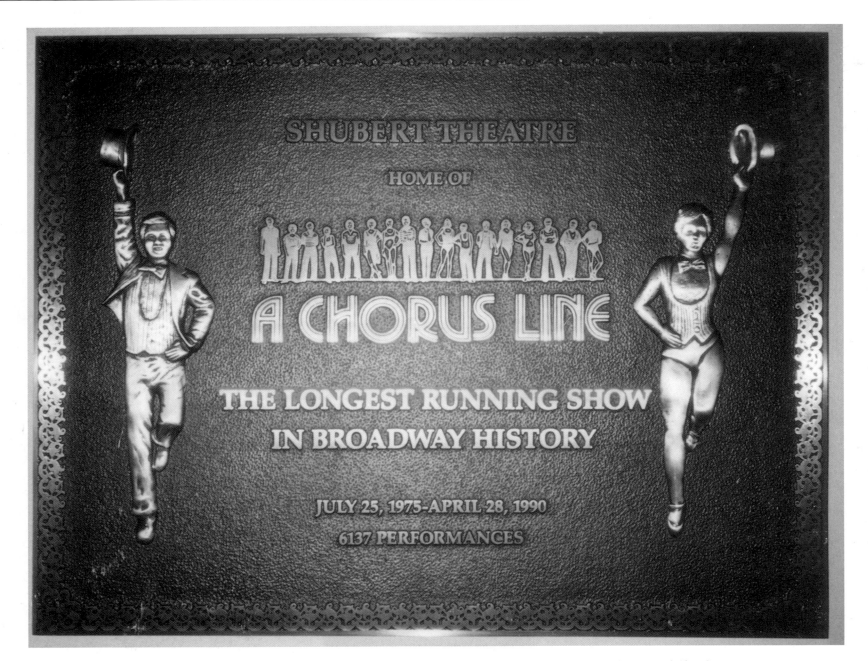

This bronze plaque, which adorns the Shubert Theatre lobby, was unveiled October 30, 1991, by Gary Stevens and Alan George.
Contributions from 198 fans made this dedication possible, and their names are attached behind it.

Index